4 ★ All-Star

Teacher's Edition

Linda Lee

Stephen Sloan ★ Grace Tanaka ★ Shirley Velasco

Teacher's Edition by Kristin Sherman

All-Star 4 Teacher's Edition

Published by McGraw-Hill ESL/ELT, a business unit of The McGraw-Hill Companies, Inc. 1221 Avenue of the Americas, New York, NY 10020. Copyright © 2005 by The McGraw-Hill Companies, Inc. All rights reserved. Permission is granted to reproduce these materials as needed for classroom use or for use by individual students. Distribution for sale is prohibited.

ISBN: 0-07-284689-5
1 2 3 4 5 6 7 8   QPD/QPD   11 10 09 08 07 06 05

Editorial director: Tina B. Carver
Executive editor: Erik Gundersen
Senior developmental editor: Mari Vargo
Developmental editor: Angela Castro
Production manager: Juanita Thompson
Interior designer: Wanda Espana of Wee Design Group
Photo credits: From the Getty Images Royalty-Free Collection: p. 213; p. 218; p. 219; p. 224; p. 226; p. 227; p. 228; From the Corbis Royalty-Free Collection: p. 217; p. 221; Other Images: p. 214: Lawrence Lawry/Getty Images; p. 215: John A. Rizzo/Getty Images; p. 222: Nancy R. Cohen/Getty Images; p. 223: Ryan McVay/Getty Images; p. 225: © Kayte M. Deioma/PhotoEdit.

Contents

WELCOME TO THE TEACHER'S EDITION

The *All-Star* Teacher's Edition provides support to teachers using the *All-Star* Student Book. Each unit of the Teacher's Edition begins with a list of the unit's lesson titles, the objective for each lesson, and the Big Picture Expansion Activities that are used with the Color Overhead Transparencies. Hundreds of additional activities are suggested throughout the Teacher's Edition to expand the use of the target language in the Student Book.

The *All-Star* Teacher's Edition offers step-by-step procedures for each lesson. Seasoned teachers can use the instructions as a quick refresher, while newer teachers, or substitute teachers, can use the step-by-step instructions as a helpful guide for conducting the Student Book activities in the classroom.

The Teacher's Edition provides:

- Step-by-step procedural notes for each Student Book activity

- More than 200 expansion activities for Student Book 4, many of which offer creative tasks tied to the Big Picture scenes in each unit

- Culture, Grammar, Pronunciation, and Academic Notes

- Worksheets for corresponding Big Picture Reading and Grammar Expansion Activities

- Two-page written tests for each unit (*Note*: Listening passages for the tests are available on the Student Book Audiocassettes and Audio CDs.)

- Audio scripts for all audio program materials

- Answer keys for Student Book, Workbook, and Tests

All-Star is a four-level, standards-based series for English learners, featuring a picture-dictionary approach to vocabulary building. Big Picture scenes in each unit provide springboards to a wealth of activities developing all of the language skills.

An accessible and predictable sequence of lessons in each unit systematically builds language and math skills around life-skill topics. *All-Star* presents family, work, and community topics in each unit, and provides alternate application lessons in its Workbooks, giving teachers the flexibility to customize the series for a variety of student needs and curricular objectives. *All-Star* is tightly correlated to all of the major national and state standards for adult instruction.

Features

★ **Accessible Big Picture scenes** present life-skills vocabulary, activities, and discussion, and provide engaging contexts for all-skills language development.

★ **Predictable sequence of nine, two-page lessons** in each unit reduces prep time for teachers and helps students get comfortable with the pattern of each lesson type.

★ **Flexible structure** allows teachers to customize each unit to meet a variety of student needs and curricular objectives, with application lessons addressing family, work, and community topics in both the Student Book and Workbook.

★ **Comprehensive coverage of key standards, such as CASAS, SCANS, EFF, and LCPs,** prepares students to master a broad range of critical competencies.

★ **Multiple assessment measures** like CASAS-style tests and performance-based assessment offer a broad range of options for monitoring and assessing learner progress.

★ **Dynamic, Interactive CD-ROM program** in Levels 1 and 2 integrates language, literacy, and numeracy skill building with computer practice.

The Complete *All-Star* Program

★ The **Student Book** features eight, 18-page units, integrating listening, speaking, reading, writing, grammar, math, and pronunciation skills with life-skill topics, critical thinking activities, and civics concepts. As in levels 1, 2, and 3, Student Book 4 addresses the themes central to the lives of adult ESL learners, making it easy to use the *All-Star* series in multi-level classrooms.

★ The **Student Book with Audio Highlights** provides students with audio recordings of all of the conversations and example dialogues in the Student Book.

★ The **Teacher's Edition with Tests** provides:
  • Step-by-step procedural notes for each Student Book activity
  • More than 200 expansion activities for Student Book 4, many of which offer creative tasks tied to the Big Picture scenes in each unit

• Culture, Grammar, Pronunciation, and Academic Notes
• Two-page written test for each unit (*Note:* Listening passages for the tests are available on the Student Book Audiocassettes and Audio CDs.)
• Audio scripts for all audio program materials
• Answer keys for Student Book, Workbook, and Tests

★ The **Interactive CD-ROM** included in Levels 1 and 2 incorporates and extends the learning goals of the Student Book by integrating language, literacy, and numeracy skill building with multimedia practice on the computer. A flexible set of activities correlated to each unit builds vocabulary, listening, reading, writing, and test-taking skills.

★ The **Color Overhead Transparencies** encourage teachers to present new vocabulary and concepts in fun and meaningful ways. This component provides a full-color overhead transparency for each of the Big Picture scenes.

★ The **Workbook** includes supplementary practice activities correlated systematically to the Student Book. As a bonus feature, the Workbook also includes alternate application lessons addressing the learner's role as worker, family member, and/or community member. These additional, optional lessons may be used in addition to, or as substitutes for, the application lessons found in Lesson 6 of each Student Book unit.

★ The **Audiocassettes** and **Audio CDs** contain recordings for all listening activities in the Student Book. Listening passages for each unit test are provided at the end of the audio section for that unit.

Overview of the *All-Star* Program

UNIT STRUCTURE

Consult the *Welcome to All-Star* guide on pages xvi–xix. This guide offers teachers and administrators a visual tour of one Student Book unit.

All-Star is designed to maximize accessibility and flexibility. Each unit contains the following sequence of nine, two-page lessons that develop vocabulary and build language, grammar, and math skills around life-skill topics:

★ Lesson 1: Talk about It

★ Lesson 2: Vocabulary in Context

★ Lesson 3: Listening and Speaking

★ Lesson 4: Reading and Critical Thinking

★ Lesson 5: Grammar

★ Lesson 6: Application

★ Lesson 7: Review and Assessment

★ Spotlight: Reading Strategy

★ Spotlight: Writing Strategy

Each lesson addresses a key adult standard, and these standards are indicated in the upper right-hand corner of each lesson in a yellow bar.

SPECIAL FEATURES OF EACH UNIT

★ *Warm Up.* This activates students' background knowledge, access their personal experience, and generate their interest in the topic of the lesson. They serve to introduce students to the lesson topic and prompt classroom discussion.

★ *Try This Strategy.* This feature presents students with learning strategies (such as identifying goals), vocabulary strategies (such as learning synonyms), and academic learning strategies (such as evaluating texts) toward the beginning of each unit so students can apply them as they proceed through the lessons. These strategies allow students to build skills to continue their lifelong learning.

★ *Communication Strategy.* This feature presents students with communication strategies that will improve their ability to communicate effectively and help them become more fluid, natural speakers. Communication strategies, such as disagreeing politely, are introduced and then practiced in real-life role-play activities called *Use the Communication Strategy.*

★ *Grammar Lessons.* Grammar is presented and practiced in Lesson 5 of each unit. These two-page lessons offer students more in-depth grammar practice than at the lower levels of the series. The essential grammar content is correlated to a variety of national and state standards. A comprehensive *Grammar Reference Guide* at the back of the book summarizes all of the structures and functions presented.

★ *Window on Math.* Learning basic math skills is critically important for success in school, on the job, and at home. As such, national and state standards for adult education mandate instruction in basic math skills. In half of the units, a blue box called *Window on Math* is dedicated to helping students develop the functional numeracy skills they need for basic math work in everyday math applications such as payroll deductions.

★ *Window on Pronunciation.* Improving pronunciation skills can greatly improve students' ability to understand others and to be understood. In half of the units, a blue box called *Window on Pronunciation* is dedicated to helping students achieve two major goals: (1) hearing and producing specific sounds, words, and minimal pairs of words so students become better listeners and speakers; and (2) addressing issues of stress, rhythm, and intonation so that the students' spoken English becomes more comprehensible.

★ *Spotlight: Reading Strategy.* After the *Review and Assessment* lesson in each unit, students and teachers will find a *Spotlight* dedicated to presenting students with academic reading strategies. These are optional, two-page lessons that offer a supplementary focus on reading skill development.

★ *Spotlight: Writing Strategy.* At the end of each unit, students and teachers will find a *Spotlight* dedicated to presenting students with academic and professional writing strategies. These are optional, two-page lessons that offer a supplementary focus on writing skill development.

TWO-PAGE LESSON FORMAT

The lessons in *All-Star* are designed as two-page spreads. Lessons 5–7 and the Spotlights employ a standard textbook layout, but Lessons 1–4 follow an innovative format with a list of activities on the left-hand page of the spread and rich textual input supporting these activities on the right-hand page. The textual input includes authentic and adapted newspaper articles, letters, and official forms and applications. The list of activities, entitled *Things To Do,* allows students and teachers to take full advantage of the visuals in each lesson, inviting students to achieve a variety of learning, by evaluating, synthesizing, and analyzing.

As in previous levels, Lessons 1–4 provide learners with the input necessary to facilitate comprehension. Student Books 3 and 4 include much of the rich visual input found in Student Books 1 and 2, but also have greater textual input in keeping with the students' more advanced abilities.

BIG PICTURE SCENES

Each unit includes one Big Picture scene. In Student Books 3 and 4, the Big Picture scene begins each unit in Lesson 1. This scene is the visual centerpiece of each unit and serves as a springboard to a variety of activities provided in the Student Book, Teacher's Edition, Color Overhead Transparencies package, and the Interactive CD-ROM program in Levels 1 and 2. The Big Picture activates background knowledge, accesses students' personal experience, increases their motivation, and serves as a prompt for classroom discussion.

The Teacher's Edition includes a variety of all-skills Big Picture Expansion activities that are tied to the Student Book scenes. For each unit, these expansion activities address listening, speaking, reading, writing, and grammar skill development, and allow teachers to customize their instruction to meet the language learning needs of each group of students.

In the Color Overhead Transparencies package, teachers will find transparencies of each Big Picture scene, which they can use to introduce the vocabulary and life-skill concepts in each unit. They can also use these transparencies to facilitate the Big Picture Expansion activities in the Teacher's Edition.

Finally, the Interactive CD-ROM program in Levels 1 and 2 highlights an additional aspect of the Big Picture scenes in its listening activities. Students working with the CD-ROM program listen to a series of new conversations taking place between characters in the Big Picture scenes. Students then work through a series of interactive activities based on these conversations and receive immediate feedback on their work.

CIVICS CONCEPTS

Many institutions focus direct attention on the importance of civics instruction for English language learners. Civics instruction encourages students to become active and informed community members. *Application* lessons provide activities that help students develop their roles as workers, parents, and community members. Those lessons targeting the students' role as a community member encourage learners to become more active and informed members of their communities.

CASAS, SCANS, EFF, LCPs, AND OTHER STANDARDS

Teachers and administrators benchmark student progress against national and/or state standards for adult instruction. With this in mind, *All-Star* carefully integrates instructional elements from a wide range of standards including CASAS, SCANS, EFF, and the Literacy Completion Points (LCPs). Unit-by-unit correlations of these standards appear in the scope and sequence on pages xii–xix. Here is a brief overview of our approach to meeting the key national and state standards:

★ **CASAS.** Many U.S. states, including California, tie funding for adult education programs to student performance on the Comprehensive Adult Student Assessment System (CASAS). The CASAS (www.casas.org) competencies identify more than 300 essential skills that adults need in order to succeed in the classroom, workplace, and community. Examples of these skills include identifying or using appropriate non-verbal behavior in a variety of settings, responding appropriately to common personal information questions, and comparing price or quality to determine the best buys. *All-Star* comprehensively integrates all of the CASAS Life Skill Competencies throughout the four levels of the series. Level 4 addresses the CASAS Level C Life Skills test items on CASAS Test Forms 35, 36, 55, and 56.

★ **SCANS.** Developed by the United States Department of Labor, SCANS is an acronym for the Secretary's Commission on Achieving Necessary Skills (www.doleta.gov/SCANS/). SCANS competencies are workplace skills that help people compete more effectively in today's global economy. The following are examples of SCANS competencies: works well with others, acquires and evaluates information, and teaches others new skills. A variety of SCANS competencies are threaded throughout the activities in each unit of *All-Star*. The incorporation of these competencies recognizes both the intrinsic importance of teaching workplace skills and the fact that many adult students are already working members of their communities.

★ **EFF.** Equipped for the Future (EFF) is a set of standards for adult literacy and lifelong learning, developed by The National Institute for Literacy (www.nifl.gov). The organizing principle of EFF is that adults assume responsibilities in three major areas of life—as workers, as parents, and as citizens. These three areas of focus are called "role maps" in the EFF documentation. In the parent role map, for example, EFF highlights these and other responsibilities: participating in children's formal education, and forming and maintaining

supportive family relationships. Each *All-Star* unit addresses all three of the EFF role maps in its *Application* lessons. Lesson 6 in each Student Book unit includes one of the three application lessons for that unit. The remaining two application lessons are found in the corresponding Workbook unit.

★ **LCPs.** Florida and Texas document the advancement of learners in an adult program through their system of Literacy Completion Points (LCPs). Community college and school districts earn an LCP each time an adult student advances to a higher proficiency level or completes a program. *All-Star* Level 4 incorporates into its instruction the vast majority of standards at LCP Level E.

NUMBER OF HOURS OF INSTRUCTION

The *All-Star* program has been designed to accommodate the needs of adult classes with 70–180 hours of classroom instruction. Here are three recommended ways in which various components in the *All-Star* program can be combined to meet student and teacher needs.

★ **70–100 hours**. Teachers are encouraged to work through all of the Student Book materials, incorporating the *Reading* and *Writing Spotlights* as time permits. The Color Overhead Transparencies can be used to introduce and/or review materials in each unit. Teachers should also look to the Teacher's Edition for teaching suggestions and testing materials as necessary.

Time per unit: 9–13 hours.

★ **100–140 hours.** In addition to working through all of the Student Book materials, teachers are encouraged to incorporate the Workbook for supplementary practice.

Time per unit: 13–18 hours.

★ **140–180 hours.** Teachers and students working in an intensive instructional setting can take advantage of the wealth of expansion activities threaded through the Teacher's Edition to supplement the Student Book and the Workbook.

Time per unit: 18–22 hours.

ASSESSMENT

★ **Purposes of Assessment:** J. Michael O'Malley and Lorraine Valdez-Pierce describe six purposes of assessment in *Authentic Assessment for English Language Learners,* similar to those listed below.

- **Screening** determines if the student is at the right level for the English language instruction that you provide. Some students may be too high for an adult ESL program, and their needs better met in an academic program or in adult high school.
- **Placement** tests determine in what level a student should be placed. Adult ESL programs with more than one class often give an entrance test of some kind to place the student. Screening and placement can be done with the same instrument. Many programs use CASAS or BEST tests for this purpose.

- **Monitoring achievement** allows the learner and the instructor to see how well particular information has been learned. An end-of-unit test can demonstrate if the student has been successful in learning specific instructional content.
- **Measuring performance** involves assessing how well learners accomplish specific tasks using prior knowledge and recent learning. Such tasks are usually productive (speaking/writing) and may involve presentations, reports, or projects.
- **Program evaluation** can involve a variety of assessments in order to determine the effectiveness of a program as a whole. Programs may look at overall improvement in test scores, examples of student projects, and surveys of students and instructors in evaluating program effectiveness.
- **Accountability** is required for programs receiving state and federal funds. Federal reporting standards (as described by the Federal Reporting System) require that programs demonstrate student progress. This progress is often measured by standardized testing (e.g., CASAS) but may also be substantiated by alternative methods of assessment.

All-Star Unit Tests

The Teacher's Edition contains a reproducible unit test for each of the eight units in *All-Star*. Each two-page test assesses students' knowledge of the vocabulary and language structures taught within the unit. Each test is worth 20 points.

Each unit test consists of four sections: Listening, Grammar, Reading/Vocabulary, and Writing. The Listening section includes two short conversations, each followed by multiple-choice questions about the conversation. The Grammar section focuses on structures learned in the unit. Students are asked to choose the correct answer to complete sentences. The Reading/Vocabulary section includes different types of reading passages and multiple-choice questions about those passages. Finally, the Writing section might ask students to write two sentences about a topic introduced in the unit, or to fill out a form or an application similar to one in the unit. The audio portion of each test is provided on the *All-Star* CDs or cassettes.

The Unit Test Listening Script and Unit Test Answer Key are included at the end of the Teacher's Edition.

The *All-Star* program offers teachers, students, and administrators the following wealth of resources for monitoring and assessing student progress and achievement:

★ **Standardized testing formats.** *All-Star* is correlated to the CASAS competencies and many other national and state standards for adult learning. Students have the opportunity to practice answering CASAS-style listening and reading questions in Lesson 7 of each unit (*What do you know?*) and in Lesson 7 of the Workbook (*Practice Test*). Students practice with the same item types and bubble-in answer sheets they encounter on CASAS and other standardized tests.

★ **Achievement tests.** The *All-Star* Teacher's Edition includes end-of-unit tests. These paper-and-pencil tests help students demonstrate how well they have learned the instructional

content of the unit. Adult learners often show incremental increases in learning that are not always measured on standardized tests. The achievement tests may demonstrate learning even in a short amount of instructional time. Twenty percent of each test includes questions that encourage students to apply more academic skills such as determining meaning from context, making inferences, and understanding main ideas. Practice with these question types will help prepare students who may want to enroll in academic classes.

★ **Performance-based assessment.** *All-Star* provides several ways to measure students' performance on productive tasks. The Teacher's Edition suggests writing and speaking prompts and rubrics that teachers can use for performance-based assessment. These prompts derive from the Big Picture scene in each unit and provide rich visual input as the basis for the speaking and writing tasks asked of the students.

★ **Portfolio assessment.** A portfolio is a collection of student work that can be used to show progress. Examples of work that the instructor or the student may submit in the portfolio include writing samples, speaking rubrics, audiotapes, videotapes, or projects. The Teacher's Edition identifies activities that require critical thinking and small group project work which may be included, as well as those that may be used as documentation for the secondary standards defined by the National Reporting System.

★ **Self-assessment.** Self-assessment is an important part of the overall assessment picture, as it promotes student involvement and commitment to the learning process. When encouraged to assess themselves, students take more control of their learning and are better able to connect the instructional content with their own goals. The Student Book includes *Learning Logs* at the end of each unit, which allow students to check off the vocabulary they have learned, and the skills and strategies they have acquired. The Workbook provides a *Practice Test Performance Record* graph where students record their number of correct answers on each practice test, encouraging them to monitor their own progress as they advance through the book.

★ **Other linguistic and non-linguistic outcomes.** Traditional testing often does not account for the progress made by adult learners with limited educational experience or low literacy levels. Such learners tend to take longer to make smaller language gains, so the gains they make in other areas are often more significant. These gains may be in areas such as self-esteem, goal clarification, learning skills, and access to employment, community involvement and further academic studies. The SCANS and EFF standards identify areas of student growth that are not necessarily language based. *All-Star* is correlated with both SCANS and EFF standards. Every unit in the student book contains a lesson that focuses on one of the EFF role maps (worker, family member, community member), and the Workbook provides alternate lessons that address the other two role maps. Like the Student Book, the Workbook includes activities that may provide documentation that can be added to a student portfolio.

About the authors and series consultants

Linda Lee is lead author on the *All-Star* series. Linda has taught ESL/ELT in the United States, Iran, and China, and has authored or co-authored a variety of successful textbook series for English learners. As a classroom instructor, Linda's most satisfying teaching experiences have been with adult ESL students at Roxbury Community College in Boston, Massachusetts.

Kristin Sherman is a contributing author on *All-Star,* Student Book 2 and a co-author on Student Book 3. Kristin has 10 years of teaching experience in both credit and non-credit ESL programs. She has taught general ESL, as well as classes focusing on workplace skills and family literacy. She has authored a number of workbooks and teacher's editions for English learners. Her favorite project was the creation of a reading and writing workbook with her ESL students at the Mecklenburg County Jail.

Stephen Sloan is Title One Coordinator at James Monroe High School in the Los Angeles Unified School District. Steve has more than 25 years of teaching and administrative experience with both high school and adult ESL learners. Steve is also the author of McGraw-Hill's *Rights and Responsibilities: Reading and Communication for Civics.*

Grace Tanaka is professor and coordinator of ESL at the Santa Ana College School of Continuing Education, in Santa Ana, California, which serves more than 20,000 students per year. She is also a textbook co-author and series consultant. Grace has 23 years of teaching experience in both credit and non-credit ESL programs.

Shirley Velasco is assistant principal at Palmetto Adult Education Center in Miami, Florida. She has been a classroom instructor and administrator for the past 24 years. At Palmetto, Shirley has created a large adult ESOL program based on a curriculum she developed to help teachers implement the Florida LCPs (Literacy Completion Points).

Teaching Strategies

Repetition: On almost every page of *All-Star*, students have the opportunity to listen to and repeat new vocabulary and structures. They need this structured practice in a low-anxiety environment before they are asked to manipulate this language in reading, writing, listening, or speaking activities. Repetition allows them to learn the pronunciation of individual words, internalize word order, and better approximate the stress and intonation pattern of native speakers. Although the audio program provides for repetition, students may need more frequent repetition drills to reinforce pronunciation or word order. One strategy is to say the new word or phrase and have the class repeat chorally, then call on individual students. You can use the Big Picture color transparencies to introduce or review new language in this way.

When students are practicing conversational structures, you can lead them through a progression of activities. First, you read one role and the students respond chorally. Then divide the class into two: one half reads one role chorally, and the other half responds chorally. Then model the conversation with a student, or have two students model the conversation for the class. Finally, students can practice with partners. In this way, they acquire confidence as they gradually become more independent in using the new language.

Modeling: Before students are asked to produce language in a new context, they need the opportunity to see it demonstrated and then to practice it in a structured setting. Whenever there is an activity that calls on students to personalize the language, the instructor should model how this is done. For example, if students are asked to talk to a partner and complete the sentence "I am wearing _____ shoes." You should point to your shoes and say, "I'm wearing . . ." You can then pause, and prompt students to say the color of your shoes. Repeat the sentence, including the color of your shoes. After you have modeled the new language, more advanced students can provide additional examples of appropriate responses (e.g., "I'm wearing brown shoes."). Less proficient students can follow their examples.

Elicitation: Elicitation is an effective tool in making the classroom more learner-centered. When students contribute their ideas, they feel more secure about their abilities in the new language and valued for what they already know. Asking questions and eliciting responses from the class will keep students more actively engaged in learning. More advanced students are often eager to respond, whereas the less proficient may be more reluctant. One way to level the playing field is to provide a sentence stem for the answer (e.g., "My name is _____ "), and then have more advanced students model appropriate responses. Less proficient students can follow the pattern set by the students before them. Another strategy is to accept partial or one-word answers and provide the rest of the sentence (e.g., "Tien," "Your name is Tien."). Allowing students to discuss the topic in small groups or pairs before you elicit responses from the whole class is also an effective strategy (see *Modeling*).

Error correction: When and how often to correct students is the subject of much debate. Research suggests that it is repeated exposure to accurate input rather than correction that helps a student internalize new language. Too much correction can cause a learner to feel insecure about his or her language ability and reluctant to take the risks necessary to becoming more fluent in a new language. When accuracy is the goal, as in the repetition of listening activities or completing a multiple-choice assessment, correction should be immediate and constructive. When fluency is the goal, as in Conversation Practice with a partner, correction should be minimized as it interrupts the conversational flow and can make students more self-conscious. In many cases, students can self-correct if you provide a model of accurate language. For example, if a student says "Hello. I Carlos," you can respond, "Hi, Carlos. I'm Isabel." By emphasizing the correct form in your response, you can help students monitor their own speech. This technique is often referred to as "counsel correction." Another strategy is to pause before the error, gesturing for students to fill in the correct form.

Pair/group work: Students at a low beginning or literacy level are often reluctant to work in pairs or small groups as they are insecure about their own language abilities and may be accustomed to a teacher-centered approach. However, pair and group work activities allow each student more opportunities to engage in conversations in English. To encourage student participation in these activities, walk around and listen to all of the pairs or small groups as they are working. Asking questions or helping with pronunciation makes students feel that the activity is purposeful and personally beneficial. Such monitoring also prepares students to speak in front of the whole group and in authentic situations outside the classroom. To maximize interaction among the students, you can vary the seating arrangements or use strategies such as counting off that match students with different partners each time. Alternatively, you can engineer the groupings so that students complement each other, perhaps placing a more communicative student with one who has stronger literacy skills.

Using the audio program: Every unit in *All-Star* includes substantive listening practice for students on realistic topics. This practice is important not only for assessment purposes, but also to help students become accustomed to listening to and comprehending voices other than that of the instructor. Such activities prepare students to navigate more successfully in the real world with other native speakers. Units are structured so that students first listen to vocabulary or conversational models as they associate the sound with the context, then they repeat the new language. When they have mastered the scripted conversation, they are then asked to personalize the new language in describing their own experiences.

Using realia: Adult students attend to and retain information when it is made relevant to their own needs and experience. Using real material such as authentic documents, maps, pictures, and objects not only helps students relate language learning to their own lives, it also appeals to a variety of learning styles. Each unit of *All-Star* includes a form that helps students develop competence with authentic documents. Wherever possible, other realistic diagrams and visuals have been included in the units to help students place the language in real world contexts. Bringing in other authentic materials related to the unit topic can make concepts more tangible and reinforce learning.

How to work with reluctant learners: Sometimes adult students enter literacy and low beginning classes having had little experience in an educational setting. Others may have had negative experiences in school or may feel that learning English at this stage in their lives is a burden rather than an opportunity. Such students may be reluctant at first to participate in class activities. Recognize that these students have a wealth of experience and knowledge on which to draw, and include activities that are relevant to their everyday lives. With every topic, be sensitive to the needs of your students. For example, those students whose families may have died or been left behind can either tell about their relatives or about the people they live with now.

Scope and Sequence

	Life Skills				
Unit	**Listening and Speaking**	**Reading and Writing**	**Critical Thinking**	**Vocabulary**	**Grammar**
Pre-Unit **Getting Started** *page 2*	• Express opinions • Introduce yourself • Interview your classmates	• Write about your classmates • Preview the book	• Evaluate • Choose the best alternative • Preview	• Introductions • Information questions	
1 **Skills and Abilities** *page 4*	• Talk about continuing education • Talk about personal and professional goals • Listen to telephone conversations and messages • Talk about telephone behavior • Talk about job interviews • Talk about importance of writing skills • Discuss success **Focus on Pronunciation:** Blending words in questions with *you*	• Complete a class registration form • Read about types of skills • Write about types of skills • Write telephone messages • Read a success story • Read about career plans • Preview a reading **Spotlight: Reading** Make inferences **Spotlight: Writing** Write business letters	• Evaluate • Apply knowledge • Analyze	• Types of courses • Educational and professional goals • Word forms	• Direct and indirect *yes/no* and *wh-* questions
2 **Getting Around** *page 22*	• Talk about types of transportation • Talk about solving transportation problems • Talk about automobile insurance • Listen to conversations regarding a traffic accident and car repair • Listen to conversations about making car and travel reservations • Get information about travel schedules **Focus on Pronunciation:** Reduction of past modals	• Read an insurance policy • Read automobile insurance terms • Read a bus schedule • Read about travel options • Take notes on transportation issues • Write synonyms • Fill out accident reports **Spotlight: Reading** Identify the topic and main idea **Spotlight: Writing** compound subjects, verbs, and objects	• Make inferences • Compare information • Analyze • Interpret	• Automobile insurance terms • Parts of an automobile • Synonyms • Car accident checklist	• Past form of *should* • Past form of *could*

Correlations to National Standards

Civics Concepts	Math Skills	CASAS Life Skill Competencies	SCANS Competencies (Workplace)	EFF Content Standards	Literacy Completion Points (LCPs)
		• 0.1.2, 0.1.4, 0.2.1, 0.2.4, 7.2.3, 7.4.6, 7.5.6	• Decision making • Sociability • Knowing how to learn	• Communicate so that others understand • Reflect on and reevaluate your opinions and ideas	• 83.03, 83.11
• Identify educational opportunities • Recognize personal and professional goals • Recognize personal job skill abilities • Recognize appropriate interviewing behavior • Ability to take and interpret telephone messages • Recognize do's and don'ts of phone use • Recognize behavior that leads to promotion		• 1: 0.2.2, 2.5.5, 4.4.5, 6.7.3, 7.1.1, 7.26, 7.5.1 • 2: 7.2.1, 7.2.4, 7.31, 7.32, 7.5.1, 7.5.6 • 3: 0.1.2, 0.1.3, 2.1.7, 4.5.4, 7.2.1, 7.2.2 • 4: 4.4.2, 4.6.2, 4.6.5, 7.2.4, 7.2.5, 7.2.6 • 5: 0.1.2, 7.2.2 • 6: 4.1.5, 4.1.7, 4.4.1, 7.2.1, 7.2.2, 7.2.3, 7.2.5 • 7: 0.1.2, 7.1.4, 7.2.4, 7.4.7 • RS: 7.2.4, 7.2.5 • WS: 0.1.2, 0.1.4, 4.6.2, 7.2.2, 7.2.3	Emphasized are the following: • Understand systems • Reasoning • Organize and maintain information • Problem solving • Self-management • Decision making • Work well with others	Emphasized are the following: • Create vision of future • Plan and renew career goals • Pursue personal self-improvement • Reflect on and reevaluate your opinions and ideas • Develop a sense of self that reflects your values	• 1: 71.01, 83.13 • 2: 70.01, 70.02, 83.06 • 3: 74.01, 74.02, 83.02, 83.04 • 4: 83.05, 83.10, 83.14 • 5: 83.16 • 6: 69.04, 70.01 • 7: 83.02, 83.18 • RS: 83.05, 83.12, 83.14 • WS: 83.15
• Compare travel schedule and cost • Interpret information about automobile insurance • Understand what to do in case of an accident • Identify basic travel signs • Interpret highway and traffic signs		• 1: 0.1.2, 1.9.1, 1.9.7, 2.2.3, 7.1.1, 7.2.4, 7.3.1, 7.3.2 • 2: 0.1.2, 1.9.7, 1.9.8, 7.2.1, 7.2.3 • 3: 0.1.2, 1.1.3, 1.9.4, 1.9.6, 1.9.7, 1.9.8, 2.2.2, 2.2.4, 2.2.5, 7.2.2, 7.2.4, 7.2.5 • 4: 0.1.2, 1.2.2, 1.9.1, 1.9.3, 1.9.4, 2.2.3, 2.2.4, 2.2.5, 5.2.4, 7.2.1, 7.2.2, 7.2.3, 7.2.5, 7.4.2 • 5: 0.1.3, 7.2.2, 7.2.4, 7.2.5 • 6: 0.1.3, 1.9.7, 1.9.8, 2.1.2, 7.2.1, 7.2.5 • 7: 0.1.2, 7.1.4, 7.2.1, 7.4.7 • RS: 0.1.2, 1.9.2, 7.2.2 • WS: 1.9.2, 1.9.7, 7.2.2	Emphasized are the following: • Participate as a member of a team • Acquire and evaluate information • Understand systems • Know how to learn • Organize and maintain information • Creative thinking • Interpret and communicate information	Emphasized are the following: • Reflect on and reevaluate opinions and ideas • Find and use community resources and services • Communicate so that others understand • Participate in group processes and decision making	• 1: 77.03, 77.04, 83.12 • 2: 77.02, 83.06 • 3: 77.01, 77.04, 83.04, 83.13 • 4: 77.01 • 5: 84.02, 83.18 • 6: 77.04, 83.13, 85.02 • 7: 66.01, 66.19 • RS: 83.05 • WS: 83.16

Scope and Sequence

Unit	Life Skills		Critical Thinking	Vocabulary	Grammar
	Listening and Speaking	**Reading and Writing**			
3 **Your Health** *page 40*	• Talk about a health emergency • Talk about types of health care professionals and specialties • Listen to phone conversations between patients and doctors' offices • Role-play phone conversations between patients and doctors' offices • Clarify information • Talk about food labels and nutrition • Talk about immunizations • Talk about healthy and unhealthy diets	• Read about health care professionals and specialties • Read nutrition labels • Read an online schedule book • Write appointments in a schedule book • Read about immunizations • Read a graph • Take notes **Spotlight: Reading** Use context clues **Spotlight: Writing** Punctuation marks	• Classify • Analyze • Make inferences • Use context clues • Prioritize	• Types of health care professionals and specialties • Nutritional labels • Words about immunization • Synonyms	• Adverb clauses of time • Adverb clauses of reason and contrast
4 **Rights and Responsibilities** *page 58*	• Talk about Washington D.C. • Talk about marches and protests • Talk about rights and responsibilities • Discuss social issues • Listen to conversations about educational system • Express agreement and disagreement • Talk about government agencies • Talk about unions	• Read about marches and protests • Read and take notes on rights and responsibilities • Read charts about education in the U.S. • Read about government agencies • Write initials of agencies to contact in emergencies • Read about acronyms vs. initials • Read and write about work unions • Scan a reading **Spotlight: Reading** Adjust your reading speed **Spotlight: Writing** Identify purpose for writing business letters	• Analyze • Rank information • Summarize • Predict • Apply knowledge to new situations	• U.S. constitutional rights and responsibilities • Educational system • Homonyms • Government agencies • Workers' rights • Unions	• Active and passive verbs • Forming the passive

Civics Concepts	Math Skills	CASAS Life Skill Competencies	SCANS Competencies (Workplace)	EFF Content Standards	Literacy Completion Points (LCPs)
• Understand when to call 911 • Understand types of health care professionals • Determine who to see for different health issues • Understand and analyze food labels • Analyze personal health habits	**Focus on Math:** Convert numbers to percentages	• **1:** 0.1.2, 2.5.1, 7.2.1, 7.2.2, 7.2.6, 7.5.1 • **2:** 0.1.2, 3.1.3, 7.2.1, 7.2.3, 7.2.5, 7.4.2 • **3:** 0.1.2, 0.1.6, 2.1.8, 3.1.2, 3.1.3, 3.2.4, 7.2.1, 7.4.2 • **4:** 0.1.2, 1.6.1, 3.5.1, 3.5.2, 6.1.1, 6.1.3, 6.1.4, 6.4.2, 7.2.3, 7.2.5, 7.3.2, 7.3.3 • **5:** 0.1.2, 7.2.2 • **6:** 1.1.3, 3.2.2, 6.4.2, 6.4.3, 6.7.1 • **7:** 0.1.2, 7.1.4, 7.2.4, 7.4.7 • **RS:** 7.2.1, 7.2.4, 7.4.1 • **WS:** 7.2.2, 7.4.1	Emphasized are the following: • Decision making • See things in the mind's eye • Self-management • Acquire and evaluate information • Organize and maintain information • Know how to learn • Reasoning • Creative thinking • Problem solving	Emphasized are the following: • Provide for physical needs • Participate in group processes and decision making • Organize and maintain information • Communicate so that others understand • Reflect on and reevaluate opinions and ideas • Find, interpret, and analyze diverse sources of information • Give and receive support outside the immediate family • Help self and others	• **1:** 75.01, 83.13 • **2:** 75.01, 83.06, 83.14 • **3:** 74.01, 83.02, 83.04, 83.13 • **4:** 75.03 • **5:** 83.16 • **6:** 75.01, 75.05 • **7:** 83.02, 83.18 • **RS:** 83.06 • **WS:** 78.01
• Identify U.S. constitutional rights and responsibilities • Understand the U.S. educational system • Identify which government agencies to use for different needs • Understand educational rights and options • Understand protests and marches	**Focus on Math:** Understand bar and line graphs	• **1:** 0.1.2, 2.7.3, 5.3.1, 5.3.2, 7.2.2, 7.5.1 • **2:** 0.1.2, 5.2.2, 5.3.2, 5.6.3, 7.2.1 • **3:** 0.1.2, 1.1.3, 6.7.2, 7.2.1, 7.2.3, 7.2.5, 7.4.2 • **4:** 1.6.2, 1.6.3, 5.3.2, 5.6.2, 7.2.1, 7.2.4 • **5:** 0.1.2, 7.2.2 • **6:** 1.1.3, 4.2.2, 4.2.3, 6.7.1, 6.7.2, 6.7.4, 7.2.1, 7.2.2 • **7:** 0.1.2, 7.1.4, 7.2.4, 7.4.7 • **RS:** 7.2.1, 7.2.2, 7.2.5, 7.4.1, 7.4.3 • **WS:** 4.6.2, 7.2.1	Emphasized are the following: • Participate as a member of a team • See things in the mind's eye • Know how to learn • Reasoning • Acquire and evaluate information • Organize and maintain information • Problem solve • Understand how systems work • Work within the system • Interpret and communicate information	Emphasized are the following: • Reflect on and reevaluate opinions and ideas • Find and use community resources and services • Recognize and understand your human and legal rights and civic responsibilities • Communicate so that others understand • Participate in group processes and decision making • Figure out how systems work	• **1:** 80.01, 83.12 • **2:** 80.01, 83.05, 83.06 • **3:** 82.01, 82.03, 83.04, 83.13 • **4:** 70.05, 80.02, 83.10, 83.14 • **5:** 84.03, 83.18 • **6:** 70.04, 83.05, 83.13 • **7:** 83.02, 83.18 • **RS:** 70.04, 83.14 • **WS:** 83.05, 83.08

Scope and Sequence

	Life Skills				
Unit	Listening and Speaking	Reading and Writing	Critical Thinking	Vocabulary	Grammar
5 **Consumer News and Views** *page 76*	• Discuss advertising • Talk about shopping and comparison shopping • Listen to conversations between customers and salespeople • Role-play conversations between customers and salespeople • Discuss food shopping tips • Talk about finding housing • Express doubt **Focus on Pronunciation:** Intonation in tag questions	• Read advertisements • Read tips for consumers and means of credit • Write definitions from context • Write a shopping list and compare ads • Read tips for food shopping • Read housing ads **Spotlight: Reading** Use a dictionary **Spotlight: Writing** Write a letter of complaint	• Analyze advertisements • Use context clues • Compare • Evaluate	• Advertisements • Shopping terms • Food shopping tips • Housing ads	• Tag questions
6 **Rules and Laws** *page 94*	• Talk about courtrooms and people in them • Summarize • Talk about a bar graph • Talk about types of crime and common laws • Listen to recorded messages • Listen to information about getting a marriage and driver's license • Talk about getting a marriage and driver's license • Paraphrase • Talk about traffic tickets • Talk about neighborhood problems **Focus on Pronunciation:** Changing stress on *that*	• Read roles of people in a courtroom • Read journal entries • Read a bar graph • Read checklists about getting a marriage and driver's license • Take notes on prerecorded instructions • Read about traffic citations • Write details about traffic citations • Read about community involvement **Spotlight: Reading** Recognize cause and effect **Spotlight: Writing** Use graphic organizers for writing	• Sequence • Summarize • Compare • Paraphrase • Interpret	• Courtroom language • Types of crimes • Word forms • Instructions to obtain a marriage license • Instructions to obtain a driver's license • Citations	• Adjective clauses

Civics Concepts	Math Skills	CASAS Life Skill Competencies	SCANS Competencies (Workplace)	EFF Content Standards	Literacy Completion Points (LCPs)
• Engage in comparison shopping • Understand impulse buying • Analyze advertisements • Analyze personal shopping behavior • Identify financial service options for making purchases		• **1:** 0.1.2, 1.2.1, 7.1.1, 7.2.3, 7.2.5 • **2:** 0.1.2, 1.3.1, 1.3.3, 1.6.3, 7.2.1, 7.2.3, 7.2.4 • **3:** 0.1.2, 1.3.3, 7.2.1, 7.2.4, 7.2.6 • **4:** 1.1.7, 1.2.1, 1.2.2, 1.2.3, 1.2.4, 7.2.3 • **5:** 7.2.2, 7.2.5, 7.2.6 • **6:** 1.4.2, 7.2.3, 7.2.6 • **7:** 0.1.2, 7.1.4, 7.2.4, 7.4.7 • **RS:** 7.2.2, 7.2.4, 7.4.5 • **WS:** 0.1.2, 1.6.3	Emphasized are the following: • See things in the mind's eye • Understand systems • Analyze and communicate information • Creative thinking • Decision making • Acquire and evaluate information • Organize and maintain information • Problem solving • Participate as a member of a team • Reasoning • Use resources wisely	Emphasized are the following: • Participate in group processes and decision making • Provide for physical needs • Identify and monitor problems • Listen to and learn from others' experiences and ideas • Communicate with others inside and outside the organization • Find and use community resources and services • Put ideas and directions into action • Teach children	• **1:** 79.03, 83.04 • **2:** 79.03, 83.06 • **3:** 83.02, 83.04 • **4:** 79.03 • **5:** 83.16 • **6:** 79.01, 83.01, 85.01 • **7:** 83.02, 83.18 • **RS:** 83.09 • **WS:** 83.14, 83.15
• Interpret basic court procedures • Understand requirements for obtaining licenses • Understand different types of crimes • Understand information about traffic tickets		• **1:** 0.1.2, 5.3.3, 5.5.3, 5.6.3, 7.2.1, 7.2.2, 7.2.3, 7.4.2, 7.4.3 • **2:** 1.1.3, 5.3.1, 5.3.7, 6.7.2, 7.2.3 • **3:** 1.9.2, 2.1.7, 2.5.7, 5.3.1, 7.2.1, 7.4.2 • **4:** 1.9.1, 5.3.5, 5.3.7, 7.2.1, 7.4.2, 7.4.3 • **5:** 0.1.2, 7.2.2, 7.2.5, 7.2.6 • **6:** 5.6.1, 5.6.2, 7.2.5 • **7:** 0.1.2, 7.1.4, 7.2.4, 7.4.7 • **RS:** 7.2.1, 7.2.4, 7.4.2 • **WS:** 7.2.3, 7.4.1, 7.4.2	Emphasized are the following: • Know how to learn • See things in the mind's eye • Analyze and communicate information • Decision making • Responsibility • Integrity and honesty • Acquire and evaluate information • Organize and maintain information • Problem solving • Work well with others	Emphasized are the following: • Participate in group processes and decision making • Identify and monitor problems, community needs, strengths, and resources • Develop a sense of self that reflects your history, values, beliefs, and roles in the larger community • Reflect on and reevaluate your opinions and ideas • Get involved in the community and get others involved • Define common values and goals and resolve conflict • Listen to and learn from others' experiences and ideas • Use technology • Recognize and understand your human and legal rights and civic responsibilities	• **1:** 80.04, 83.07 • **2:** 80.01, 83.06, 83.13 • **3:** 74.01, 77.02, 83.01, 83.02, 83.04 • **4:** 77.02, 77.03, 83.05 • **5:** 83.16, 84.02 • **6:** 80.02, 85.01 • **7:** 83.02, 83.18 • **RS:** 83.05, 83.15 • **WS:** 83.13, 83.14, 83.15

Scope and Sequence

Unit	Life Skills		Critical Thinking	Vocabulary	Grammar
	Listening and Speaking	Reading and Writing			
7 **Career Paths** *page 112*	• Talk about workplace situations • Talk about workplace responsibilities and behavior • Talk about interviews • Listen to job interviews • Roleplay job interviews • Discuss ideal employees and employers • Describe workplace tasks • Expand responses to questions	• Read work rules • Read online job postings • Write a job description • Write job tasks • Read an employment application • Read a company profile **Spotlight: Reading** Identify a sequence of events **Spotlight: Writing** Understand the writing process	• Solve problems • Analyze • Evaluate • Rank job benefits • Solve problems based on new information	• Workplace skills and behavior • Prefixes • Word forms • Classified job postings	• Past perfect • Past unreal conditional
8 **Money Matters** *page 130*	• Talk about household budgets • Talk about expenses • Listen to conversations about banking • Talk about protecting your money • Talk about financial terms • Give advice	• Read questions about money issues • Read about credit cards • Read about ways to save and invest • Take notes • Write a budget **Spotlight: Reading** Compare and contrast **Spotlight: Writing** Use transition words	• Evaluate • Analyze • Apply knowledge • Compare banking alternatives	• Expenses and budgeting • Banking • Credit cards	• Quoted speech • Reported speech

Appendices

Correlations to National Standards

Civics Concepts	Math Skills	CASAS Life Skill Competencies	SCANS Competencies (Workplace)	EFF Content Standards	Literacy Completion Points (LCPs)
• Understand and analyze appropriate workplace behavior • Understand how to interview effectively • Understand and rank job benefits • Identify job performance in an employee evaluation form	**Focus on Math:** Compute averages	• **1:** 0.1.3, 4.4.1, 4.8.2, 7.2.5, 7.2.7, 7.3.2 • **2:** 4.1.3, 4.1.6, 7.2.1, 7.2.3 • **3:** 0.1.2, 0.2.4, 4.1.2, 4.1.5, 4.1.7, 7.2.2, 7.2.5 • **4:** 0.1.3, 4.4.2, 4.4.4, 7.2.3, 7.2.4, 7.2.5, 7.2.6 • **5:** 7.2.2, 7.2.6 • **6:** 1.1.8, 4.2.1, 6.7.5, 7.2.1, 7.2.2, 7.2.4, 7.2.7 • **7:** 0.1.2, 7.1.4, 7.4.7 • **RS:** 7.2.3, 7.2.5, 7.4.2 • **WS:** 7.2.3, 7.2.6, 7.4.2	Emphasized are the following: • Interpret and communicate information • See things in the mind's eye • Reasoning • Work well with others • Know how to learn • Acquire and evaluate information • Organize and maintain information • Self-management • Creative thinking • Use resources wisely • Self esteem	Emphasized are the following: • Participate in group processes and decision making • Pursue personal self-improvement • Create a vision of the future • Plan and renew career goals • Balance and support work, career, and personal goals • Organize, plan, and prioritize work and use resources • Reflect on and reevaluate your opinions and ideas • Find and get a job • Communicate with others inside and outside the organization	• **1:** 69.01, 70.01, 70.02 • **2:** 69.01, 69.02, 83.06 • **3:** 69.03, 70.01, 83.02, 83.04 • **4:** 69.01, 70.01, 71.02, 83.14 • **5:** 83.16, 83.18, 84.01 • **6:** 71.01, 83.05, 83.14 • **7:** 83.02, 83.18 • **RS:** 83.07, 83.17 • **WS:** 83.13, 83.15
• Interpret credit card applications • Understand the use of credit • Understand a budget • Understand interest rates • Understand banking services	**Focus on Math:** Understand rates	• **1:** 1.5.1, 6.0.3, 6.0.4, 6.4.3, 7.1.1, 7.2.6, 7.4.3 • **2:** 1.3.2, 1.8.3, 6.7.2, 7.2.1, 7.2.5, 7.3.2 • **3:** 0.1.6, 1.2.2, 1.8.1, 1.8.5, 7.2.3, 7.2.5 • **4:** 1.6.2, 7.2.5, 7.3.2 • **5:** 0.1.2, 7.2.2 • **6:** 1.2.4, 4.2.1, 6.1.3 • **7:** 0.1.2, 7.1.4, 7.2.4, 7.4.7 • **RS:** 7.2.3, 7.4.2 • **WS:** 7.2.2, 7.2.6	Emphasized are the following: • See things in the mind's eye • Acquire and evaluate information • Reasoning • Problem solving • Analyze and communicate information • Use resources wisely • Understand how systems work	Emphasized are the following: • Manage resources • Provide for physical needs • Educate self and others	• **1:** 76.02, 83.13 • **2:** 76.01, 83.06, 83.13, 83.14 • **3:** 76.01, 83.02, 83.04 • **4:** 83.05, 83.06, 83.14 • **5:** 83.02, 83.04, 83.18 • **6:** 69.05, 83.13 • **7:** 83.02, 83.18 • **RS:** 83.05, 83.13, 83.14 • **WS:** 83.16, 83.18

OBJECTIVE

Getting to Know Your Classmates

1. Evaluate, page 2

★ Introduce yourself to the class. Explain that in the first activity students will learn about introductions and greetings.

★ Have students look at the first photo. Ask questions (*Who do you see? What is he doing? What is he saying?*).

★ Have students look at the photos and read what the people are saying. Then have them check *Good start* or *Not a good start.*

★ Have students check their answers with a partner.

★ Go over the example. Call on students to share their answers with the class and tell what they liked and disliked about each conversation.

ANSWER KEY:

Answers may vary.
  1. Good start;
  2. Not a good start (no information);
  3. Good start;
  4. Not a good start (we don't usually ask about marital status right away)

Culture Notes:

★ Your students may have different responses to the introductions.

★ In less formal introductions, we sometimes give our first names only, although it is always polite to give both first and last name.

★ Some of your students might be surprised that several responses asked questions. Point out that we often "make small talk" to keep the conversation going and show polite interest.

★ Make sure students are aware that we don't usually ask about marital status or other personal questions right away. We do often talk about the weather or where someone lives or goes to school.

2. Talk About It 🎧, page 3

★ Have students read the conversation silently while you read the conversation or play the tape or CD.

★ Ask comprehension questions (*Do the speakers know each other? How do you know? What are 3 questions that were asked? What else did they talk about?*).

★ Go over the directions. Remind students to use the conversation as a model.

★ Have students stand and move around the room to ask and answer questions and complete the chart.

★ When everyone has talked to 3 classmates, call on students to tell the class about one classmate.

3. Look It Over, page 3

★ Tell students that previewing, or looking over, a textbook can often tell them a lot about the course.

★ Go over the directions.

★ Have students look at the book and answer the questions.

★ Have students check their answers with a partner.

★ Go over the answers with the class.

ANSWER KEY:

1. 8; 2. Consumer News and Views; 3. 53; 4. 7; 5. Glossary; 6. Map; 7. Grammar Reference Guide

EXPANSION ACTIVITY: Scavenger Hunt

★ Put students in pairs to create 10 more questions about information in the book. Walk around to monitor the activity and provide help as needed.

★ Have each pair exchange sentences with another pair and complete.

★ Have the group of four go over the answers with each other.

★ Call on students to tell the class about something else in the book.

Skills and Abilities

UNIT OVERVIEW

LESSON	OBJECTIVE	TEACHER'S EDITION PAGE NUMBER
1. What skills do you want to learn?	Exploring Continuing Education	p. 5
2. What skills do you need?	Identifying Job Skills	p. 7
3. Please leave a message.	Analyzing Telephone Skills	p. 9
4. Writing Skills	Evaluating Writing Skills	p. 13
5. Do you know if Maria is married?	Asking Indirect Questions	p. 15
6. Job Interview Questions	Describing Skills and Abilities	p. 17
7. What do you know?	Review and Assessment	p. 20
Spotlight: Reading Strategy	Making Inferences	p. 23
Spotlight: Writing Strategy	Writing Business Letters	p. 24

Big Picture Expansion Activities

FOCUS	ACTIVITY	SUGGESTED USE
Speaking	Which class is it?	Lesson 3
Reading	Course Catalog	Lesson 6
Grammar	Do you know?	Lesson 5
Writing	Describing Skills and Activities	Lesson 7
Speaking Assessment	Talking about the Big Picture	Lesson 7

Big Picture Expansion Activity Worksheets

WORKSHEET NUMBER/FOCUS	TITLE	TEACHER'S EDITION PAGE NUMBER
1. Grammar	Do you know?	p. 181
2. Reading	Course Catalog	p. 182

OBJECTIVE

Exploring Continuing Education

TRY THIS STRATEGY

Setting Goals

1. Warm Up, page 4

★ Put the Big Picture color transparency for Unit 1, Lesson 1 on the overhead projector, or have students look at the Big Picture in their books.

★ To set the context, ask questions about the picture (*Who do you see in the picture? What's happening?*).

★ Direct students' attention to the course schedule and ask comprehension questions (*When is the photography course? How much does it cost to take tai chi? How long is the interviewing skills class?*).

★ As students talk about the Big Picture, write key vocabulary words on the board.

★ Read the questions aloud.

★ Put students in pairs or small groups and have them discuss the questions.

★ Call on students to tell the class about their pair or small group discussion.

EXPANSION ACTIVITY: Partner Interview

★ Write on the board: *name, country, greatest learning experience to date.*

★ Model the activity. Introduce yourself by name and tell where you were born. Describe your greatest learning experience to date and how it helped your personal growth.

★ Put students in pairs to share names, countries, and greatest learning experiences.

★ Call on students to introduce their partners to the class.

2. Identify, page 4

★ Go over the directions.

★ Direct students' attention to the Big Picture. Ask students to list 6 activities they see in the pictures.

★ Have students check the activities they know how to do or would like to learn to do.

★ Call on students to share their ideas with the class.

★ Have students talk to their classmates to find a partner who wants to learn to do the same things. Then have partners list 3 ways they could learn the skill.

★ Call on students to share their ideas with the class.

ANSWER KEY:

Answers will vary but may include:
using a computer, writing, repairing/fixing an engine, cooking, making pottery, making speeches, speaking in public

EXPANSION ACTIVITY: Find Someone Who

★ Explain that students should find a classmate who already has one of the skills listed in Activity 2. Remind students that they can only write down each person's name once.

★ Model the activity. Write a skill on the board (*repair computers*). Call on a student and ask about the skill (*Do you know how to repair computers?*). If the student answers in the affirmative, write the student's name next to the skill on the board.

★ Have students stand and walk around the room asking classmates about the skills (*Do you know how to take photographs?*) and writing down names.

★ Call on students to tell the class about a skill someone has.

3. Write, page 4

★ Go over the directions.

★ Have students complete the registration form.

★ Put students in pairs to share their ideas.

★ Call on students to tell the class about the classes they want to take.

Culture/Civics Notes:

★ You may want to point out that adults frequently take classes for personal growth or to enhance job skills, even after their formal education is completed.

★ Students may be surprised to discover all the places that offer classes for personal growth: continuing education programs, park and recreation departments, museums, theaters, community arts organizations, and community colleges. The Expansion Activity below will help students explore these options.

EXPANSION ACTIVITY: Research

★ Brainstorm a list of places where adults can take classes for personal growth in your community. Write the ideas on the board.

★ For an out-of-class assignment, have students go online or in person to find out about classes for adults at one of the places on the board. Have students list 3 classes that are available that they find interesting.

★ Call on students to share their ideas with the class.

OBJECTIVE

Identifying Job Skills

VOCABULARY

affect	encourage
behavior	essential
clearly	interact
come up with	interpersonal
comprehend	leave out
concentrate	personal responsibility
concisely	proficient
cooperative	resolve
distracted	share

1. Warm Up, page 6

★ Have students look at the pictures. Ask: *What are some skills you need at work?*

★ Read the questions aloud.

★ Put students in pairs or small groups and have them discuss the questions.

★ Call on students to tell the class about their pair or small group discussion.

EXPANSION ACTIVITY: Free Write

★ Tell students that you are going to give them a phrase. They should write for 5 minutes on that phrase.

★ Explain the rules of this free write: students shouldn't worry about spelling or grammar, they shouldn't correct, single words or phrases are fine, it's okay to stray from the topic, they need to keep the pen or pencil moving.

★ Write a phrase on the board (*a good parent, a good student, a great teacher, a best friend*).

★ Set a time limit of 5 minutes. After 5 minutes, have students underline a phrase or sentence in their writing that they like.

★ Put students in pairs to talk about what they wrote.

★ Call on students to share their ideas with the class.

2. Read and Respond, page 6

★ Go over the directions.

★ Have students read the information and circle their answers.

★ Have students rank the skills from very good (1) to not very good (6).

★ Call on students to share their ideas with the class.

ANSWER KEY:

Answers will vary.

EXPANSION ACTIVITY: Skill Sort

★ Write ideas such as the following on slips of paper, enough so each student gets one slip: *asks others for their ideas, encourages others, gives constructive feedback, asks questions if he or she doesn't understand, maintains good eye contact, uses good grammar, sticks to the point, pays attention to the feelings of others, is polite, has good ideas, can analyze a situation, is clear, doesn't use unnecessary words, gives credit to others.*

★ Point out that each of these skills belongs to a larger category such as *interpersonal skills* or *problem-solving skills.* Have students stand and walk around to find classmates who represent the same types of skills. Point out that some examples may represent more than one type of skill.

★ Have students stand with students who belong to the same category.

★ When students have sorted themselves, ask them to tell the class the specific skill they have and how it demonstrates the job-skill category they represent. Encourage discussion and allow students to move to another category.

3. Evaluate, page 6

★ Go over the directions.

★ Have students read the situations and identify the skill that is needed in each situation and whether or not the person has it.

★ Put students in pairs to compare their answers. Have students talk in pairs about what they would do in that situation.

★ Call on students to share their ideas with the class.

★★★★★★★★★★★★★★★★★★★★★★★★★★★★★★★★★★★★★

TRY THIS STRATEGY: Setting Goals
★★★★★★★★★★★★★★★★★★★★★★★★★★★★★★★★★★★★★

★ Read the strategy aloud.

★ Have students number the goals in order from most useful (1) to least useful (5).

★ Put students in pairs to compare their ideas with a partner.

★ Call on students to share their ideas with the class.

ANSWER KEY:

1. Laura did not have good oral-communication skills.
2. Charles did not show good interpersonal skills/team skills.
3. Violet is showing good interpersonal skills.
4. Sean does not have good problem-solving skills.

OBJECTIVE

Analyzing Telephone Skills

COMMUNICATION STRATEGY

Stating Your Purpose

EXPANSION ACTIVITY:
Telephone Etiquette Sort

★ Have students close their books.

★ Put students in pairs or small groups to brainstorm some things they should and shouldn't do on the telephone.

★ Or enlarge and photocopy the list below (enough so each pair or small group has a set). Cut along the lines and distribute to pairs or small groups.

★ Have students sort the behaviors into *dos* and *don'ts*.

★ Call on students to share their ideas with the class.

Speak clearly.	Keep someone on hold for a minute.
Hang up without saying goodbye.	Speak softly when you use a cell phone in a public place.
Be concise when you leave a message.	Leave a message with as much detail as possible.
Use a cell phone in a restaurant.	Use a cell phone at school.
Avoid using filler words such as "you know," "like," and "you guys."	Forget whom you are calling.
Identify yourself when you leave a phone message.	Identify yourself on your answering machine message.
State your purpose for calling.	Say negative things on a message.
Turn your cell phone off in libraries.	Interrupt one phone call to take another.
Talk to other people when you are leaving a message.	

1. Warm Up, page 8

★ Have students look at the picture on page 8. To set the context, ask questions (*What do you see on page 8? When do we use this?*)

★ Read the questions aloud and have students repeat.

★ Put students in pairs or small groups and have them discuss the questions.

★ Call on students to tell the class about their pair or small group discussion.

Culture Notes:

★ You may want to point out that cell phone etiquette is the subject of much discussion. You could begin the discussion by asking students if they have had experiences where cell phone use seemed rude.

★ Point out that in most places where cell phone use is not allowed, it is usually posted (movies, libraries, hospitals). Explain that if students are unsure whether it is appropriate to use a cell phone in a particular place, they should probably avoid it.

2. Listen for General Information 🎧, page 8

★ Go over the directions.

★ Have students read the sentences.

★ Have students listen and read the sentences again while you read the conversations or play the tape or CD.

★ Have students write the appropriate number next to each sentence.

★ Have students check their answers with a partner.

★ Read the conversation or play the tape or CD again if necessary.

LISTENING SCRIPT

2. Listen for General Information, page 8

Listen to 6 telephone calls and number them in order from first (1) to last (6).

Telephone call #1

A: You have reached the Smith residence. Please leave a message.

B: Hi, Pat. This is Leila calling. I just wanted to ask if you could give me a ride to the meeting tomorrow. My car isn't working again! Call when you can. 555-8724. Thanks. Bye.

Telephone call #2

Woman: You have reached the Continuing Education Office at Redwood High. Our office hours are Monday through Friday from 10:00 to 7:00 and on Saturday from 10:00 to 2:00. We are closed on Sunday. Please call during our business hours. Thank you for calling. Goodbye.

Telephone call #3

A: The Paper Shop.

B: Hi. Can I speak to Mr. Takase, please?

A: I'm sorry, but Mr. Takase just left the office. Can I take a message?

B: Well, this is John Lee with Safe Software. I'm returning Mr. Takase's call.

A: I see. Do you want him to call you back?

B: Well, I'm going to be in and out today. Do you know when he'll be back in the office?

A: He should be here between 2:00 and 5:00 today.

B: Well, I'll try to call him back this afternoon then.

A: Okay. I'll tell him you called.

B: Thank you.

A: You're welcome. Goodbye.

B: Goodbye.

Telephone call #4

A: Hello.

B: Hi. Could I speak to Jan, please?

A: I'm sorry, but she's not at home right now.

B: Do you know when she'll be back?

A: No, I'm not sure.

B: Well, could you tell her that Maria called? I just wanted to apologize for missing the meeting today.

A: Okay. Do you want her to call you back?

B: No, that's not necessary. Tell her I'll see her next week.

A: Okay. Will do.

B: Thanks.

A: You're welcome. Bye.

B: Bye.

Telephone call #5

A: Metro Supply. This is Joe speaking.

B: Could I speak with Tom Field, please?

A: I'm sorry, but he's in a meeting now. Can I take a message?

B: Sure. Could you tell him that Betty Grand called to invite him to a lunch meeting next Wednesday at noon?

A: Could you spell your last name, please?

B: Yes, that's G-r-a-n-d.

A: And you want to invite him to a lunch meeting next Tuesday at noon?

B: Ah, that was Wednesday not Tuesday.

A: Yes, of course. Next Wednesday at noon. Does Mr. Field have your phone number?

B: Well, I think so. But let me give it to you anyway. It's 555-3345.

A: Ah, sorry. Could you repeat that?

B: Sure. 555-3345.

A: Thanks. I'll give him your message, Ms. Grand.

B: Thank you. Bye bye.

A: Bye now.

Telephone call #6

A: Southwest Cartage. This is Ginger speaking.

B: Hello. My name is Sam Sellers, and I'm calling about the sales job advertised in the newspaper.

A: Yes, you need to speak to Ms. Parker. Let me see if she's in her office. Can you hold for a second?

B: Sure.

A: I'm sorry, but she isn't in her office. Can I have her call you back?

B: Sure, when it's convenient for her.

A: Your name again, please?

B: Sam Sellers. S-e-l-l-e-r-s.

A: Thanks. And you're calling about the sales job?

B: Yes, that's right. I've been in sales and marketing for over 7 years.

A: And your phone number?

B: It's 555-6688.

A: 555-6688.

B: Yes, that's right.

A: Okay. I'll have her call you back.

B: Thank you.

A: You're welcome. Goodbye.

B: Bye.

ANSWER KEY:

6, 4, 1, 2, 5, 3

3. Listen for Specific Information 🎧, page 8

★ Go over the directions.

★ Have students read the telephone messages.

★ Have students write the missing information while you read the conversations or play the tape or CD.

★ Have students check their answers with a partner.

★ Read the conversations or play the tape or CD again if necessary.

★ Go over the answers with the class.

ANSWER KEY:

1. give her a ride to the meeting tomorrow/ 8724
2. 10–7/10–2/closed
3. Mr. John Lee/call this afternoon
4. apologize for missing the meeting
5. Grand/Tom Field/invite him to lunch/next Wednesday/12:00/3345
6. Sellers/555-6688/❑ Please Call/get information about the sales job

EXPANSION ACTIVITY: Real Messages

★ Check out a list of places that students could call after business hours and get information from a recorded message. Such places might include an adult school, a public school, a museum, a library, and an amusement center. Write down the phone numbers.

★ Assign students one or more of the places on your list. Tell them to write down the information they hear (hours, location, prices, services).

★ Have students compare information with classmates who called the same place.

★ Call on students to tell the class what they found out.

4. Use the Communication Strategy: Stating Your Purpose 🎧, page 8

★ Go over the directions.

★ Direct students' attention to the Communication Strategy box. Go over the information in the box.

★ Say each example and have students repeat.

★ Model the activity with a student. Have the student read the message on the answering machine. Demonstrate how to substitute a different message using your own ideas.

★ Have students work in pairs to practice leaving messages, substituting their own ideas for the underlined words.

★ Walk around to make sure students understand the activity and provide help if needed.

★ Call on volunteers to say their messages to the class. Elicit feedback on the message from the other students.

BIG PICTURE EXPANSION ACTIVITY: SPEAKING—Which class is it?

★ Put the Big Picture color transparency for Unit 1, Lesson 1, on the overhead projector, or have students look at the Big Picture in their books.

★ Put students in pairs. Walk around the room and quietly assign each pair of students a character in the Big Picture.

★ Have students create a telephone conversation in which that character is making a telephone call to his or her teacher. Remind them to use the communication strategy in the conversation.

★ Have students perform their conversations for the class. Have the class guess which class the student is in.

OBJECTIVE

Evaluating Writing Skills

VOCABULARY

according to
accuracy
assess
complex
promotion
sought after
up to

1. Warm Up, page 10

★ Have students look at the pictures on page 10. To set the context, ask questions about the pictures (*What do you see in the pictures? What do they have in common?*)

★ Read the questions aloud. Remind students that when they skim, they should look over the reading quickly to find main ideas or facts.

★ Put students in pairs or small groups and have them discuss the questions.

★ Call on students to tell the class about their pair or small group discussion.

ANSWER KEY:

Title: How Well Do You Write?
Source: Netscape Network
Topic: How well employees need to write

EXPANSION ACTIVITY: Guessing Meaning from Context

★ Review strategies for guessing meaning from context (*using synonyms, comparison or contrast, examples, description, or cause and effect*).

★ Have students look at the highlighted words and write possible definitions. Remind students to use the strategies you reviewed if appropriate.

★ When students are finished, put them in pairs to compare their definitions.

★ Call on students to read definitions only and have the class guess which words the students are defining.

2. Read and Respond, page 10

★ Go over the directions.

★ Have students read the article. Ask comprehension questions (*What are some examples of writing people do on the job? What are some problems people have with writing?*).

★ Read the first question aloud and elicit the answer. Have students answer the questions.

★ Have students check their answers with a partner.

★ Go over the answers with the class.

ANSWER KEY:

1. writing requirements of their jobs;
2. director of the education initiative for the Business Roundtable/because she is an expert;
3. because the demand is greater;
4. It's important for most jobs, and employers often assess writing skills when they hire and promote;
5. *Answers will vary.*

EXPANSION ACTIVITY: Rate Yourself

★ Have students look at the 6 top writing problems on page 11 and put them in order from what they do least well (1) to what they do best (6).

★ Give students a writing prompt such as *What is something you have done that you are proud of?* and have them write a paragraph on that topic.

★ Put students in pairs to exchange paragraphs. Have them rate their partner's writing according to the six problem areas (1 is the greatest problem, 6 is the smallest problem). Point out that self-evaluations may be different from peer evaluations.

★ Have students share their ratings with their partners.

★ Call on students to tell the class about how their ratings compared to their partner's ratings of their writing.

3. Evaluate, page 10

★ Go over the directions.

★ Read each question aloud. Have students answer *yes* or *no* for each email.

★ Have students circle the mistakes and underline the unclear portions. Then have students compare their answers with a partner.

★ Call on students to share their ideas with the class.

ANSWER KEY:

	Email #1	Email #2
1.	yes	no
2.	yes	yes
3.	yes	yes
4.	no	yes
5.	no	yes

EXPANSION ACTIVITY: Revise

★ Have students rewrite email #1 to correct and improve the writing.

★ Have students compare ideas with a partner.

★ Call on students to share their ideas with the class.

ANSWER KEY:

Email 1: Corrections are underlined; information in italics is not essential.
Hi Joe,
Joyce P. just called to say that we <u>should</u> meet on Monday at 3. I'm busy on Monday<u>,</u> so I was wondering if you could go for me<u>.</u> *By the way,* the meeting is about the new dress code<u>,</u> *so I think it's important for someone to go.* <u>I'm</u> sorry to ask you on such short notice, *but my schedule on Monday is really full.* Let me know as soon as you can if you *are available to attend this meeting*/can go on Monday at 3:00<u>.</u>
Ted

Email 2:
Paul<u>,</u>
The next meeting of the Open Space Committee is on December 12th at 7 P.M.
<u>I</u> hope you can attend.
Barbara

4. Write, page 10

★ Go over the directions.

★ Put students in pairs. Have students write email messages to their partners.

★ Have students evaluate their partner's message.

★ Call on students to tell the class one thing they could improve in their email messages.

Culture Notes:

★ This may be a good time to introduce the concept of *netiquette*. Explain to students that netiquette is the set of rules we should follow in writing emails in order to be polite.

★ Point out that employee emails can be read by supervisors, so they should be polite and professional.

EXPANSION ACTIVITY: Take It Online

★ Have students use their favorite search engines and enter the key word "netiquette." Have students write down three things they learn about proper netiquette.

★ Call on students to share their ideas with the class. Write the ideas on the board.

★ Have students email you (or each other) following the netiquette guidelines the class discussed.

OBJECTIVE

Asking Indirect Questions

Indirect *Yes/No* Questions, page 12

★ Have students look at the notes in the box. Read the information and examples aloud.

★ Ask comprehension questions (*What word do you use with yes/no indirect questions? How is the word order in indirect questions different from the order in direct questions? What are some ways to begin an indirect question?*).

Grammar Notes:

★ Students have seen *if* used in conditional clauses. Make sure they understand its different use here.

★ Students may have heard *whether* used in indirect questions also. You could point out that that is another way to make indirect questions, but you do not need to teach that grammar point here.

★ Make sure students notice that the indirect question is in clause form, not question form (*Do you know <u>what her name is?</u>*, not *Do you know <u>what is her name?</u>*).

1. Write the Question, page 12

★ Read the directions aloud.

★ Go over the first question. Point out that *Do you know if* has been added to the direct question, and the order has been changed.

★ Have students rewrite the questions.

★ Have students check their answers with a partner.

★ Go over the answers with the class.

ANSWER KEY:

1. Do you know/Can you tell me if Hanh is a good writer?
2. Do you know/Can you tell me if Tom has good problem-solving skills?
3. Do you know/Can you tell me if the President of the U.S. is married?
4. Do you know/Can you tell me if Sam called?
5. Do you know/Can you tell me if Jan apologized to Chandra?
6. Do you know/Can you tell me if Lilia registered for a computer class?
7. Do you know/Can you tell me if Miguel has good communication skills?

Indirect *Wh-* Questions, page 13

★ Have students look at the notes in the box. Read the information and examples aloud.

★ Ask comprehension questions (*Does the subject go before or after the verb in indirect questions? In direct questions?*).

2. Write and Ask, page 13

★ Read the directions aloud.

★ Go over the first question. Elicit how to rewrite it as an indirect question.

★ Have students rewrite the questions.

★ Have students compare their answers with a partner.

★ Go over the answers with the class.

★ Put students in pairs to take turns asking and answering the questions.

ANSWER KEY:

1. Do you know/Can you tell me who the President of the United States is?
2. Do you know/Can you tell me where San Diego is?
3. Do you know/Can you tell me how old the President of the U.S. is?
4. Do you know/Can you tell me what time it is?
5. Do you know/Can you tell me what street the post office is on?
6. Do you know/Can you tell me when the teacher's birthday is?
7. Do you know/Can you tell me where Arizona is?
8. Do you know/Can you tell me when class started?
9. Do you know/Can you tell me who wrote this book?
10. Do you know/Can you tell me what the teacher just said?

EXPANSION ACTIVITY: Role Play

★ Write situations on slips of paper (*at a travel agency, train station, bank, registration office at a community college, car dealership*), enough so each pair of students gets one.

★ Put students in pairs and have each pair take a slip.

★ Have students work in pairs to list direct questions people might ask in those situations. Elicit examples and write them on the board (*Do I need a Social Security number to open an account? When does the train for Miami leave? Do I need to pay when I register?*).

★ Model the activity. Ask a volunteer to come to the front of the room. Have the student play the role of a bank teller. Demonstrate how to ask an indirect question (*Can you tell me if I need a Social Security number to open an account?*).

★ Have pairs create conversations for the situations using indirect questions.

★ Call on pairs of students to perform their role plays for the class.

BIG PICTURE EXPANSION ACTIVITY: GRAMMAR—Do you know?

★ Make copies of **Worksheet #1** and distribute them to students.

★ Put the Big Picture color transparency for Unit 1, Lesson 1, on the overhead projector, or have students look at the Big Picture in their books.

★ Instruct students to complete the activities and then check their answers with a partner.

★ Go over the answers with the class.

ANSWER KEY:

Answers will vary.

A.

1. Do you know how long the defensive driving class is?

2. Can you tell me where the public speaking class is?

3. Can you tell me how much the tai chi class costs?

4. Do you know/Can you tell me if the photography class has started?

5. Do you know how long/how many weeks the writing II class is?

6. Do you know/Can you tell me if I will make a pot in the pottery class?

7. Can you tell me if there are any classes that start at 4 P.M.?

8. Do you know/Can you tell me where the basic computer skills class is?

B.

1. Do you know/Can you tell me the location of the pottery class?

2. Do you know/Can you tell me the time of the small engine repair class?

3. Do you know/Can you tell me the number of weeks for/in the photography course?

OBJECTIVE

Describing Skills and Abilities

VOCABULARY

incredibly
overcome
overview

WINDOW ON PRONUNCIATION

Blending words in questions with *you*

1. Warm Up, page 14

★ Go over the directions.

★ Read each question aloud.

★ Put students in pairs or small groups to answer the questions.

★ Call on students to share their ideas with the class.

Culture/Civics Notes:

★ Point out that there are many resources available to practice interviewing skills. Students can go online and research interview questions and tips (as in the Expansion Activity that follows the Window on Pronunciation), or they can find information at career centers on college campuses and in libraries.

EXPANSION ACTIVITY: Compare and Contrast

★ Put students in pairs or small groups according to their country of origin.

★ Have students compare and contrast interview questions typically asked in their country of origin with those asked in the U.S.

★ Call on students to share their ideas with the class.

2. Read and Respond, page 14

★ Go over the directions.

★ Have students read the article and complete the chart.

★ Put students in pairs to compare their charts.

★ Go over the answers with the class.

ANSWER KEY:

Answers are in italics.

Interview question	Do's	Don'ts
Tell me about yourself.	*Give a summary of your work and school background.*	*Tell about your personal life, hobbies, or personal problems.*
What is your greatest strength?	*Identify ways a strength is useful in a work situation.*	*Focus on your strengths at home.*
What is your greatest weakness?	*Focus on the positive not the negative. Tell what you did or are doing to overcome the weakness.*	*Focus on the negative.*

EXPANSION ACTIVITY: Silver Linings

★ Point out that our greatest strengths are often our greatest weaknesses.

★ Model the activity by describing one of your weaknesses/strengths (*I am sometimes too direct in expressing my opinions.*). Elicit ways in which this is both a weakness and a strength (*You might offend people/You are honest and don't waste time.*).

★ Have students write down one of their weaknesses/strengths on a slip of paper. Ask students to write their names on the back of the paper.

★ Collect the slips and redistribute.

★ Give examples of how you could work on your weakness (*I try to be tactful in expressing myself and make sure others have an opportunity to express their ideas.*).

★ Have students rewrite the weakness on the slip as a possible strength.

★ Have students return the slips to the original writers.

★ Call on students to share the ideas with the class.

3. Apply, page 15

★ Go over the directions.

★ Have students read the situations and check the answer they like best.

★ Put students in pairs to share what they liked and disliked about each answer. Call on students to share their answers with the class.

ANSWER KEY:

1. Answer 1, because it focuses on work and education

2. Answer 2, because it discusses the strength in a general way rather than talking about situations at home

3. Answer 2, because it talks about how the person addressed the problem

EXPANSION ACTIVITY: Role Play

★ Put students in pairs to practice asking and answering the questions. Tell students that they should answer the questions about themselves. Have the interviewer evaluate the applicant's responses.

★ Call on volunteers to role play in front of the class. Elicit feedback on the answers from the other students.

BIG PICTURE EXPANSION ACTIVITY: READING—Course Catalog

★ Make copies of **Worksheet #2** and distribute them to students.

★ Put the Big Picture color transparency for Unit 1, Lesson 1 on the overhead projector, or have students look at the Big Picture in their books.

★ Instruct students to complete the activities and then check their answers with a partner.

★ Go over the answers with the class.

ANSWER KEY:

A.

1. Photography; 2. Pottery; 3. Writing; 4. Tai Chi; 5. Italian Cooking; 6. Public Speaking

B.

__6__ sales and marketing assistant

__5__ stay-at-home dad

__1__ newsletter photographer

__3__ secretary

WINDOW ON PRONUNCIATION: Blending Words in Questions with *You*

A. Sometimes when two consonants 🎧, page 15

★ Go over the directions.

★ Have students look at the words in the box while you read them or play the tape or CD.

★ Read the phrases or play the tape or CD a second time, pausing after each phrase to have students repeat.

LISTENING SCRIPT

Window on Pronunciation: Blending Words in Questions with *You*, page 15

A. Sometimes when two consonants are next to each other we blend the sounds together. Listen to the phrases. Listen again and repeat.

can't you	could you
did you	don't you
haven't you	should you
shouldn't you	would you

B. Write the phrases from Activity A in the correct column below 🎧, page 15

★ Have students complete the chart.

★ Read the sentences or play the tape or CD again if necessary. Have students check their answers with a partner.

★ Go over the answers with the class.

ANSWER KEY:

Underlined letters sound like *j* (as in *juice*)
  did <u>y</u>ou
  coul<u>d y</u>ou
  shoul<u>d y</u>ou
  woul<u>d y</u>ou

Underlined letters sound like *ch* (as in *change*)
  can'<u>t y</u>ou
  haven'<u>t y</u>ou
  shouldn'<u>t y</u>ou
  don'<u>t y</u>ou

C. Listen to the sentences 🎧, page 15

★ Go over the directions.
★ Have students look at the sentences and write the missing phrases while you read them or play the tape or CD.
★ Go over the answers with the class.
★ Put students in pairs to practice asking and answering the questions.

LISTENING SCRIPT

C. Listen to the sentences. Write the missing words. Use the correct spelling.

1. <u>Did you</u> have any supervisory experience in your last position?
2. <u>Could you</u> tell me what your greatest strength is?
3. <u>Would you</u> describe your duties in your last job?
4. <u>Would you</u> like to study something new?

ANSWER KEY:

1. Did you; 2. Could you; 3. Would you; 4. Would you

EXPANSION ACTIVITY: Research It

★ For an out-of-class or lab assignment, have students use their favorite search engine and enter "job interview questions."
★ Have students write down 3 new questions (not variations on the 3 in this lesson) that they find online.
★ Call on students to tell the class what other interview questions they found online.

OBJECTIVE

Review and Assessment

1. Listening Review 🎧, page 16

★ Go over the directions for items 1–5 with the class.

★ Read items 1–5 or play the tape or CD. Have the students mark their answers in the Answer Sheet box.

★ Walk around to monitor the activity and help students stay on task.

★ Go over the directions for items 6–10 and repeat the procedure.

★ Have students check their answers for 1–10 with a partner.

★ Go over the answers with the class.

ANSWER KEY:

1. b; 2. a; 3. b; 4. c; 5. a; 6. c; 7. a; 8. b; 9. c; 10. a

LISTENING SCRIPT

1. Listening Review, page 16

Listen and choose the statement that is closest in meaning to the statement you hear. Use the Answer Sheet.

1. Juanita did her share of the work.
2. Bill came up with a solution to the problem.
3. He is a proficient writer.
4. John returned my call.
5. I'm calling about the job in sales.

Listen to each conversation and choose the best answer to the question you hear. Use the Answer Sheet.

6.
A: How is your new employee?
B: Do you mean Sam?
A: Yes. Is he working out okay?
B: Yes, I think so. He seems to work well with everyone on the team.

Question: What does Sam's supervisor say about him?

7.
A: Do you need some help, John?
B: Yes. I could use some help writing this report.
A: Let me ask Jane if she can help. She's a great writer.
B: Thanks.

Question: What is one of Jane's work skills?

8.
A: Johnson Wood Supply. Can I help you?
B: Yes. Is Mr. Taylor in?
A: He's in a meeting right now. Can I take a message?
B: Yes. Could you ask him to call Mike Jones?
A: Does he have your number, Mr. Jones?
B: I think so, but let me give it to you just in case.
A: Okay.
B: It's 555-7993.
A: That's 555-7993.
B: That's right.
A: Okay. I'll give him the message.
B: Thank you.
A: Sure. Bye bye.
B: Bye.

Question: What message did the man leave for Mr. Taylor?

9.
A: Ashwood Town Hall.
B: Can I speak to Cindy Harris, please?
A: She's not in the office right now. Can I take a message?
B: Could you just tell her that Jan Smith called and I'll call back later?
A: Certainly.
B: Thanks, bye.
A: Bye.

Question: What telephone message did the woman leave?

10.

A: Excuse me.

B: Yes.

A: Do you know what time it is?

B: Sure, it's almost one.

A: Thanks.

Question: What did the man want to know?

2. Dictation, page 16

★ Go over the directions.

★ Have students write the sentences as you read the sentences or play the tape or CD.

★ Put students in pairs to compare sentences.

★ Go over the sentences with the class.

LISTENING SCRIPT

2. Dictation, page 16

Listen and write the sentences you hear.

1. He expresses his ideas clearly.
2. Do you have good listening skills?
3. Bob called to get information.

3. Vocabulary Review, page 17

★ Have students look at the chart. Go over the directions and the example.

★ Have students complete the chart and then compare charts with a partner.

★ Go over the answers with the class.

★ Have students choose 6 words and use them to write 6 questions.

★ Put students in pairs to practice asking and answering the questions.

ANSWER KEY:

Noun	Verb
behavior	behave
comprehension	*comprehend*
concentration	*concentrate*
cooperation	cooperate
demand	*demand*
encouragement	*encourage*
distraction	*distract*
interaction	*interact*
promotion	promote
resolution	*resolve*

Adjective	Adverb
clear	*clearly*
concise	*concisely*
cooperative	cooperatively
responsible	responsibly
essential	essentially
proficient	*proficiently*
personal	personally
accurate	*accurately*
soft	*softly*
incredible	*incredibly*

LEARNING LOG, page 17

★ Point out the two sections of the Learning Log: *I know these words* and *I practiced these skills, strategies, and grammar points.*

★ Ask students to check the words they know and what they practiced.

★ Walk around to note what students don't know or didn't practice. Use this information to review areas of difficulty.

BIG PICTURE EXPANSION: SPEAKING ASSESSMENT—Talking about the Big Picture

★ You can use the Big Picture as an individual assessment to place new students in classes, to diagnose difficulties, or to measure progress.

★ Work with one student. Show the Big Picture to the student. Ask: *What do you see in the picture?* Or say: *Tell me about the picture.* Tell the student to speak for as long as possible. Wait a moment for the student to prepare an answer.

★ If the student has difficulty, you can use prompts (*Who do you see? What are the people doing? Where are they?*).

★ You can use a scoring rubric like the one below to rate speakers.

4	Exhibits confidence; begins speaking without prompting Uses some complex sentences, although may make mistakes with irregular forms Can use several tenses
3	Uses sentences, although form may be incorrect Uses more than one tense Can speak for a sustained length of time Responds to prompts, but doesn't need them to begin speaking
2	Can use nouns and verbs in sentences Uses one tense most of the time Answers informational questions Limited vocabulary
1	Can name objects Uses single words Can answer yes/no questions
0	Cannot say anything independently May be able to point to objects when prompted

★ Review areas of difficulty.

TEACHER NOTES:

Things that students are doing well:

_____

_____

_____

_____

Things students need additional help with:

_____

_____

_____

_____

Ideas for further practice or for the next class:

_____

_____

_____

_____

BIG PICTURE EXPANSION ACTIVITY: WRITING—Describing Skills and Activities

★ Put the Big Picture color transparency for Unit 1, Lesson 1 on the overhead projector, or have students look at the Big Picture in their books.

★ Ask the class: *What activities do you see? What skills will students learn?*

★ Have students brainstorm ideas to prepare to write.

★ Have students write a paragraph about the skills that students might need or learn in different courses.

★ Put students in pairs to exchange and read paragraphs. Ask students to provide feedback to their partners.

★ Have students revise paragraphs as necessary.

OBJECTIVE

Making Inferences

VOCABULARY

fulfilled
turn around

Making Inferences, page 18

★ Direct students' attention to the information in the box. Explain the strategy.

★ Go over the examples.

★ Check comprehension by asking questions (*How is an inference different from a fact?*).

1. Read each fact below, page 18

★ Go over the directions.

★ Read the first fact. Elicit the logical inference (*The test was very difficult*). Discuss why this inference is more logical than the other.

★ Have students check the logical inferences for the other facts.

★ Have students check their answers with a partner.

★ Go over the answers with the class.

ANSWER KEY:

1. The test was very difficult.
2. It takes about 4 hours to drive from Boston to New York.
3. Carlos's grandmother understands Spanish.
4. Taka wants to improve her computer skills.
5. Manuel has good interpersonal skills.

2. Read the article, page 19

★ Go over the directions.

★ Have students read the article individually, or have volunteers read it aloud. Then have students answer the questions.

★ Have students check their answers with a partner.

★ Go over the answers with the class.

ANSWER KEY:

1. (*Answer depends on current year.*) 2. having children and getting good jobs; 3. They spoke little English. 4. They own 2 restaurants.
5. expand the dining space and restaurant hours

3. Give an inference, page 19

★ Have students give an inference based on the factual information in the article.

ANSWER KEY:

Answers will vary.
2. They probably worked very hard. 3. They may have felt discouraged. 4. The Trieus felt that their customers' opinions were important. 5. They like living in the U.S.

EXPANSION ACTIVITY:
Newspaper Hunt

★ Have students bring in newspaper articles, or bring some in yourself.

★ Put students in pairs and give each pair an article.

★ Have students write 3 logical inferences based on information stated in the article.

★ Have each pair exchange articles and inferences with another pair and identify the facts that support the inferences.

★ Call on students to share their ideas with the class.

OBJECTIVES

Writing Business Letters

Writing Business Letters, page 20

★ Go over the information in the box.

★ Check comprehension by asking questions (*What does the inside address include? Where does the writer's signature go? What goes in the body?*).

1. Label the parts, page 20

★ Go over the directions.

★ Direct students' attention to the 2 letters and ask questions (*Who wrote Letter A? Who is Letter B to?*).

★ Have students label the parts of each letter. Then have students compare answers with a partner.

★ Go over the answers with the class.

ANSWER KEY:

Letter A: heading, inside address, salutation, body, closing, signature

Letter B: heading, inside address, salutation, body, closing, signature

2. How is the semi-block style different, page 21

★ Go over the directions.

★ Have students answer the question. Then have students compare answers with a partner.

★ Go over the answers with the class.

ANSWER KEY:

Possible answers include:
Heading, closing, and signature in the semiblock are on the right; in the fullblock, they're on the left; paragraphs in the semiblock are indented.

EXPANSION ACTIVITY: Take It Online

★ For an out-of-class or lab assignment, have students use a search engine and enter the words "sample business letter."

★ Have students write down three things they learn.

★ Put students in pairs or small groups to share information.

★ Call on students to share their information with the class.

3. Write a sample business letter 🗀, page 21

★ Go over the directions.

★ Have students write letters. Walk around to monitor the activity and provide help as needed.

★ Have students exchange their letters with a partner, to read and provide feedback.

★ Call on students to read their letters to the class.

EQUIPPED FOR THE FUTURE ROLE

Family

OBJECTIVE

Evaluating Parenting Skills

A. For each category below, Workbook page 12

★ Direct students' attention to the chart. Go over the directions and examples.

★ Have students add two more examples to each category and then compare their answers with a partner.

★ Call on students to share their ideas with the class.

ANSWER KEY:

Answers will vary.

B. Read the article below, Workbook page 12

★ Go over the directions.

★ Have students read the article and write *VI* (very important), *SI* (somewhat important), or *NI* (not important) next to each thing to indicate how important they think it is.

★ Put students in pairs to talk about their answers.

★ Call on students to share their answers with the class.

ANSWER KEY:

Answers will vary.

C. Which of the suggestions, Workbook page 13

★ Go over the directions and the example.

★ Have students write answers and then check their answers with a partner.

★ Go over the answers with the class.

ANSWER KEY:

1. She provides resources at home for learning.
2. She sets a good example.
3. They encourage their daughter to do her best in school.
4. She is involved.
5. He called the teacher early because he thought there might be a problem.

D. Choose the correct form, Workbook page 13

★ Go over the directions.

★ Read the first question and elicit that *involvement* should be written on the line.

★ Have students complete the questions and then check their answers with a partner.

★ Go over the answers with the class.

★ Put students in pairs to practice asking and answering the questions.

ANSWER KEY:

1. involvement; 2. successful; 3. active;
4. enjoyable; 5. encourage; 6. education;
7. support; 8. discipline

 Take It Online, Workbook page 13

★ Go over the directions.

★ Have students use a search engine to find out information about parenting skills.

★ Tell students to write down three interesting things they learn.

★ Call on volunteers to share the information with the class.

EXPANSION ACTIVITY: Tell a Story

★ Put students in pairs to tell a story about a positive experience they had in school.

★ Call on students to tell the class about their partner's positive experience.

★ Have students write a paragraph about their own experience and then exchange paragraphs with a partner for feedback.

★ Ask students to revise if necessary.

★ Collect the paragraphs and compile them into a class booklet about positive school experiences.

★ Have students share their stories with family members.

EQUIPPED FOR THE FUTURE ROLE

Community

OBJECTIVE

Interacting with Community Services

A. Read questions 1 and 2, Workbook page 14

★ Direct students' attention to the photo and article and ask: *What do you think this article is about?*

★ Go over the directions.

★ Have students answer the questions and check their answers with a partner.

★ Call on students to share their answers with the class.

ANSWER KEY:

1. When she was in second grade, someone told her she could be a doctor. She heads a health clinic. She volunteers 3 hours a week in the second grade.

2. It helps people like Dr. Gomez get connected with children in school. It orients volunteers. It places volunteers in a school convenient for them. It follows up to make sure placements are successful. 2,000 volunteers are placed every year. The program needs volunteers who have second-language ability in Chinese or Spanish.

B. Answer the questions, Workbook page 15

★ Go over the directions.

★ Have students answer the questions and compare their answers with a partner.

★ Go over the answers with the class.

ANSWER KEY:

1. She is a doctor. 2. The purpose is to connect volunteers with schools. 3. they listen to a child read, use beads or cubes to reinforce math concepts, assist in the computer lab.

C. Read the Community Bulletin Board, Workbook page 15

★ Go over the directions.

★ Have students add ideas to the chart and then compare their ideas with a partner.

★ Call on students to share their ideas with the class.

ANSWER KEY:

Possible answers include:
Cleaners/Painters
  climb a ladder
  follow instructions
  do physical work
Meal Delivery
  drive a car
  have a driver's license
  be friendly
Santa Claus
  be friendly
  be good with children
Manicurist
  give a manicure
  work with older people

Take It Outside, Workbook page 15

★ Go over the directions.

★ Have students bring in information about volunteer opportunities.

★ Call on students to share the information with the class.

 Take It Online, Workbook page 15

★ Go over the directions.

★ Have students use a search engine to find out information about volunteer opportunities.

★ Tell students to write down three things they could volunteer to do.

★ Call on volunteers to share the information with the class.

EXPANSION ACTIVITY:
Why Should I?

★ Point out that although there are lots of volunteer opportunities, not many people volunteer. Put students in small groups to brainstorm a list of advantages and disadvantages of volunteering.

★ Call on students to share their ideas with the class.

★ Have the small groups create a flyer, poster, or brochure to encourage people to volunteer, using the list of advantages as a starting point.

★ Have representatives present the flyer or poster to the class.

2 Getting Around

UNIT OVERVIEW

LESSON	OBJECTIVE	TEACHER'S EDITION PAGE NUMBER
1. It happened during rush hour.	Describing Transportation Problems	p. 30
2. My insurance will cover it.	Understanding Insurance Terms	p. 32
3. Could you tell me the arrival time?	Understanding Transportation Issues	p. 34
4. Planning a Trip	Evaluating Travel Options	p. 38
5. I should have stayed home.	Using Past Forms of Modals	p. 40
6. What To Do In a Car Accident	Dealing with Emergencies	p. 42
7. What do you know?	Review and Assessment	p. 44
Spotlight: Reading Strategy	Identifying the Topic and Main Idea	p. 47
Spotlight: Writing Strategy	Using Compound Subjects, Verbs, and Objects	p. 48

Big Picture Expansion Activities

FOCUS	ACTIVITY	SUGGESTED USE
Speaking	Who said it?	Lesson 3
Reading	Safe Driving Tips	Lesson 2
Grammar	He could have watched the news.	Lesson 5
Writing	Analyzing Problems	Lesson 7
Speaking Assessment	Talking about the Big Picture	Lesson 7

Big Picture Expansion Activity Worksheets

WORKSHEET NUMBER/FOCUS	TITLE	TEACHER'S EDITION PAGE NUMBER
3. Reading	Safe Driving Tips	p. 183
4. Grammar	He could have watched the news.	p. 184

OBJECTIVE

Describing Transportation Problems

TRY THIS STRATEGY

Setting Goals

VOCABULARY

flat tire
rush hour

1. Warm Up, page 22

★ Put the Big Picture color transparency for Unit 2, Lesson 1 on the overhead projector, or have students look at the Big Picture in their books.

★ To set the context, ask questions about the picture (*Who do you see in the picture? What's happening?*).

★ As students talk about the Big Picture, write key vocabulary words on the board.

★ Read the questions aloud.

★ Put students in pairs or small groups and have them discuss the questions.

★ Call on students to tell the class about their pair or small group discussion.

Culture Notes:

★ You may want to use this opportunity to talk about cultural differences regarding traffic laws and behavior during rush hour.

★ Your students may not know that in some states, talking on a cell phone while driving is against the law. Discuss the other things in the picture that are illegal in your state or are unsafe.

EXPANSION ACTIVITY: Venn Diagrams

★ Brainstorm different types of transportation and write them on the board.

★ Draw a Venn diagram like the one below on the board. Write one mode of transportation above each circle.

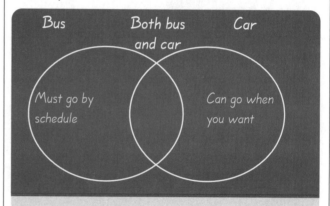

★ Elicit an example for each part, including the overlap, and write the examples on the diagram.

★ Have students complete Venn diagrams for two modes of transportation.

★ Put students in pairs to share their ideas.

2. Make Inferences, page 22

★ Go over the directions. Remind students that they learned this strategy in the Reading Spotlight for Unit 1.

★ Go over the first item. Elicit that *He likes to drive fast* is a better inference. Have students check the logical inferences and then compare their answers with a partner.

★ Go over the answers with the class.

★ Have students choose another person in the Big Picture, write three facts about the person, and then write two inferences for each fact.

★ Call on students to read their inferences to the class. Have the class guess who the person is.

ANSWER KEY:

He likes to drive fast; He's not very happy now.

EXPANSION ACTIVITY: Prove It

★ Divide the class into two teams.

★ Model the activity. Say an inference you can make about someone or something in the picture (*Tito might be late.*). Elicit the information that supports that inference (*He has a flat tire.*).

★ Have each team write logical inferences about the people in the picture, enough so that every team member can read an inference.

★ Call on a representative from each team. Have one read an inference and the other provide the information that supports the inference. Then have them switch roles. A team earns a point for each inference that is clearly supported.

★ Continue until everyone has had a chance to participate.

3. Analyze, page 22

★ Go over the directions. Read each statement aloud.

★ Have students write the action they would take for each situation.

★ Put students in pairs and have them share their ideas.

★ Call on students to tell the class about their partner's answers.

EXPANSION ACTIVITY: Role Play

★ Put students in pairs.

★ Assign each pair one of the situations. Explain that they are both in the car facing the problem together.

★ Have students create conversations in which they discuss what they should do. Walk around to monitor the activity and provide help as needed.

★ Call on volunteers to perform their role plays for the class.

TRY THIS STRATEGY: Setting Goals, page 22

★ Read the strategy aloud.

★ Have students write 1, 2, or 3 next to each action.

★ Put students in pairs to compare their ideas with a partner.

★ Call on students to share their ideas with the class.

EXPANSION ACTIVITY: 30-Second Speeches

★ Write topics related to transportation issues on slips of paper. Topics could include: *talking on cell phone while driving, causes of accidents, advantages of riding the train, disadvantages of taking the bus.*

★ Tell students that they will each draw a slip of paper and will speak on that topic continuously for at least 30 seconds.

★ Model the activity. Draw a topic and speak for 30 seconds.

★ Reassure students that this activity is to promote fluency and they do not have to be perfect.

★ Assign a student the role of timekeeper.

★ Call on students to draw topics and speak.

★ If you think your students need a little time to compose their thoughts, let them draw a topic when they are next in line to speak.

OBJECTIVE

Understanding Insurance Terms

TRY THIS STRATEGY

Learning Synonyms

VOCABULARY

actual cash value	liability
claim	policy
collision	policyholder
comprehensive	premium
coverage	reimbursement
deductible	uninsured
depreciate	vehicle
effective	

1. Talk about it, page 24

★ Have students look at the information on pages 24–25. Ask: *What do you think you will learn in this lesson?*

★ Read the questions aloud.

★ Put students in pairs or small groups and have them discuss the questions.

★ Call on students to tell the class about their pair or small group discussion.

EXPANSION ACTIVITY: Tell a Story

★ Model the activity. Tell the class a story about an accident you have had or know about. Explain how it happened and what kind of damage resulted.

★ Put students in pairs. Set a time limit of 3 minutes. Have one student tell a story while the partner takes notes.

★ Have students switch roles.

★ Have students write a paragraph summarizing their partner's story.

★ Call on students to read their paragraphs to the class.

2. Write *True* or *False*, page 24

★ Go over the directions.

★ Go over the first statement. Read the sentence aloud and elicit if it is true or false. Have students write *True* on the line.

★ Have students study the insurance policy, write *True* or *False* next to each sentence, and then check their answers with a partner.

★ Go over the answers with the class.

★ Have students correct the false statements. Go over the answers with the class.

ANSWER KEY:

1. True; 2. False, he owns a Porsche; 3. True; 4. False, it's good for a year; 5. False, he pays $256.80 + $92.00 ($348.80); 6. True; 7. True; 8. False, it comes to $1,211.55; 9. True; 10. False, it's in Virginia.

Culture Notes:

★ Students may not know that insurance rates are also based on gender and age. For example, insurance for an 18-year-old male with a sports car would typically be much higher than for a 40-year-old woman with a minivan.

★ Insurance rates also vary according to where the driver lives. Some areas have much higher accident or theft rates and so have higher premiums.

EXPANSION ACTIVITY: Dictation

★ Tell students that you will dictate 3 sentences. They should write the sentence and then write if it is true or false. Use the following sentences or create your own.

1. *Thomas Rideout lives in Tampa, Florida.*

2. *He is covered for $50,000 in property damage for each accident.*

3. *His car is a four-door sport utility vehicle.*

★ Read each sentence 3 times at normal speed.

★ Have students compare sentences with a partner.

★ Ask volunteers to write the sentences on the board. Elicit corrections if necessary from the class.

★ Call on students to tell you if the sentences are true or false.

ANSWER KEY:

1. False, he lives in Miami; 2. True; 3. False, it's a two-door coupe.

3. Apply, page 24

★ Go over the directions.

★ Have students read the situations and answer the questions.

★ Have students compare ideas with a partner.

★ Call on students to share their ideas with the class.

ANSWER KEY:

1. comprehensive; 2. collision; 3. yes

Grammar Note:

★ Your students may notice the use of *would* in situations 1 and 2. If appropriate, point out that this is a use of the conditional (*If you were in this situation. . .*).

 EXPANSION ACTIVITY: Go Online

★ Write the following website address on the board: http://www.pueblo.gsa.gov/cic_text/cars/autoinsu/autoinsu.htm.

★ Have students go to the website and click on one of the links.

★ Have students write down 3 things they learn about reducing insurance costs.

★ Call on students to share their ideas with the class.

TRY THIS STRATEGY: Learning Synonyms, page 24

★ Read the strategy aloud.

★ Have students find synonyms on pages 24–25 and write them next to the words.

★ Put students in pairs to compare their ideas with a partner.

★ Call on students to share their ideas with the class.

ANSWER KEY:

yearly: annual; car or truck: vehicle; driver: motorist; belongings: property; payment: premium; crash: collision

---

 BIG PICTURE EXPANSION ACTIVITY: READING—Safe Driving Tips

★ Make copies of **Worksheet #3** and distribute them to students.

★ Put the Big Picture color transparency for Unit 2, Lesson 1 on the overhead projector, or have students look at the Big Picture in their books.

★ Instruct students to complete the activities and then check their answers with a partner.

★ Go over the answers with the class.

ANSWER KEY:

1. No, Takeshi is driving aggressively (honking the horn), and that is not safe.
2. *Answers will vary.*
3. No. Kyle is reading a map, so he is distracted.
4. *Answers will vary.*

OBJECTIVE

Understanding Transportation Issues

COMMUNICATION STRATEGY

Pausing Expressions

VOCABULARY

antenna
bumper
hood
trunk
windshield

1. Warm Up, page 26

★ Have students look at the pictures on pages 26 and 27. To set the context, ask questions (*Who do you see in each picture? What do you think is going on?*).

★ Read the questions aloud.

★ Put students in pairs or small groups and have them discuss the questions.

★ Call on students to tell the class about their pair or small group discussion.

EXPANSION ACTIVITY: Chronological connectors

★ Brainstorm a list of chronological connectors with the class, and write their ideas on the board. Ideas should include: *first, next, then, after that, before that, finally.*

★ Put students in pairs. Have them take turns telling stories about the pictures. Remind students to use chronological connectors.

★ Walk around to monitor the activity. Provide help as needed.

★ Call on volunteers to tell their stories to the class.

2. Put in Sequence 🎧, page 26

★ Go over the directions.

★ Have students number the pictures in order from 1 to 5.

★ Read the conversations or play the tape or CD while students check their guesses.

★ Go over the answers with the class.

LISTENING SCRIPT

2. Put in Sequence, page 26.

Number the pictures about Tom and his accident in order from 1 to 5. Then listen to 5 conversations and check your guesses.

1.

Officer:	Can I see your license and registration, please?
Tom:	My registration?
Officer:	Yes. Your car registration. I need to see proof of insurance, too.
Tom:	Yes, of course. Just a minute. Oh, good, yes, here they are.
Officer:	Okay. Why don't you tell me what happened.
Tom:	Well, I, uh, I was driving along, but I wasn't speeding or anything.
Officer:	Of course.
Tom:	And then suddenly the car in front of me stopped. I mean, it all happened in an instant. I slammed on my brakes, but there was nothing I could do.
Officer:	I see. Good thing you were wearing your seat belt.
Tom:	Hmm. You're right. Oh, and officer?
Officer:	Yes.
Tom:	Could I get your name, please?
Officer:	Yes, of course. I'm Officer Bee Goode.
Tom:	Officer Bee Goode?
Officer:	Yes, that's right.
Tom:	Thank you for your help, Officer Goode.

2.

Recording: You have reached Unified Insurance Company. If you have a question about a bill, press 8. If you need to make a claim, press 7.

Recording: Please press the 15-digit number of your policy, then press the pound key.

Agent: Hello. This is Yumiko Sazaki speaking. How can I help you?

Tom: I'm calling to report an accident.

Agent: Your name, please.

Tom: Tom. Tom Rideout.

Agent: Okay, Mr. Rideout. Could you please verify your policy number, address, and Social Security number?

Tom: Yes, my policy number is 00044 44 244 4443 5. My address is 564 Philips Street in Miami, Florida, and my Social Security number is 123-45-6789.

Agent: First of all, I'm sorry to hear about your accident. Please tell me who was driving the car.

Tom: I was.

Agent: Were there any injuries?

Tom: No. Only damage to my car.

Agent: And this was your 2000 Porsche Boxster?

Tom: Yes.

Agent: Okay. And what day did the accident happen?

Tom: Today. This morning.

Agent: And where did the accident take place?

Tom: I was on interstate 95 in Miami.

Agent: And the weather conditions when the accident happened?

Tom: The weather? Uhm, well, it was clear and sunny.

Agent: And how did the accident happen?

Tom: Well, I was driving along, and suddenly the driver in the car in front of me slammed on his brakes.

Agent: I see.

Tom: Yes, and then my car hit the back of his car. It was terrible! The police came, and I talked with Officer Bee Goode.

Agent: Okay, Mr. Rideout. Can you give me a number where I can reach you?

Tom: Yes. You can call my cell phone. The number is 555-3465.

Agent: Thank you, Mr. Rideout. I'll be back in touch with you within the next 24 hours.

Tom: Okay. Thanks.

Agent: You're welcome. Bye bye.

3.

Tom: So what do you think? Do you think you can fix it today?

Mechanic: Today? I don't think so.

Tom: I can't believe this. I just can't believe this. So how long *is* it going to take?

Mechanic: Well, it depends.

Tom: Depends! Depends on what?

Mechanic: Well, you're going to need a new bumper and two new headlights and then there's that crack in your windshield. It's really a question of how quickly I can get the parts.

Tom: So there's no chance it could be fixed by tomorrow?

Mechanic: Don't think so. But I might have it for you by next Tuesday.

Tom: Oh, but that's too late.

Mechanic: You have to be somewhere?

Tom: Yes, somewhere important. And it's a day's drive away—in Tampa.

Mechanic: Can't help you there, but I can take you to the bus station. It's just down the road.

Tom: Would you? Thank you so much.

4.

Ticket Agent: Next, please.

Tom: I need to get to Tampa as quickly as possible.

Agent: Let's see. Yes, the next bus to Tampa is at 4:10.

Tom:	4:10? But it's only 2 o'clock now.
Agent:	Yes, well, I'm afraid you just missed the 1:45 bus to Tampa.
Tom:	This is terrible. So when does that bus get into Tampa?
Agent:	The 4:10?
Tom:	Yes.
Agent:	Hold on a minute. Okay, that bus gets into Tampa at 12:10.
Tom	12:10 in the morning? Oh, boy. Great.
Agent:	So do you want to buy a ticket?
Tom	Well, I, well, yes, I guess so.
Agent:	One way or round trip?
Tom:	Round trip.

5.

Bill:	Hello.
Tom:	Bill. It's Tom.
Bill:	Tom? Where are you?
Tom:	I'm in Miami.
Bill:	You're in Miami? What are you doing there?
Tom:	It's a long story. I'm at the bus station.
Bill:	Where's your car?
Tom:	It's a long story.
Bill:	Are you okay?
Tom:	Yes, I'm fine.
Bill:	Are you going to get here in time?
Tom:	Yeah, I think so. I was just wondering if I could ask three favors?
Bill:	Whatever you want.
Tom:	First, could you pick me up at the bus station at midnight tonight?
Bill:	Yeah. Sure. No problem.
Tom:	And can I borrow your car to get to the wedding tomorrow?
Bill:	Anything you want, Brother.
Tom:	And then could you drive Sara and me to the airport?
Bill:	Of course. Boy, I can't wait to hear the whole story. Does Sara know?
Tom:	Not yet. See you tonight.
Bill:	Bye, Tom.

ANSWER KEY:

From left to right, top to bottom
Picture 1: 4; Picture 2: 3; Picture 3: 1;
Picture 4: 2; Picture 5: 5

3. Listen for Specific Information 🎧, page 26

★ Go over the directions.

★ Have students listen and look at the pictures while you read the conversations or play the tape or CD.

★ Have students check *True* or *False*.

★ Have students compare their answers with a partner.

★ Read the conversations or play the tape or CD again if necessary.

★ Have students correct the false statements.

★ Go over the answers with the class.

LISTENING SCRIPT

3. Listen for Specific Information, page 26
Read the statements below. Then listen to the conversations again and check (✓) *True* or *False*. Next, correct the false statements.

NOTE: See conversations from Activity 2 above.

ANSWER KEY:

1. True; 2. False; 3. True; 4. False; 5. False;
6. False; 7. False; 8. True; 9. False; 10. True;
11. False; 12. False

Culture Notes:
★ You may want to point out that we should be very polite in speaking to police officers.

★ Students may not know that they should not do anything until the police officer asks them to, including getting their license and registration.

4. Use the Communication Strategy 🎧, page 26

★ Go over the directions.

★ Have students read the conversation, or read the conversation aloud line by line and have students repeat.

★ Have students practice reading the conversation in pairs.

★ Direct students' attention to the Communication Strategy box. Go over the information in the box.

★ Say each example and have students repeat.

★ Model the conversation with a student. Have the student read A's lines. Demonstrate how to substitute using your own ideas. Elicit appropriate responses from the student.

★ Have students work in pairs to practice the conversation, substituting their own ideas for the underlined words.

★ Walk around to make sure students understand the activity. Provide help if needed.

BIG PICTURE EXPANSION ACTIVITY: SPEAKING—Who said it?

★ Put the Big Picture color transparency for Unit 2, Lesson 1 on the overhead projector, or have students look at the Big Picture in their books.

★ Put students in pairs. Walk around the room and quietly assign each pair of students a character in the Big Picture interacting with someone else later in the day.

★ Have students create a conversation for their characters. One character should tell the other about his or her experience on the highway. Encourage students to use the communication strategy in the conversation if possible.

★ Have students perform their conversations for the class. Have the class guess who in the picture is speaking.

OBJECTIVE

Evaluating Travel Options

VOCABULARY

check into
in advance
nonrefundable
option
standard fare

1. Warm Up, page 28

★ Have students look at the pictures on page 28. To set the context, ask questions about the pictures (*What do you see in the pictures? Which ones do you use?*).

★ Read the questions aloud and have students repeat.

★ Put students in pairs or small groups and have them discuss the questions.

★ Call on students to tell the class about their pair or small group discussion.

EXPANSION ACTIVITY: Sort

★ Post signs around the room for different modes of transportation (*car, train, bus, subway, plane, bicycle*).

★ Have students stand. If your class is large, you may want to have one group at a time stand. Tell students you are going to ask a series of questions and they should stand by the appropriate sign to answer the question about themselves.

★ Ask questions. Create your own or use the ones below.
Which form of transportation do you use most often?
Which one did you use to come to class today?
Which is your favorite?
Which one is the safest? the cleanest? the most fun?
If you could only have one type of transportation in this city, what would it be?

★ Whenever possible, stop and ask students to tell you more about why they are standing where they are.

2. Read and Compare, page 28

★ Go over the directions.

★ Have students read the information and take notes in the chart. Ask comprehension questions (*Who is sending the first email? Where does Jackie want to go? What do you think their relationship is?*).

★ Have students compare their charts with a partner.

★ Go over the answers to the chart with the class.

★ Read the questions aloud and have students answer them.

★ Go over the answers with the class.

Academic Notes:

★ Remind students that comparing and contrasting are skills that help us evaluate or make decisions.

★ Point out that we can choose the criteria on which to base decisions. So, for example, if we must arrive at a destination by tomorrow, travel time may be the most important criteria.

ANSWER KEY:

Travel Options	Travel Time	Cost of Ticket (Round Trip)	Other Expenses
Plane	8 hours	$300	Bus to airport $100 to change ticket
Bus	2 days and 15 hours	$240–296	
Train	2 days and 14 hours	$266	
Car	40 hours (3 or 4 days)	$120–160	Hotel each night Gas Tolls

1. fastest: plane; slowest: car
2. The advantages of taking the train is that it's cheaper than flying; the disadvantage is that it takes a long time.
3. She would have to pay for her hotel and for any tolls.
4. *Answers will vary.*
5. She's thinks she's going to go the cheapest way—by bus.

EXPANSION ACTIVITY: Take It Online

★ Put students in pairs or small groups. Assign each a destination at some distance from your city.

★ Have students research various ways to travel to their assigned destination. Ask students to note advantages and disadvantages, including time, cost, and other factors. Brainstorm factors to consider as needed.

★ Ask the pairs or groups to tell the class what they found out.

3. Interview, page 28

★ Go over the directions.

★ Model how to make questions about the items (*Have you rented a car?*). Call on a student and ask the question. If the person answers *yes*, point out that you could write his or her name down. Ask other questions (*Where were you? Where were you going? What kind of car was it? Do you remember how much it cost?*).

★ Have students stand and walk around the room, asking and answering questions.

★ When students have completed the chart, ask question about their answers (*Who did you find out has taken a long bus trip? How many people have booked a flight on the Internet?*).

EXPANSION ACTIVITY: Have you ever?

★ Ask students what tense is used in most of the items in Activity 3 (present perfect). Review the formation of the present perfect if necessary.

★ Have students write 5 questions with *Have you ever* that ask about common transportation experiences.

★ Arrange all the chairs in a circle, or have each student stand on a piece of paper in a circle.

★ Explain the activity. You will stand in the middle and ask a question beginning *Have you ever* (*flown to another country?*). All students who can answer *yes* must leave their chairs or papers and move around the circle until they find a new spot. Tell them the rule is they cannot move to a place next to the one they have now. Point out that you will also need to find a spot. This will leave someone without a spot; that person will go to the middle of the circle.

★ Ask the question and have the students move. Take a spot so that a student is in the middle of the circle. The person in the middle asks the next question. Encourage the student to ask a question that most people can answer *yes* to. If necessary, let students check their list of questions.

★ Continue playing until most or all students have asked a question.

OBJECTIVE

Using Past Forms of Modals

The Past Form of *Should*, page 30

★ Have students look at the notes in the box. Read the information and examples aloud.

> **Grammar Notes:**
> ★ You may want to review the formation of regular vs. irregular past participles. Remind students that while regular verbs have the same form in the simple past and the past participle, irregular verbs have different forms.
> ★ Point out that this structure has 3 parts (modal + *have* + past participle) and that none of the parts changes form.

1. Complete the Sentences, page 30

★ Read the directions aloud.

★ Go over the first sentence. Elicit that students should write *should have taken* on the line.

★ Have students complete the sentences.

★ Have students check their answers with a partner.

★ Go over the answers with the class.

ANSWER KEY:

1. should have taken; 2. should have bought; 3. should have made; 4. should have slowed down; 5. should have gotten; 6. should have stopped

2. What's Your Advice?, page 30

★ Read the directions aloud. Point out that students should write sentences using *should have* or *shouldn't have*.

★ Go over the first sentence. Elicit ideas.

★ Have students write advice for each situation.

★ Have students compare their sentences with a partner.

★ Call on students to share their answers with the class.

EXPANSION ACTIVITY: Write Your Own

★ Model the activity. Tell a story about a mistake you made that led to a transportation problem. Do not describe what you should have done. When you are finished, elicit ideas from the class for what you should or shouldn't have done.

★ Have students write about a mistake they made in the past that led to a transportation problem.

★ Put students in pairs to exchange stories and write sentences in response, using *should have* or *shouldn't have*.

ANSWER KEY:

Answers will vary.
1. Nan should have put the emergency brake on.
2. Jamal shouldn't have waited until the day before to buy his ticket.
3. Keiko shouldn't have lost her wallet./Keiko should have looked for her wallet earlier.

The Past Form of *Could*, page 31

★ Have students look at the notes in the box. Read the information and examples aloud.

3. Write, page 31

★ Read the directions aloud.

★ Go over the first question and elicit other possible answers.

★ Have students answer the questions.

★ Have students take turns asking and answering questions with a partner.

★ Call on students to share their answers with the class.

ANSWER KEY:

Answers will vary.

BIG PICTURE EXPANSION ACTIVITY: GRAMMAR—He could have watched the news.

★ Make copies of **Worksheet #4** and distribute them to students.

★ Put the Big Picture color transparency for Unit 2, Lesson 1 on the overhead projector, or have students look at the Big Picture in their books.

★ Instruct students to complete the activities and then check their answers with a partner.

★ Go over the answers with the class.

ANSWER KEY:

A.
1. He shouldn't have driven so fast.
2. He should have picked a quieter spot.
3. He should have tied the plants down.
4. He shouldn't have hitch-hiked on the highway.
5. She shouldn't have been talking on her cell phone.

B. *Possible answers include:*
1. He could have watched the news.
2. He could have followed the rules of the road.
3. He couldn't have had a good day because he had an accident.
4. He could have put the roof up.
5. She could have taken a class/test.
6. She could have had engine trouble/run out of gas.

OBJECTIVE

Dealing with Emergencies

VOCABULARY

oncoming
shoulder (of a road)
warn
witness

WINDOW ON PRONUNCIATION

Reduction of Past Modals

1. Warm Up, page 32

★ Go over the directions.

★ Read each item aloud.

★ Put students in pairs or small groups to answer the questions.

★ Call on students to share their ideas with the class.

EXPANSION ACTIVITY: What should you have done?

★ Have students write at least 3 sentences about a car accident they have seen or been in. Ask students to use past forms of modals to describe what they could have or should have done differently.

★ Put students in pairs to read their sentences.

★ Call on students to read their sentences to the class.

2. Read and Respond, page 32

★ Go over the directions.

★ Have students read the checklist and then answer the questions.

★ Put students in pairs to check their answers.

★ Go over the answers with the class.

ANSWER KEY:

Address: 564 Philips Street, Miami, FL 33136
Make/Model/Year: Porsche/Boxster/2000
Driver's Name: Thomas Rideout

1. Things you should do (list 3): stop immediately, remain calm, move cars if possible to the shoulder, warn oncoming traffic, call for medical assistance, call law enforcement, get information.
   Things you shouldn't do (list 3): argue, accuse anyone, make any admission of blame, leave the scene.

2. *Answers will vary.*

3. *Answers will vary.*

4. You could injure the person further.

5. You should get the names of witnesses in case there is any disagreement about what happened.

EXPANSION ACTIVITY: Real Event

★ Put students in pairs. Have students interview each other and complete the form in Activity 2 with the information from a real accident (perhaps the accident they talked about in Activity 1). Point out that they should be able to write in most of the accident facts and can use their own vehicle information.

★ Call on students to tell the class 2 pieces of information that they learned from their partners.

3. Apply, page 33

★ Go over the directions.

★ Read the situations aloud, or have students read the situations. Have students answer the questions and then compare answers with a partner.

★ Call on students to share their answers with the class.

ANSWER KEY:

Answers will vary.

WINDOW ON PRONUNCIATION: Reduction of Past Modals

A. Listen to the words 🎧, page 33

★ Say the phrases or play the tape or CD while the students look at the phrases in the book.

★ Say the phrases or play the tape or CD a second time, and have the students repeat.

B. Listen to the sentences 🎧, page 33

★ Go over the directions.

★ Direct students' attention to the sentences. Have students write the missing words as you say the sentences or play the tape or CD. Play the tape or CD a second time if necessary.

★ Put students in pairs to check their answers.

★ Go over the answers with the class.

ANSWER KEY:

1. should have; 2. could have; 3. couldn't have; 4. should have; 5. shouldn't have; 6. should have

C. Work with a partner, page 33

★ Go over the directions.

★ Read the questions aloud and have students repeat. Use the reduced form.

★ Put students in pairs to take turns asking and answering the questions.

★ Call on students to tell the class their partner's answers.

EXPANSION ACTIVITY: Advice Call-in

★ Model the activity. Tell a story about a problem situation you had that resulted from your own actions or inaction (*My mother's birthday was last week, and I forgot to send her a present. I didn't even call. Now she is upset with me.*). Ask: *What do you think I should have done?* Elicit examples using past modals. Then ask for advice about what you should do now.

★ Put students in pairs. Explain that they will role play a radio call-in show. One student will be the "advice doctor" and the other will be the caller. The caller should describe a problem resulting from his or her actions. The "advice doctor" should use past modals in the response.

★ Call on volunteers to role play their conversations for the class.

OBJECTIVE

Review and Assessment

1. Listening Review 🎧, page 34

★ Go over the directions for items 1–5 with the class.

★ Read items 1–5 or play the tape or CD and have the students mark their answers in the Answer Sheet box.

★ Walk around to monitor the activity and help students stay on task.

★ Go over the directions for items 6–10 and repeat the procedure.

★ Have students check their answers for 1–10 with a partner.

★ Go over the answers with the class.

┌╴**LISTENING SCRIPT:** ╴┐

1. Listening Review, page 34

Listen to each conversation and choose the best answer to the question you hear. Use the Answer Sheet.

1.

A: Can you tell me when the next bus leaves for Miami?

B: Hmm. Let's see. Yes, there's a bus at 3:15.

A: There's nothing before that?

B: No, that's the next bus to Miami.

Question: Where does the man want to go?

2.

A: This is Aubrey Road Assistance. Can I help you?

B: Yes, I'm having a problem with my car.

A: Where are you now?

B: I'm on Route 19 just outside of Bedford.

A: What exactly is the problem?

B: I'm not sure. The engine just died, and it won't start.

A: Okay. I should have a truck out there within 30 minutes.

Question: What did the man call to get?

3.

A: Unified Automobile Insurance. How can I direct your call?

B: I have a billing question.

A: Just a moment, please.

C: Billing Department. Can I have your policy number, please?

B It's 45405504034004.

C: Your name, please.

B: Jane Tucker.

C: How can I help you, Ms. Tucker?

B: Yes, I'm calling about the insurance bill I just received.

C: Just a minute. Let me bring it up on my screen. Okay, I have it in front of me.

B: I usually get a discount for a good driving record, but I don't see it on my most recent bill.

C: Hmm. Yes, it looks as though it's missing from your bill. Let me correct that, and we'll send you a new bill.

B: Thanks.

C: You're welcome. Bye now.

B: Bye.

Question: What did the woman call her insurance company to get?

4.

A: Hello.

B: Sandi. Hi. It's Joe.

A: Joe, hi. So what did you decide to do?

B: I've decided to take the train instead of flying.

A: Really?

B: Well, I have the time. And I think it'll be interesting to see some of the country.

A: Makes sense. And it's cheaper than flying.

Question: Why does Joe decide to take the train?

5.

A: What happened to your car?

B: Oh, someone ran into me.

A: How fast were you going?

B: Well, actually, my car wasn't moving. I had to stop suddenly, and the guy behind me couldn't stop in time.

B: Sounds like he was driving too close to you.

A: I'm not sure about that, but I know he was driving too fast.

Question: What does the woman think caused the accident?

Listen and choose the sentence that is closest in meaning to the sentence you hear. Use the Answer Sheet.

6. My car has depreciated a lot since I bought it.
7. My insurance policy is effective on August 1.
8. She bought her plane ticket 7 days in advance.
9. She should have bought liability insurance.
10. I could have taken the train instead of the bus.

ANSWER KEY:

1. C; 2. A; 3. B; 4. C; 5. A; 6. C; 7. A; 8. B;
9. C; 10. B

2. Vocabulary Review, page 35

★ Direct students' attention to the crossword puzzle.

★ Go over the directions. Make sure students understand how to fill in the crossword puzzle. Remind them to use words from the unit.

★ Have students check their answers with a partner.

★ Go over the answers with the class.

ANSWER KEY:

Across:
  2. collide; 3. shoulder; 6. policy;
  9. reimburse; 10. premium;
  11. windshield; 12. witness

Down:
  1. depreciate; 4. oncoming;
  5. warnings; 6. vehicle; 7. option

LEARNING LOG, page 35

★ Point out the two sections of the Learning Log: *I know these words* and *I practiced these skills, strategies, and grammar points.*

★ Ask students to check the words they know and what they practiced.

★ Walk around to note what students don't know or didn't practice. Use this information to review areas of difficulty.

🖼 BIG PICTURE EXPANSION: SPEAKING ASSESSMENT—Talking about the Big Picture

★ You can use the Big Picture as an individual assessment, to place new students in classes, to diagnose difficulties, or to measure progress.

★ Work with one student. Show the Big Picture to the student. Ask: *What do you see in the picture?* Or say: *Tell me about the picture.* Tell the student to speak for as long as possible. Wait a moment for the student to prepare an answer.

★ If the student has difficulty, you can use prompts (*Who do you see? What are the people doing? Where are they?*).

★ You can use a scoring rubric like the one below to rate speakers.

4	Exhibits confidence; begins speaking without prompting Uses some complex sentences, although may make mistakes with irregular forms Can use several tenses
3	Uses sentences, although form may be incorrect Uses more than one tense Can speak for a sustained length of time Responds to prompts, but doesn't need them to begin speaking
2	Can use nouns and verbs in sentences Uses one tense most of the time Answers informational questions Limited vocabulary
1	Can name objects Uses single words Can answer yes/no questions
0	Cannot say anything independently May be able to point to objects when prompted

★ Review areas of difficulty.

TEACHER NOTES:

Things that students are doing well:

_____

_____

_____

_____

_____

_____

Things students need additional help with:

_____

_____

_____

_____

_____

_____

_____

Ideas for further practice or for the next class:

_____

_____

_____

_____

_____

> **BIG PICTURE EXPANSION ACTIVITY:**
> **WRITING—Analyzing Problems**
>
> ★ Put the Big Picture color transparency for Unit 2, Lesson 1 on the overhead projector, or have students look at the Big Picture in their books.
> ★ Ask the class: _What problems do you see? How could they have been avoided?_
> ★ Have students brainstorm ideas to prepare to write.
> ★ Have students write a paragraph about the problems they see and what the people could have done to avoid the problems. Remind students to use past modals in their paragraphs.
> ★ Put students in pairs to take turns reading their paragraphs to their partners.

OBJECTIVE

Identifying the Topic and Main Idea

Identifying the Topic and Main Idea, page 36

★ Direct students' attention to the information in the box. Explain the strategy.

★ Go over the examples.

★ Check comprehension by asking questions (*How is a main idea different from a topic? How can you find the main idea?*).

1. Think of a main idea, page 36

★ Go over the directions.

★ Read the first topic and elicit examples of main ideas (*driving too fast is dangerous, you can get a ticket for driving too fast*).

★ Have students complete the chart and then compare ideas with a partner.

★ Call on students to share their ideas with the class.

ANSWER KEY:

Answers will vary.

2. Read paragraphs 1–4, page 36

★ Go over the directions.

★ Have students read the paragraphs individually, or read them aloud.

★ Have students identify the topic and the main idea of each paragraph.

★ Have students check their answers with a partner.

★ Go over the answers with the class.

ANSWER KEY:

1. Topic: different types of travelers
   Main Idea: The way people travel differs greatly.
2. Topic: driver's license
   Main Idea: A driver's license is necessary to drive a car and as identification.
3. Topic: how to get a driver's license in California
   Main Idea: To get a driver's license you have to take a four-part test.
4. Topic: how to buy a pre-owned car
   Main Idea: Be sure to do your homework if you're buying a pre-owned car.

EXPANSION ACTIVITY: News Shorts

★ Have students bring in short news articles, or bring some in yourself. Cut the headlines off. Put the headlines on a table.

★ Put students in pairs. Give each pair one or more articles. Have students write the main idea.

★ Have students select the headlines they think match their articles.

★ Call on students to read their main ideas and headlines to the class.

OBJECTIVE

Using Compound Subjects, Verbs, and Objects

Using Compound Subjects, Verbs, and Objects, page 38

★ Direct students' attention to the information in the box. Go over the examples.

★ Write a sentence on the board (*Luis and I pack and seal boxes and envelopes in the mail room*), and have students identify the compound subject, verb, and object.

1. Complete these sentences, page 38

★ Go over the directions and the example. Elicit that *my friend* completes the compound subject.

★ Have students complete the sentences and then compare their answers with a partner.

★ Call on students to share their ideas with the class.

ANSWER KEY:

Answers will vary.

Writing Compound Sentences, page 39

★ Direct students' attention to the information in the box. Go over the examples.

Grammar Notes:
★ You may want to point out that we often use a pronoun in the second simple sentence if the subject is the same. For example, we could write *Even-numbered interstates run east-west; odd-numbered ones run north-south.*

★ Remind students that we use commas before coordinating conjunctions that join sentences.

2. Join each pair of sentences, page 39

★ Go over the directions.

★ Read the first pair of sentences. Elicit ideas for how they could be combined (*Hitchhiking is not common in the U.S., and in many parts of the country, it is illegal.*).

★ Have students combine the sentences to make compound sentences.

★ Put students in pairs to read their sentences aloud.

★ Call on volunteers to write their sentences on the board.

ANSWER KEY:

Possible answers include:
1. Hitchhiking is not common in the U.S., and in many parts of the country, it is illegal.
2. Taxis are more expensive than most other kinds of public transportation, but they take you exactly where you want to go.
3. In some states, you can make a right turn at a red light, but you must come to a complete stop first.
4. Each state has different rules for getting a driver's license, but they all require you to take a driving test.
5. Driving across the country takes a lot of time, but it allows you to see more than if you fly.

3. Choose a topic 📁, page 39

★ Go over the directions.

★ Have students write paragraphs. Walk around to monitor the activity and provide help as needed.

★ Have students read their paragraphs to a partner.

★ Call on students to read their paragraphs to the class.

EQUIPPED FOR THE FUTURE ROLE

Family

OBJECTIVE

Interpreting Information about Recreation

A. Read the Calendar of Events, Workbook page 32

★ Direct students' attention to the information and ask questions: *What is a calendar of events? Where would you see one? What kinds of things are listed?*

★ Have students read the information and circle the 3 most interesting activities.

★ Have students write a sentence about each activity describing why it is interesting.

★ Put students in pairs to read their sentences to a partner.

★ Call on students to read their sentences to the class.

ANSWER KEY:

Answers will vary.

B. Use the information, Workbook page 33

★ Go over the directions. Read each question aloud.

★ Have students answer the questions and then check their answers with a partner.

★ Go over the answers with the class.

ANSWER KEY:

1. Three are listed as free; 2. two; 3. five; 4. $19.00; 5. The family concert because it is at a good time and might interest all ages

C. The activities in the calendar, Workbook page 33

★ Go over the directions.

★ Have students complete the chart and then compare their ideas with a partner.

★ Go over the answers with the class.

Activities on Friday	Activities on Saturday	Activities on Sunday
Schoolhouse Rock, Live The King and I "Lapsit" "Books at Bedtime"	Wayne from Maine family concert Youth Symphony orchestra Schoolhouse Rock, Live The Tamborines Storytime "The Masked Bandit"	Circle Comedy Clowns "An afternoon of Humor" "Summer Insects"

Take It Outside, Workbook page 33

★ Go over the directions.

★ Have students bring in listings to the class.

★ Put students in pairs to share their ideas.

★ Call on students to share their ideas with the class.

 Take It Online, Workbook page 33

★ Go over the directions.

★ Have students use a search engine and enter the name of your town or city and "library." Have them write down the website address.

★ Ask students to look at the library's calendar of events and write down 3 things they learn.

★ Call on students to share their ideas with the class.

EXPANSION ACTIVITY: Tour Guide

★ Put students in pairs or small groups.

★ Explain the activity: Each group will plan several activities for their "clients" this weekend. Groups should find out what events are happening and plan a schedule. They should also suggest ways the clients can get to the event.

★ Create a list of "clients" or use the one below. Assign each group one of the client descriptions.

An American family of four from out of town, the son is 8, the daughter is 5

Three teenagers from a nearby town (ages 15–17)

A group of college students from Italy

A couple from England in their 70s, retired college professors

Four politicians from Africa

Five women who went to college together 20 years ago

A group of 7th graders

A newly married couple from the other side of the country

★ Have each group present their itinerary for their clients to the class. Groups should tell why they selected each activity.

EQUIPPED FOR THE FUTURE ROLE

Work

OBJECTIVE

Interpreting Maps

A. Study the map below, Workbook page 34

★ Have students look at the map. Ask comprehension questions (*What cities and towns do you see? What are some major highways? What state is it?*).

★ Have students circle the answer to complete the sentence.

★ Put students in pairs and have them take turns asking and answering the questions.

★ Call on students to share their answers with the class.

ANSWER KEY:

1. c; 2. c; 3. a; 4. a; 5. c; 6. c

B. Read each situation below. Workbook page 35

★ Go over the directions. Read each situation aloud.

★ Have students complete the directions by circling the answer.

★ Have students compare their answers with a partner.

★ Go over the answers with the class.

ANSWER KEY:

1. north/right/left; 2. south/Route 29/ west/Route 1; 3. north/1/east/195/north

C. Write the directions, Workbook page 35

★ Go over the directions.

★ Have students write the directions and then compare their ideas with a partner.

★ Have students take turns asking and answering the questions with a partner.

ANSWER KEY:

Answers will vary but may include:
Take a left onto White Horse Avenue and follow it north until you come to Route 195. Head west and stay on that road when it becomes Route 29. Take Route 1 north. Just after you pass Chambers Street on your right you'll see Prospect Park ahead on the left. Weber Park is just behind Prospect Park.

Take It Outside, Workbook page 35

★ Go over the directions.

★ Put students in pairs to interview each other.

★ Have students write the directions and then check their directions with their partners.

★ Call on students to read their directions to the class.

 Take It Online, Workbook page 35

★ Go over the directions.

★ Have students use a search engine to find a map of their area. You may want to suggest that they enter the town name and "map." Make sure students are able to locate sites that provide maps and directions.

★ Tell students to enter their partner's address in the "from" address and the school's in the "to" address. They may need to click on "get directions." If students do not want to give their real address, provide the actual address of a public building such as the library as the "from" address.

★ After students have obtained directions, have them compare their directions with their partner's directions.

★ Call on students to tell the class if the directions were the same.

EXPANSION ACTIVITY: Phone Call

★ Point out that we often have to get directions over the phone.

★ Have students call a local business and ask for directions from their homes. Point out that people will often ask "Where are you coming from?" before they decide how to give directions. Students should be ready to respond to this question with a major intersection near where they are.

★ Have students write the directions.

★ Have students check the directions against a map or by using a map website as in the Take It Online activity.

Your Health

UNIT OVERVIEW

LESSON	OBJECTIVE	TEACHER'S EDITION PAGE NUMBER
1. Call 911!	Describing a Health Emergency	p. 54
2. Who's your doctor?	Identifying Health Care Professionals	p. 56
3. That was the 22nd not the 28th.	Calling for Information	p. 59
4. Food Labels	Interpreting Nutritional Information	p. 63
5. It hurts when I breathe.	Using Adverb Clauses	p. 64
6. FAQs about Immunizations	Learning about Immunizations	p. 66
7. What do you know?	Review and Assessment	p. 68
Spotlight: Reading Strategy	Using Context Clues	p. 71
Spotlight: Writing Strategy	Identifying Punctuation Marks	p. 72

Big Picture Expansion Activities

FOCUS	ACTIVITY	SUGGESTED USE
Speaking	What did you say?	Lesson 3
Reading	FAQs about Heart Attacks	Lesson 6
Grammar	What did he do when he saw the bill?	Lesson 5
Writing	Describing Activities	Lesson 7
Speaking Assessment	Talking about the Big Picture	Lesson 7

Big Picture Expansion Activity Worksheets

WORKSHEET NUMBER/FOCUS	TITLE	TEACHER'S EDITION PAGE NUMBER
5. Grammar	What did he do when he saw the bill?	p. 185
6. Reading	FAQs about Heart Attacks	p. 186

OBJECTIVE

Describing a Health Emergency

VOCABULARY

pass out
revive
vital signs

1. Warm Up, page 40

★ Put the Big Picture color transparency for Unit 3, Lesson 1 on the overhead projector, or have students look at the Big Picture in their books.

★ To set the context, ask questions about the picture (*What do you see in the pictures? What's the story about?*).

★ As students talk about the Big Picture, write key vocabulary words on the board.

★ Read the questions aloud.

★ Put students in pairs or small groups and have them discuss the questions.

★ Call on students to tell the class about their pair or small group discussion.

Culture Note:
★ Some students may not be sure when they should call 911. Point out that 911 should be reserved for real emergencies (life-threatening medical situations, serious crimes where there is a threat of harm, and fires).

EXPANSION ACTIVITY: Non-emergency Numbers

★ Put students in small groups, and have them brainstorm a list of serious situations that require help but are probably not emergencies.

★ Have students use a telephone directory to find numbers that might be helpful in each situation.

★ Call on students to describe a situation and identify a possible resource.

★ Have students work in groups to create a poster or brochure addressing the non-emergency situations.

2. Put in Sequence, page 40

★ Go over the directions.

★ Read the sentences aloud, or have students take turns reading them aloud.

★ Have students match each picture to a sentence and then check their answers with a partner.

★ Go over the answers with the class.

ANSWER KEY:

1. Oscar and Rita were at home playing cards.
2. Suddenly he felt a sharp pain in his chest.
3. Oscar passed out and fell to the floor. His wife ran to the phone and called 911.
4. The ambulance took him to the emergency room.
5. In the emergency room, the doctors were able to revive him.
6. While he was in the hospital, the nurses took his vital signs frequently.
7. Oscar got out of the wheelchair and went home.
8. A month later, a bill from the hospital arrived in the mail.
9. When Oscar and Rita saw the hospital bill, they suddenly felt a sharp pain in their chests.

EXPANSION ACTIVITY: Story Strips

★ Give each student sheets of paper or index cards.

★ Have students write a story about a medical emergency that they experienced or know about. Tell them to write one sentence on a line or card.

★ Have students cut the story into strips of one sentence each.

★ Put students in pairs to exchange story strips. Each student should recreate the story and check it with their partner.

★ Call on students to read their partner's stories to the class.

3. Write, page 40

★ Go over the directions.

★ Have students match the synonyms and then check their answers with a partner.

★ Go over the answers with the class.

★ Have students rewrite the story in their own words.

★ Put students in pairs to take turns reading their stories.

★ Call on students to read their stories to the class.

ANSWER KEY:

1. e; 2. a; 3. g; 4. f; 5. d; 6. c; 7. b

**EXPANSION ACTIVITY:
Diminishing Returns**

★ Put students in small groups.

★ Explain the activity: the first student will whisper a short story to the second, who will retell the story in a whisper to the third, and so on, until everyone has had a chance to tell the story. The last person will retell the story aloud to the group.

★ Have the first student in each group begin with a story. Walk around the room to monitor the activity and provide help as needed.

★ Continue the activity until several stories have been told and retold in each group.

★ Elicit from the class the ways in which the stories changed through the retelling.

OBJECTIVE

Identifying Health Care Professionals

VOCABULARY

blood vessel	obstetrician
cardiologist	optometrist
cardiopulmonary	pediatrician
cardiovascular	perform
death	physical therapist
dental hygienist	preparation
depressed	procedure
dermatologist	psychiatrist
diagnose	psychologist
dietician	refer
FYI	respiratory therapist
general practitioner	specialize
gynecologist	specialty
nutrition	treat
nutritionist	vision

TRY THIS STRATEGY

Learn Word Forms

1. Warm Up, page 42

★ Have students look at the pictures, and ask: *Who do you see in the photos?*

★ Read the questions aloud.

★ Put students in pairs or small groups and have them discuss the questions.

★ Call on students to tell the class about their pair or small group discussion.

EXPANSION ACTIVITY:
Expand Your List

★ Put students in pairs or small groups to list all the medical professionals they or someone they know have used.

★ Call on students to share their ideas with the class and write them on the board. The list might include: *surgeon, nurse, ophthalmologist, dentist, oral surgeon, orthodontist, plastic surgeon, anesthesiologist.*

★ Go over what each type of medical professional does.

★ Have students write 1 sentence about each of 3 medical professionals listed on the board.

2. Read and Take Notes, page 42

★ Go over the directions. Read the occupations aloud, and have students repeat.

★ Have students read the information, complete the chart, and then check their answers with a partner.

★ Have students answer the questions.

★ Go over the answers with the class.

Vocabulary Notes:

★ Your students are probably more familiar with using the term *doctor* to refer to a physician. You may want to point out that we also use the term *physician* for a medical doctor.

★ Anyone with a doctorate degree may be called a doctor, although we identify specialties with certain abbreviations: *MD* for a medical doctor, *DD* for a dentist, *OD* for a doctor of optometry, *DVM* for a veterinarian, and *PhD* for most other doctorates.

Pronunciation Notes:

★ Sometimes students have difficulty locating the stress in multi-syllabic words, especially when prefixes or suffixes have been added. You may want to point out that the addition of many suffixes does not change the stress (*treat* — *treatment*).

★ When we add some suffixes (*-tion, -sion, -ian, -ic, -logy, -ity, -ial*), stress moves to the syllable just before the suffix (*psyche* — *psychologist*).

ANSWER KEY:

(possible answers)

Health care professional	Specialty
Cardiologist	treats heart diseases
Dental hygienist	cleans teeth
Dermatologist	treats skin problems
Dietician/Nutritionist	plans meals and nutrition programs
General practitioner	treats common health problems
Obstetrician/ Gynecologist	deals with women's health, pregnancy, and childbirth
Physical therapist	helps patients use body parts after an illness
Optometrist	diagnoses vision problems and diseases
Respiratory therapist	treats breathing problems
Pediatrician	takes care of children
Psychiatrist/Psychologist	treats emotional problems

1. Medical doctors: cardiologist, dermatologist, general practitioner, obstetrician, gynecologist, pediatrician, psychiatrist

2. Neither a respiratory nor a physical therapist is a medical doctor, although both help patients with medical problems. Both a psychiatrist and a psychologist treat emotional problems, but a psychiatrist can prescribe medicines because he or she is a medical doctor, whereas a psychologist is not.

EXPANSION ACTIVITY: Stress It

★ Review the concept of word stress. Remind students that words can have more than one stressed syllable, although one syllable receives primary stress.

★ Distribute small markers of 3 different sizes (paper circles, coins, hard candy) to each student, enough so that each student has several markers of the 3 sizes.

★ Say a medical profession (*pediatrician*), and have students use the markers to indicate the stress pattern of each word (••●••). Go over the pattern.

★ Repeat with other medical professions.

3. Apply, page 42

★ Go over the directions.

★ Put students in pairs to discuss the situations.

★ Call on students to share their ideas with the class.

EXPANSION ACTIVITY: Team Toss Challenge

★ Model the activity. Call on a student, and toss a ball or beanbag as you ask a question (*Who should I see if I think I need glasses?*). Elicit the appropriate health care professional (*optometrist*).

★ Divide the class into 2 teams. Ask each student to think of a question about a health care problem to which the answer is the name of a health care professional.

★ Toss the ball to students on alternating teams to pose a question to a student on the other team. Continue until everyone has had a chance to participate. In a variation, the 2 teams stand and face each other in 2 lines, and students ask the questions going down the line.

★ ★

TRY THIS STRATEGY: Learn Word Forms, page 42

★ ★

★ Read the strategy aloud.

★ Have students complete the chart.

★ Put students in pairs to compare their ideas with a partner.

★ Call on students to share their ideas with the class.

ANSWER KEY:

Answers are in italics.

Noun	Verb
specialist	*specialize*
treatment	*treat*
death	die
performance	*perform*
preparation	prepare
diagnosis	*diagnose*
prescription	*prescribe*

EXPANSION ACTIVITY:
Medical Specialties

★ Put students in pairs to list related word forms for the medical professionals listed in this lesson.

★ Put two pairs together to compare answers.

★ Call on students to share their ideas with the class.

OBJECTIVE

Calling for Information

COMMUNICATION STRATEGY

Correcting Someone

1. Warm Up, page 44

★ Have students look at the photo and information on page 44. To set the context, ask questions (*What do you think you will learn about? Have you been to a doctor's office recently?*).

★ Read the questions aloud.

★ Put students in pairs or small groups and have them discuss the questions.

★ Call on students to tell the class about their pair or small group discussion.

Culture Note:
★ Remind students that we write numerical dates with the month first (10/1/06), rather than with the day first.

EXPANSION ACTIVITY: Whip It

★ Remind students that we always say and read dates aloud as ordinal rather than cardinal numbers (*January twenty-second*, not *January twenty-two*).

★ Have students stand in a circle. Turn to the student on your right and say a date as a series of number (4/15/07). Elicit the date as the name of the month with an ordinal number (April fifteenth, two thousand and seven).

★ Have the first student turn to the student on his or her right and say a numerical date.

★ Continue until everyone has had a chance to participate. This should be a very fast-paced activity, lasting only a couple of minutes.

2. Listen and Take Notes 🎧, page 44

★ Go over the directions.

★ Have students listen and take notes in the chart while you read the conversations or play the tape or CD.

★ Have students compare notes with a partner.

★ Read the conversations, or play the tape or CD again if necessary.

★ Go over the answers with the class.

★ Have students add the new information to the appointment book on page 45 and then check their answers with a partner.

LISTENING SCRIPT

2. Listen and Take Notes, page 44

1. Listen to Conversation #1 and take notes in the chart.

Appointment Desk:	Redfield Medical Clinic. How can I help you?
Male Patient:	I'm calling to make an appointment with Dr. McCoy.
Desk:	Do you need to see her right away?
Patient:	No. I'm just making an appointment for my annual exam.
Desk:	All right. Can you hold for a minute?
Patient:	Sure.
Desk:	OK, let's see, Dr. McCoy has an opening on November 15th at noon.
Patient:	Uhm, the 15th will work, but 1:00 would be better. Do you have an opening then?
Desk:	Yes, you're in luck. She does have an opening at 1:00. Your name, please?
Patient:	It's Jeff Bartell.
Desk:	How do you spell that?
Patient:	It's B-a-r-t-e-l-l.
Desk:	Okay. And your telephone number, Mr. Bartell?
Patient:	It's 555-4834.
Desk:	555-4843.

Patient:	Excuse me, but that's 4834.
Desk:	Okay, 4834. Thank you. Well, Mr. Bartell, we'll see you on the 15th.
Patient:	Okay. See you then. Thank you very much.
Desk:	You're welcome. Bye bye.

2. Listen to Conversation #2 and take notes in the chart.

Appointment Desk:	Redfield Medical Clinic. Can I help you?
Patient:	This is Shirley Bao calling. I have an appointment with Dr. McCoy on the 15th that I need to cancel.
Desk:	Okay. Just a minute, please. Yes, I see. Your appointment is at 2:30. Would you like to reschedule that?
Patient:	No, not right now, thank you. I'll call back next week.
Desk:	Okay. I've canceled your appointment on the 15th. Anything else we can do for you?
Patient:	No, that's it for now. Thank you.
Desk:	Sure. Goodbye now.

3. Listen to Conversation #3 and take notes in the chart.

Appointment Desk:	Redfield Medical Clinic. Can I help you?
Maria:	Redfield Medical Clinic?
Desk:	Yes, that's right.
Maria:	I'm sorry. I must have dialed the wrong number. Is this 555-3312?
Desk:	No, I'm sorry it's not. But you're close.
Maria:	Okay. Sorry to bother you.
Desk:	No problem. Bye bye.
Maria:	Bye.

4. Listen to Conversation #4 and take notes in the chart.

Appointment Desk:	Redfield Medical Clinic. How can I help you?
Patient:	Yes, I need to change an appointment with Dr. McCoy.
Desk:	And when's your appointment?

Patient:	It's on the 12th at 2:30.
Desk:	And your name?
Patient:	Hong, Jim Hong. H-o-n-g.
Desk:	Okay, Mr. Hong. When would you like to reschedule that for?
Patient:	Anytime after the 14th would be fine.
Desk:	Can you come in on the 15th at 9:00?
Patient:	Hmm, that might be hard. Do you have anything later in the day?
Desk:	What about 4:30?
Patient:	Ah, yes. That would be great.
Desk:	Okay, Mr. Hong. We'll see you on the 15th at 3:30.
Patient:	Excuse me, but that should be 4:30. I can't come in at 3:30.
Desk:	Yes, of course. I'm sorry, Mr. Hong. We'll see you on the 15th at 4:30.
Patient:	Okay. Goodbye now.
Desk:	Goodbye.

5. Listen to Conversation #5 and take notes in the chart.

Appointment Desk:	Redfield Medical Clinic. How can I help you?
Patient:	I'm calling about a bill I just received from Dr. McCoy.
Desk:	Can I have your name, please?
Patient:	It's June Waite.
Desk:	White?
Patient:	No, it's Waite. W-a-i-t-e. It rhymes with gate.
Desk:	Okay, Ms. Waite. Thank you. And your date of birth?
Patient:	8-12-84.
Desk:	8—12—74.
Patient:	Excuse me. That's 84, not 74.
Desk:	Sorry. I'm having a little trouble hearing you. And you said there was a problem with your bill?
Patient:	Yes, that's right. I just received a second bill for the check up I had in August, but I already paid that bill. I paid it in September.
Desk:	Well, it's probably just a mix up. Let me look into it, and I'll get back to you.
Patient:	Thank you. Bye bye.

6. Listen to Conversation #6 and take notes in the chart.

Appointment Desk: Redfield Medical Clinic. How can I help you?

Patient: I'm just calling to check on the time of my appointment with Dr. McCoy.

Desk: Your name, please?

Patient: Coralia Torres. T-o-r-r-e-s.

Desk: Do you know what day your appointment is?

Patient: Yes. It's on the 15th, sometime in the morning.

Desk: Just a minute, please. Okay, Ms. Torres, you have a follow-up appointment at 11:30 on the 15th.

Patient: Seven-thirty? That can't be. I know I wouldn't make an appointment for 7:30.

Desk: I'm sorry, Ms. Torres. I said 11:30 not 7:30.

Patient: Okay, that's much better. Sorry about that.

Desk: No problem. See you on the 15th.

Patient: See you then. Thanks.

ANSWER KEY:

Answers are in italics.

Name of caller	Purpose for calling
1. *Jeff Bartell*	*make an appointment —1:00*
2. *Shirley Bao*	*cancel appointment at 2:30 on 15th*
3. *Maria*	*wrong number*
4. *Jim Hong*	*reschedule appointment to the 15th at 4:30*
5. *June Waite*	*problem with bill*
6. Coralia Torres	*confirm appointment time*

Students should add Jeff Bartell/Exam/ 555-4834 to 1:00, add Jim Hong to 4:30, and cross out Shirley Bao at 2:30.

Culture Note:
★ You may want to point out that when someone calls our home phone by mistake, we usually ask what number they intended to call. We then confirm or deny if that is the number they indeed called.

3. Use the Communication Strategy 🎧, page 44

★ Go over the directions.

★ Have students read the conversation, or read the conversation aloud line by line and have students repeat.

★ Have students practice reading the conversation in pairs.

★ Direct students' attention to the Communication Strategy box. Go over the information in the box.

★ Say each example and have students repeat.

★ Model the conversation again with a student. Have the student read B's lines. Demonstrate how to substitute, using your own ideas. Elicit appropriate responses from the student.

★ Have students work in pairs to practice the conversation, substituting their own ideas for the underlined words.

★ Walk around to make sure students understand the activity. Provide help if needed.

EXPANSION ACTIVITY: Role Play

★ Put students in pairs. Tell Student A to play the role of the doctor's administrative assistant and Student B to play the role of patient June or John Waite.

★ Have students role play a conversation about the bill on page 45. The patient should call to ask about the bill. The administrative assistant should make mistakes (*The due date is March 15.*) that the patient should correct (*Excuse me, but the due date on this bill is March 5.*).

★ Walk around to monitor the activity and provide help as needed.

BIG PICTURE EXPANSION ACTIVITY: SPEAKING—What did you say?

★ Put the Big Picture color transparency for Unit 3, Lesson 1 on the overhead projector, or have students look at the Big Picture in their books.

★ Have students work individually to list alternative ideas for each picture frame. For example, in the first frame, ideas might include *watching TV, reading a book*, or *playing the piano.*

★ Model the activity. Say a sentence about the first picture: *Oscar was at home playing the piano.* Elicit a correction (*Excuse me, but he was playing <u>cards</u>.*).

★ Put students in pairs. Have students take turns telling the story with incorrect information. Remind them to use the communication strategy to correct their partner's story.

★ Walk around the room to monitor the activity. Encourage students to practice all the phrases used to correct someone.

★ Have students tell a chain story. The first student will say an alternate version of the first picture. The second student will correct the first student and then add an alternate version of the second picture. Continue until all the students have had a chance to participate.

OBJECTIVE

Interpreting Nutritional Information

VOCABULARY

calorie
container
cut back on
energy

1. Warm Up, page 46

★ Have students look at the information on page 46. To set the context, ask questions about the labels (*What do you see? Where can you find this information?*).

★ Read the questions aloud.

★ Put students in pairs or small groups and have them discuss the questions.

★ Call on students to tell the class about their pair or small group discussion.

EXPANSION ACTIVITY: Student Sort

★ Have students stand. Tell them that you will ask a question, and they should talk to their classmates and then stand next to people with the same or a similar answer.

★ Ask questions. Create your own or use these:
What's your favorite vegetable?
What's your favorite type of restaurant?
How often do you go grocery shopping?
How often do you read nutritional labels?
What piece of information on a nutritional label is the most important?

★ After students respond to the question by sorting themselves, call on students in each group to tell the class about their group.

2. Read and Compare, page 46

★ Go over the directions.

★ Have students read the food labels. Ask comprehension questions (*What are the 2 foods? What is a serving size of peanuts? How many ingredients are in each package?*).

★ Have students read the sentences and check peanuts or spinach.

★ Have students check their answers with a partner.

★ Go over the answers with the class.

ANSWER KEY

1, 2, 4, 6, 7, 8 peanuts, 3, 5, 7 spinach

EXPANSION ACTIVITY: Reading Labels

★ Bring in food labels or have students bring them in.

★ Put students in small groups. Distribute labels to each group.

★ Have the groups compare the labels and note which food has the fewest calories, the highest fat content, the highest amount of sodium, the most protein per serving.

★ Call on students to tell the class what they discovered.

3. Apply, page 46

★ Go over the directions.

★ Put students in pairs to answer the questions.

★ Call on students to share their ideas with the class.

ANSWER KEY:

1. 340; 2. 17; 3. No, vegetables typically have a low fat content; 4. It's not a good idea because peanuts have little or no vitamins; 5. fewer peanuts

EXPANSION ACTIVITY: Research Project

★ Assign students research topics (a mineral found in food, a vitamin, the food pyramid), and have them go online to gather information.

★ Have students prepare presentations with visuals and present the information to the class.

OBJECTIVE

Using Adverb Clauses

Adverb Clauses of Time, page 48

★ Have students look at the notes in the box. Read the information and examples aloud.

★ Direct students' attention to the tip box. Make sure students understand the time expressions.

1. Find It, page 48

★ Read the directions aloud.

★ Go over the first sentence. Ask students how they can tell which clause is the adverb clause (*it begins with* as soon as).

★ Have students underline the adverb clauses and add commas where necessary.

★ Have students check their answers with a partner.

★ Go over the answers with the class.

ANSWER KEY:

1. <u>As soon as the ambulance arrived,</u> the nurses rushed out through the main door.
2. <u>When she saw the bill from the hospital,</u> she passed out.
3. <u>Whenever you have a question about your diet,</u> you should talk to a nutritionist.
4. <u>After his GP looked at the results of the tests,</u> she referred him to a cardiologist.
5. The cardiologist called <u>as soon as he got the results of the test.</u>
6. The doctor couldn't make a diagnosis <u>until she saw the blood test.</u>
7. Julia had to stay in bed for a month <u>while she was pregnant.</u>
8. <u>After Jean saw her GP,</u> she had to go to a specialist.

2. Complete the Sentences, page 48

★ Read the directions aloud. Go over the first sentence. Elicit ideas to complete the sentence.

★ Have students complete the sentences.

★ Have students compare their answers with a partner.

★ Call on students to share their answers with the class.

EXPANSION ACTIVITY: Find Your Match

★ Model the activity. Begin a sentence with an adverb clause (*Because I was late for class*) and elicit possible completions (*I drove faster than usual/I took a cab/I didn't eat breakfast*).

★ Have students write an adverb clause on an index card or a slip of paper. Tell them to memorize the clause they wrote. Collect the clauses and redistribute.

★ Have students write clauses to complete the sentences beginning with the adverb clause that they received (*I didn't eat breakfast*).

★ Call on students to read their new clauses aloud. Have classmates say their original adverb clause aloud if they think it matches the new clause (*because I was late for class/before I took a shower/although I was hungry*).

ANSWER KEY:

Answers will vary.

Adverb Clauses of Reason and Contrast, page 49

★ Have students look at the notes in the box. Read the information and examples aloud.

★ Direct students' attention to the tip box. Make sure students understand the expressions.

3. Write, page 49

★ Read the directions aloud.

★ Go over the first sentence.

★ Have students combine the sentences and then compare sentences with a partner.

★ Call on students to share their answers with the class.

BIG PICTURE EXPANSION ACTIVITY: GRAMMAR—What did he do when he saw the bill?

★ Make copies of **Worksheet #5** and distribute them to students.

★ Put the Big Picture color transparency for Unit 3, Lesson 1 on the overhead projector, or have students look at the Big Picture in their books.

★ Instruct students to complete the activities and then check their answers with a partner.

★ Go over the answers with the class.

ANSWER KEY:

A.
1. e; 2. a; 3. b; 4. g; 5. j; 6. c; 7. f; 8. h; 9. i; 10. d

B. *Possible answers include:*
1. Rita was worried when Oscar had his first heart attack.
2. After Oscar got to the hospital, the doctor examined him, and the nurse gave him medicine.
3. Oscar and Rita yelled because the bill was so high.
4. He should sue the hospital because it gave him another heart attack.

OBJECTIVE

Learning about Immunizations

VOCABULARY

immunization	serious reaction
immunize	side effect
measles	susceptible
mumps	vaccinate
recommended	

WINDOW ON MATH

Converting Numbers to Percentages

1. Warm Up, page 50

★ Go over the directions.

★ Put students in pairs or small groups to answer the questions.

★ Call on students to share their ideas with the class.

EXPANSION ACTIVITY: Compare Experiences

★ Put students in small groups of diverse national origins if possible.

★ Write questions on the board: *What shots did you get when you were a child? At what age did you get those shots?*

★ Have students talk about the differences between their vaccination histories. If everyone in the group is from the same home country, have them compare that country with the U.S.

★ Call on students to share their ideas with the class.

---

2. Read and Respond, page 50

★ Go over the directions.

★ Have students read the article and answer the questions.

★ Put students in pairs to check their answers.

★ Go over the answers with the class.

ANSWER KEY:

Answers will vary.
1. they get antibodies from their mothers;
2. measles/mumps; 3. it depends, sometimes immunity fades over time; 4. it is extremely unusual; 5. fever, soreness at the site of the injection, rash

---

EXPANSION ACTIVITY: Meaning from Context

★ Write the following words from the reading on the board:

> *immune   immunize   antibodies*
> *fade   susceptible*

★ Review ways to determine meaning from context. Have students work in pairs to write definitions for each word. Tell students not to write the word they are defining.

★ Have pairs exchange definitions and match them with the words on the board.

★ Call on students to read the words and definitions to the class.

---

3. Read a Graph, page 51

★ Go over the directions.

★ Put students in pairs or small groups to talk about the graph and answer the question.

★ Call on students to share their answers with the class.

ANSWER KEY:

Answers will vary.
The measles vaccine seems to be very effective because the number of cases dropped dramatically.

EXPANSION ACTIVITY: Compare Vaccines

★ Write a list of diseases for which vaccines are available on the board (*measles, mumps, pertussis, diphtheria, polio, tetanus*).

★ Have students use a search engine to enter the name of a disease and "graph." Have them visit sites to find graphs illustrating the incidence of the disease over time.

BIG PICTURE EXPANSION ACTIVITY: READING—FAQs About Heart Attacks

★ Make copies of **Worksheet #6** and distribute them to students.

★ Put the Big Picture color transparency for Unit 3, Lesson 1 on the overhead projector, or have students look at the Big Picture in their books.

★ Instruct students to complete the activities and then check their answers with a partner.

★ Go over the answers with the class.

ANSWER KEY:

A.
A. 3; B. 4; C. 2, 9; D. possibly 9; E. 5; F. 9

B.
1. False; 2. False; 3. False; 4. False; 5. False

WINDOW ON MATH: Converting Numbers to Percentages

A. Read the information, page 51

★ Have students read the information.

★ Model how to read the information in the box.

B. Calculate the percentages, page 51

★ Have students calculate the percentages and then check their answers with a partner.

★ Go over the answers with the class.

ANSWER KEY:

1. 50%; 2. 14%

EXPANSION ACTIVITY: Check the Label

★ Direct students' attention to the food labels from Lesson 4. Have students calculate the following information: *percentage of protein in each food based on a 2,000-calorie diet and based on a 2,500-calorie diet.*

★ Go over the answers with the class.

ANSWER KEY:

Peanuts: 16% and 12.3%
Spinach: 4% and 3.1%

OBJECTIVE

Review and Assessment

1. Listening Review 🎧, page 52

★ Go over the directions for items 1–5 with the class.

★ Read items 1–5 or play the tape or CD, and have the students mark their answers in the Answer Sheet box.

★ Walk around to monitor the activity and help students stay on task.

★ Go over the directions for items 6–10, and repeat the procedure.

★ Have students check their answers for 1–10 with a partner.

★ Go over the answers with the class.

LISTENING SCRIPT:

1. Listening Review, page 52

Listen to each conversation and choose the best answer to the question you hear. Use the Answer Sheet.

1.

A: We're going out for lunch at 1:00 today, Silvia. Can you join us?

B: Thanks, Bob, but I can't. I have an appointment to get my eyes checked today.

A: You're having problems with your eyes?

B: Well, it's nothing unusual. I'm just getting older.

Question: Who does the woman have an appointment to see?

2.

A: Did you have a good day?

B: Yeah. Pretty good.

A: Did you see Dr. Heinsle?

B: Yeah.

A: Well, what did he say?

B: He doesn't think it's anything serious, but he wants me to see a dermatologist.

A: A dermatologist? Why?

B: She can do some tests just to be sure.

Question: What kind of exam does he need?

3.

A: Dr. Jones' office. Can I help you?

B: Yes. I'd like to make an appointment with Dr. Jones.

A: Are you a patient of Dr. Jones?

B: No, I'm not. But Dr. Smith said I needed to see a cardiologist. He referred me to Dr. Jones.

A: I see. Can you come in on March 16th at 2:00?

B: March 16th at 2:00?

A: Yes.

B: That would be fine.

Question: What kind of doctor is Dr. Jones?

4.

A: Dr. Jones' office. Can I help you?

B: Yes. I need to cancel my appointment on February 18th.

A: Your name, please.

B: Hernandez. Sandra Hernandez.

A: And what time was your appointment on the 18th?

B: At 10:00.

A: Okay. And do you want to reschedule that?

B: Ah, no. I'll call back later to reschedule.

A: Okay. Bye now.

B: Bye.

Question: Why did the woman call the doctor's office?

5.

A: Did you look at the label on this cereal?

B: No. Why?

A: It says it has 300 calories per serving.

B: Mmm. That's a lot.

A: Yeah. I don't think we should buy it.

B: Okay. Let's choose something different.

Question: What doesn't the man like about the cereal?

Listen and choose the statement that is closest in meaning to the statement you hear. Use the Answer Sheet.

6. A GP refers patients to specialists.
7. Your appointment is on Monday the 5th at 4:00 P.M.
8. She felt sick when she woke up in the morning.
9. John has high blood pressure even though he exercises a lot.
10. Sandra went to the doctor because she had a high fever.

ANSWER KEY:

1. C; 2. C; 3. A; 4. B; 5. A; 6. A; 7. A; 8. A;
9. B; 10. C

2. Dictation 🎧, page 52

★ Go over the directions.
★ Have students write the sentences as you read the sentences or play the tape or CD.
★ Put students in pairs to compare sentences.
★ Go over the sentences with the class.

LISTENING SCRIPT:

2. Dictation, page 52

Listen and write the sentences you hear.

1. Do you know the name of a good pediatrician?
2. A cardiologist specializes in diseases of the heart.

3. Vocabulary Review, page 53

★ Direct students' attention to the crossword puzzle, and ask what it is.
★ Go over the directions. Make sure students understand how to fill in the crossword puzzle. Remind them to use words from the unit.
★ Have students check their answers with a partner.
★ Go over the answers with the class.

ANSWER KEY:

Across:
  7. psychiatrist; 8. specialists; 10. nutritionists;
  11. cardiologist; 12. preparation

Down:
  1. diagnose; 2. pass; 3. revive; 4. containers;
  5. vital; 6. refer; 7. pediatrician; 9. vision

LEARNING LOG, page 53

★ Point out the two sections of the Learning Log: *I know these words* and *I practiced these skills, strategies, and grammar points.*
★ Ask students to check the words they know and what they practiced.
★ Walk around to note what students don't know or didn't practice. Use this information to review areas of difficulty.

BIG PICTURE EXPANSION: SPEAKING ASSESSMENT—Talking about the Big Picture

★ You can use the Big Picture as an individual assessment to place new students in classes, to diagnose difficulties, or to measure progress.

★ Work with one student. Show the Big Picture to the student. Ask: *What do you see in the picture?* Or say: *Tell me about the story.* Tell the student to speak for as long as possible. Wait a moment for the student to prepare an answer.

★ If the student has difficulty, you can use prompts (*Who do you see? What are the people doing? Where are they?*).

★ You can use a scoring rubric like the one below to rate speakers.

4	Exhibits confidence; begins speaking without prompting Uses some complex sentences, although may make mistakes with irregular forms Can use several tenses
3	Uses sentences, although form may be incorrect Uses more than one tense Can speak for a sustained length of time Responds to prompts, but doesn't need them to begin speaking
2	Can use nouns and verbs in sentences Uses one tense most of the time Answers informational questions Limited vocabulary
1	Can name objects Uses single words Can answer yes/no questions
0	Cannot say anything independently May be able to point to objects when prompted

★ Review areas of difficulty.

TEACHER NOTES:

Things that students are doing well:

_____

_____

_____

_____

Things students need additional help with:

_____

_____

_____

_____

Ideas for further practice or for the next class:

_____

_____

_____

_____

BIG PICTURE EXPANSION ACTIVITY: WRITING—Describing Activities

★ Put the Big Picture color transparency for Unit 3, Lesson 1 on the overhead projector, or have students look at the Big Picture in their books.

★ Ask the class: *What happened in the story?*

★ Have students brainstorm ideas to prepare to write.

★ Have students write a paragraph retelling the story. Remind them to use adverb clauses.

★ Put students in pairs to take turns reading their paragraphs to their partners.

OBJECTIVE

Using Context Clues

Using Context Clues, page 54

★ Direct students' attention to the information in the box. Explain the strategy.

★ Go over the examples.

★ Check comprehension by asking questions (*What is a synonym? What is an example of a contrast?*).

1. Use context clues, page 54

★ Go over the directions. Read the first sentence. Ask how students can tell that *melanoma* is bad (*Her grandmother died from it*).

★ Have students read the sentences and write *G* or *B* to indicate if the underlined word is something good or bad for one's health.

★ Have students check their answers with a partner.

★ Go over the answers with the class.

ANSWER KEY:

1. B; 2. B; 3. G; 4. G; 5. B; 6. G; 7. B; 8. B; 9. B; 10. G

2. Use context clues, page 55

★ Go over the directions and the example.

★ Have students read the sentences individually, or read them aloud.

★ Have students write the general meaning of the underlined words.

★ Have students check their answers with a partner.

★ Go over the answers with the class.

ANSWER KEY:

Answers will vary.

1. unwanted effects from a medicine; 2. bad, harsh; 3. thing, ingredient in food; 4. eaten, drunk, taken by mouth; 5. a local law officer; 6. addition; 7. lot; 8. painkilling drug; 9. easier to swallow and easier on the stomach; 10. a condition which blocks airflow and makes breathing difficult; 11. getting

EXPANSION ACTIVITY: Real World Reading

★ For an out-of-class assignment, have students select a text in English with at least one example of an unfamiliar word or phrase whose meaning is easy to determine from context clues.

★ Have students underline the word or phrase in the text they brought in. Tell students to make a photocopy of the page if the text is one that they cannot write on.

★ Put students in pairs to exchange examples of text. Ask the partners to write definitions for the underlined word or phrase.

★ Call on students to read the word and their definitions aloud.

OBJECTIVE

Identifying Punctuation Marks

Identifying Punctuation Marks, page 56

★ Direct students' attention to the information in the box. Read each word aloud and have students repeat.

★ Ask comprehension questions (*When do we use a period? Quotation marks?*).

1. Count and identify, page 56

★ Go over the directions.

★ Have students count and identify the punctuation marks.

★ Go over the answers with the class.

ANSWER KEY:

1. 4 commas and 1 period; 2. 1 comma, 2 periods, 1 hyphen/dash, and 1 set of parentheses; 3. 1 colon, 2 slashes, 2 periods, 2 dots, and 1 pair of quotation marks; 4. 2 commas, 1 set of quotation marks, 1 pound sign, and 1 period; 5. 1 underscore, 1 colon, 2 bullets, and 2 periods

2. Write the correct punctuation, page 56

★ Go over the directions.

★ Have students add the punctuation marks.

★ Go over the answers with the class.

ANSWER KEY:

1. The doctor's patient didn't arrive on time.
2. Can you email me at drfranklin.help.net.
3. My next appointment is on 03/21/07. That's the first day of spring.
4. You can find information about immunizations at http://www.cdc.gov.
5. When she saw the child run into the street, she yelled, "Stop!"

Using Commas, page 57

★ Direct students' attention to the information on page 57.

★ Explain the ways we use commas. Go over the examples.

★ Check comprehension by asking questions (*What are some times we use commas?*).

3. Add commas, page 57

★ Go over the directions.

★ Have students read the paragraphs and add commas where appropriate.

★ Put students in pairs to compare their answers.

★ Go over the answers with the class.

ANSWER KEY:

Stop Smoking

In 1960, the Surgeon General of the U.S. announced that smoking was bad for your health. Since then, many Americans have stopped using tobacco products. Recently, however, there has been an increase in the number of young people who smoke. Some people think that movies are influencing young people to start smoking.

Get Moving

According to the U.S. Surgeon General, people aren't getting enough exercise, and this is causing serious health problems. There are some easy ways to get more exercise. For example, you can walk up the stairs instead of taking the elevator. You can also take an exercise class, join a gym, or take up a sport.

EXPANSION ACTIVITY: Punctuation Practice

★ Bring in articles from newspapers or magazines, or have students bring them in.

★ Distribute an article to each student.

★ Have students white out all the punctuation in the article, or recopy the article without punctuation.

★ Put students in pairs to exchange and repunctuate the articles.

★ Have students check their answers with their partners.

EQUIPPED FOR THE FUTURE ROLE

Work

OBJECTIVE

Identifying Hazards at Work

A. Test your knowledge, page 52

★ Have students answer the questions in the quiz. Point out that they may not know the answers, but they should make their best guess.

★ Put students in pairs to talk about their answers.

★ Go over the answers with the class.

ANSWER KEY:

1. to remove uncomfortable safety equipment; 2. sprains, strains; 3. false; 4. construction; 5. false

B. Read questions 1 to 5, Workbook page 52

★ Have students read the questions, or read the questions aloud. Point out that reading the questions first will help students pay attention to important information as they read.

★ Have students read the story to answer the questions and then check their answers with a partner.

★ Go over the answers with the class.

ANSWER KEY:

1. He fell off a ladder; 2. His injuries were very serious—he's paralyzed; 3. He is 24 now; 4. He says that if workers don't feel safe, they should tell their boss and ask for training; 5. *Answers will vary.* He may have felt embarrassed/afraid/shy.

Vocabulary Note:

★ Your students may be unfamiliar with certain expressions (*as it stands now, miss out on, at the snap of your fingers*), but they should be able to guess the meaning from context clues. If not, go over the meaning of any unfamiliar expressions.

EXPANSION ACTIVITY: Write Questions

★ Have students write 3 more questions about the story.

★ Put students in pairs to exchange and answer questions.

★ Call on students to read their questions aloud and elicit answers from the class.

Take It Outside, Workbook page 53

★ Read each question aloud and have students repeat.

★ If you do this in class, students can interview classmates. If students do this as an out-of-class assignment, they can interview family members, friends, or coworkers.

★ Call on volunteers to share the information with the class.

 Take It Online, Workbook page 53

★ Have students use a search engine and enter "OSHA." Tell students to write down 3 things they learn from the website.

★ Call on volunteers to share the information with the class.

EQUIPPED FOR THE FUTURE ROLE

Community

OBJECTIVE

Recognizing Addiction Problems

A. Read questions 1 to 4, Workbook page 54

★ Have students read the questions, or read the questions aloud. Remind students that reading the questions first will help students pay attention to important information as they read.

★ Have students read the story to answer the questions and then check their answers with a partner.

★ Go over the answers with the class.

ANSWER KEY:

1. something you do all the time even when it causes problems; 2. She spent hours and hours on the computer, even though she knew she should do her homework; 3. poor grades, incomplete work; 4. sell your computer, set a time limit, talk to a counselor, don't go to places where there is a computer, etc.

B. Use the graph below, Workbook page 55

★ Point out that bar graphs are another visual way to show numerical information. In this graph, students can see the different percentages of problems that are alcohol-related. Ask comprehension questions: *What is being measured? What categories are listed? Which problem has the greatest percentage of cases related to alcohol?*

★ Have students complete the sentences and then compare their answers with a partner.

★ Go over the answers with the class.

ANSWER KEY:

1. 50%; 2. half, 3/4, 80% [lots of answers]; 3. 75%; 4. 40%

C. What kinds of problems, Workbook page 55

★ Go over the directions.

★ Have students complete the chart and then compare their answers with a partner.

★ Go over the answers with the class.

ANSWER KEY:

[possible ideas]

Drinking Alcohol
car accidents
accidents at work
fires
bad health
bad parenting
domestic violence
marital problems
jail

Gambling
debt
marital problems
crime

Smoking
bad health
bad breath
smelly clothes
bad example for children

Taking Illegal Drugs
car accidents
accidents at work
fires
bad health
bad parenting
domestic violence
marital problems
crime
jail

 Take It Online, Workbook page 55

★ Go over the directions.

★ Have students use a search engine to find information about addiction.

★ Have students write the facts and opinions, as well as the Internet source in the chart.

★ Call on volunteers to share the information with the class.

EXPANSION ACTIVITY: Project

★ Put students in small groups. Have each small group select an addiction they would like to research. You may want to brainstorm other addictions or compulsive behaviors (*overeating, addiction to prescription drugs*).

★ Have the groups present their research to the class. Encourage them to make an educational poster or brochure to inform people about the problems associated with the behavior.

Rights and Responsibilities

UNIT OVERVIEW

LESSON	OBJECTIVE	TEACHER'S EDITION PAGE NUMBER
1. They marched on Washington.	Describing an Event	p. 77
2. It's your right.	Identifying Rights and Responsibilities	p. 79
3. Should high school be compulsory?	Understanding the U.S. Educational System	p. 81
4. Government Agencies	Learning about Government Agencies	p. 85
5. He was elected in 1789.	Using Active and Passive Verbs	p. 87
6. The Purpose of a Union	Understanding Workers' Rights	p. 89
7. What do you know?	Review and Assessment	p. 91
Spotlight: Reading Strategy	Adjusting Your Reading Speed	p. 94
Spotlight: Writing Strategy	Identifying Your Purpose for Writing	p. 95

Big Picture Expansion Activities

FOCUS	ACTIVITY	SUGGESTED USE
Speaking	Agree or Disagree	Lesson 3
Reading	Peaceful Protests	Lesson 2
Grammar	We aren't paid overtime.	Lesson 5
Writing	Express Your Opinion	Lesson 7
Speaking Assessment	Talking about the Big Picture	Lesson 7

Big Picture Expansion Activity Worksheets

WORKSHEET NUMBER/FOCUS	TITLE	TEACHER'S EDITION PAGE NUMBER
7. Reading	Peaceful Protests	p. 187
8. Grammar	We aren't paid overtime.	p. 188

OBJECTIVE

Describing an Event

VOCABULARY

march
participate
protest

1. Warm Up, page 58

★ Put the Big Picture color transparency for Unit 4, Lesson 1 on the overhead projector, or have students look at the Big Picture in their books.

★ To set the context, ask questions about the picture (*Who do you see in the picture? What's happening?*).

★ As students talk about the Big Picture, write key vocabulary words on the board.

★ Read the questions aloud.

★ Put students in pairs or small groups and have them discuss the questions.

★ Call on students to tell the class about their pair or small group discussion.

Culture/Civics Notes:

★ You may want to discuss the functions of some of the famous buildings in the mall area of Washington, DC:

White House — where the president lives (the executive branch)

Capitol — where Congress meets (the legislative branch)

Supreme Court (judicial branch)

Smithsonian — museum with many buildings devoted to particular subjects

★ Your students might also be interested to know that protest marches were very popular in Washington in both the civil rights and anti-war movements. Martin Luther King, Jr., made his famous "I Have a Dream" speech at the Lincoln Memorial during the 1963 March on Washington.

 EXPANSION ACTIVITY: That's a capital idea.

★ For an out-of-class or lab activity, assign students specific topics related to Washington, DC to research. Topics could include important buildings: *the White House, the Capitol, the Smithsonian, the Lincoln Memorial, the Washington Monument, the Jefferson Memorial, the Library of Congress.* Or you could assign specific events: *the 1963 March on Washington, the Million Man March, anti-war protests during the Vietnam war, inaugurations, the Bicentennial.*

★ Have students prepare a 1-minute speech on their topic and present it to the class.

2. Check *True* or *False*, page 58

★ Go over the directions.

★ Direct students' attention to the Big Picture. Read the first statement aloud and ask students if it is true or false. Ask students to use evidence from the picture to support their answers. Have students check *True*.

★ Have students check *True* or *False* for each statement and then write 2 more true sentences.

★ Put students in pairs to check their answers with a partner.

★ Go over the answers with the class.

ANSWER KEY:

1. True; 2. True; 3. False; 4. True; 5. False; 6. False

EXPANSION ACTIVITY: Memory Game

★ Divide the class into two teams.

★ Have teams write false statements about the picture, enough so that each team member can say or read one statement.

★ With books closed, have a member of Team A read a statement to a member of Team B

(*This is a picture of New York City*). B should correct the statement (*No, it's a picture of Washington, DC.*).

★ A team earns a point when it can stump the opposing team. Continue, alternating teams, until everyone has had a chance to read and correct at least one statement.

3. Give Opinions, page 58

★ Go over the directions. Read each question aloud.

★ Put students in pairs to answer the questions.

★ Call on students to share their ideas with the class.

ANSWER KEY:

Answers will vary.

EXPANSION ACTIVITY: Fact vs. Opinion

★ Review the differences between a fact and an opinion.

★ Model the activity: state an opinion about something in the Big Picture (*The Capitol is more beautiful than the Washington Monument*). Elicit a factual statement about the picture (*A police car is on the street.*).

* On pieces of paper, have students write 5 statements of opinion and 5 factual statements about the Big Picture.

* Put students in pairs or small groups. Have them take turns reading statements aloud and eliciting from their partners whether the statement is factual or an opinion.

EXPANSION ACTIVITY: Make a Choice

★ Write *agree* on one side of the board and *disagree* on the other.

★ Have a group of students stand and come to the board.

★ Tell students at the board that you will read a statement, and they should move to stand next to the word that expresses their opinion.

★ Read a statement that refers to the topics of the unit (*It is more important to discuss the responsibilities of citizens than it is to learn about the U.S. educational system.*). Remind students to move.

★ Call on students to explain their position on the issue.

★ Repeat with other statements and students.

OBJECTIVE

Identifying Rights and Responsibilities

TRY THIS STRATEGY

Understanding Homonyms

VOCABULARY

authorities	honestly
compulsory	peaceful
constitution	register
discriminate	religious
election	respect
get together	tolerant

1. Identify, page 60

★ Go over the directions.

★ Have students read the information and complete the chart.

★ Put students in pairs to compare charts.

★ Go over the answers with the class.

ANSWER KEY:

(possible answers)

Rights
   to be treated equally
   to vote in elections
   to a free education through high school
   to speak freely
   to get together in public to protest
   to follow any religious belief

Responsibilities
   to report unfair treatment
   to register to vote
   to keep informed about issues
   to make sure children go to school and
     do their homework
   to pay taxes honestly and on time
   to protest peacefully
   to respect people with different opinions
   to be tolerant of the religious beliefs
     of others

EXPANSION ACTIVITY: Compare and Contrast

★ Draw a Venn diagram on the board. Over one circle write *U.S.* Over the other, write *Other:* _____. Instruct students to write the name of their home country or another country they know well on the line. Remind students how to complete a Venn diagram.

★ If possible, put students in pairs according to national origin, and have them complete the Venn diagrams to show the similarities and differences between their home country and the U.S. in terms of rights.

★ Call on students to share their ideas with the class.

★ For a greater challenge, have students use the information on the Venn diagram to write a paragraph comparing and contrasting the 2 countries.

2. Use the Vocabulary, page 60

★ Go over the directions.

★ Have students complete the chart and then check their answers with a partner.

★ Have students write 5 *wh-* questions.

★ Put students in pairs to take turns asking and answering their questions.

ANSWER KEY:

Answers are in italics. Additional possible answers are in brackets.

Noun	Verb	Adjective
1. discrimination	*discriminate*	discriminatory
2. *election*	elect	—— [elected]
3. registration	*register*	—— [registered]
4. tolerance	tolerate	*tolerant*
5. requirement	*require*	—— [required, requisite]
6. *authority*	authorize	—— [authorized]

EXPANSION ACTIVITY: Use the Glossary

★ Have students look up the highlighted words from this lesson in the glossary.

★ Put students in pairs to list synonyms and antonyms for as many of the words as possible. Allow students to use dictionaries. Point out that students may not be able to find antonyms and synonyms for all words.

★ Model the activity. Write a word from the lesson on the board (*peaceful*). Then write an antonym (*violent*) and a synonym (*calm*) for the word. Call on a student, and say a word and either *antonym* or *synonym* (*peaceful, synonym*). Elicit the answer (*calm*).

★ For more practice, put 2 pairs together in groups of 4. Have each pair take turns reading their own synonyms or antonyms to prompt the correct vocabulary word from the other pair.

★ Walk around the room to monitor the activity and provide help as needed.

3. Interview, page 60

★ Go over the directions.

★ Have students walk around and talk to classmates to complete the chart.

★ Call on students to tell the class something they found out.

EXPANSION ACTIVITY: Sort

★ For a more kinesthetic activity, have students stand.

★ Tell them that you will ask questions and they should stand with classmates who have the same or a similar answer.

★ Ask *How many elections have you voted in?*, and remind students to move around until they are standing with classmates who have voted in the same number of elections. If needed, set up ranges such as 0, 1–2, 3–5, more than 6.

★ Continue asking questions. Create your own, or use the ones below:
How many children do you have in school?
What type of discrimination have you faced?
How much education should children have?
How likely would you be to report a problem with discrimination?

★ ★

TRY THIS STRATEGY: Understanding Homonyms, page 60

★ ★

★ Read the strategy aloud.

★ Have students write homonyms next to each word.

★ Put students in pairs to compare their answers with a partner.

★ Go over the answers with the class.

ANSWER KEY:

Additional answers not in the lesson are in italics.
right/*rite*; to/*too*; their/*they're*; do/*dew*

BIG PICTURE EXPANSION ACTIVITY: READING—Peaceful Protests

★ Make copies of **Worksheet #7** and distribute them to students.

★ Put the Big Picture color transparency for Unit 4, Lesson 1 on the overhead projector, or have students look at the Big Picture in their books.

★ Instruct students to complete the activities and then check their answers with a partner.

★ Go over the answers with the class.

ANSWER KEY:

A. 1. False; 2. True; 3. True; 4. False; 5. False; 6. False

B. 1. the Constitution; 2. any opinion that does not advocate violence or libel someone; 3. pornography, threats of violence or harm, or libel

OBJECTIVE

Understanding the U.S. Educational System

COMMUNICATION STRATEGY

Agreeing and Disagreeing

VOCABULARY

coeducational	physical punishment
elect	required
elective	spank
extracurricular activity	

1. Warm Up, page 62

★ Have students look at the pictures on page 63. To set the context, ask questions about the picture (*What do the pictures have in common? What is the graph showing?*).

★ Read the questions aloud.

★ Put students in pairs or small groups and have them discuss the questions.

★ Call on students to tell the class about their pair or small group discussion.

EXPANSION ACTIVITY: Venn Diagram

★ Draw a Venn diagram on the board. Write *U.S.* above one circle.

★ Have students complete a Venn diagram comparing the school system in the U.S. with the educational system in another country.

★ Put students in pairs to share their ideas.

---

2. Listen and Take Notes 🎧, **page 62**

★ Go over the directions.

★ Have students listen and look at the pictures while you read the statements or play the tape or CD.

★ Have students summarize each opinion in the chart.

★ Have students compare their notes with a partner.

★ Read the statements or play the tape or CD again if necessary.

★ Then ask students to decide if they agree or disagree with each opinion and to check their answer in the chart.

┌ **LISTENING SCRIPT:** ┐

2. Listen and Take Notes, page 62

Listen to 6 peoples' opinions about education. Summarize each opinion.

1.

Woman: The biggest problem with schools today is that parents aren't involved. Maybe it's because they're too busy with work and other things, but the truth is, parents need to be more involved. I mean, they can volunteer and attend school meetings. And they can make sure their children do their school work. That's a parent's job.

2.

Man: I think students today spend too much time in extracurricular activities. When I was a child, we didn't have extracurricular activities. School was all about studying and learning. It wasn't about playing sports and having parties.

3.

Woman: I think children need to start school at a younger age. Why do we wait until they are 5 years old? A child's brain develops quickly from the time he or she is born. There are so many things they can learn before age 5.

4.

Man: I think it's a good thing that teachers can't physically punish their students. In the old days teachers could hit their students and maybe things were quieter in class, but I think students then were afraid to think for themselves and ask questions. And what's education if you can't think for yourself and ask questions?

5.

Woman: I really don't think schools should be coeducational, especially for teenagers. When girls and boys are together in class, they don't think about studying. And when girls study with boys, they don't talk as much. Well, that's my opinion anyway.

6.

Man: I just heard that students at the high school in my area can take dancing as an elective course. I think that's crazy. I mean, my tax money is paying for schools, and I don't think I should be paying for young people to learn to dance. Their parents can pay for dance classes, not me.

ANSWER KEY:

Answers will vary.

Speaker's opinion
1. Parents should be involved in their child's school and education.
2. Students should focus on school, not on extracurricular activities.
3. Children should start school before age 5.
4. Teachers shouldn't use physical punishment.
5. Schools shouldn't be coeducational.
6. Electives such as dancing shouldn't be paid for with tax money.

Culture Notes:

★ You may want to discuss the differences between policies in public schools and private schools. Point out that many parents send their children to private schools, some of which are religious. These schools are not bound by the rules affecting public schools.

★ Although some public schools are single-sex, the majority are coeducational. Many private schools are single-sex. Some educators believe that restricting certain classes or even the entire school to one gender fosters better learning.

EXPANSION ACTIVITY:
How do you know? 🎧

★ Point out that we often signal an opinion through the use of certain words or phrases. Elicit examples and write them on the board (*I think, I believe, people should*).

★ Tell students to write down the phrases that signal the opinions about education.

★ Have students listen and write phrases as you read the statements or play the tape or CD.

★ Call on students to share their ideas with the class.

ANSWER KEY:

I think, I don't think, that's my opinion, the biggest problem, that's crazy

3. Listen and Circle Your Answer 🎧, page 62

★ Go over the directions.

★ Have students listen while you read the conversations or play the tape or CD.

★ Have students check the answers and then compare answers with a partner.

★ Read the conversation, or play the tape or CD again if necessary.

LISTENING SCRIPT:

3. Listen and Circle Your Answer, page 62

Listen to 5 conversations. Decide if the two people agree or disagree. Check (✓) the correct box.

1.

A: Do you think school should be compulsory?

B: Hmm. That's an interesting question. To be honest, I *don't* think it should be compulsory.

A: Yeah. Neither do I. I mean, when it's compulsory, kids don't value it.

2.

A: Do you think students should have more time for physical education?

B: Yes, yes, yes. It's not good for children to sit in a chair all day. They need exercise. They need to move around.

A: Why can't they get exercise after school? That would be better.

B: Well, they can do that, too. But most kids are in school for at least 6 hours, and that's too much time to be sitting.

3.

A: Do you think our high school should have a school newspaper?

B: Yes. That's a great idea.

A: Really? Why do you think so?

B: Well, it gives students a real purpose for writing. I think they learn a lot from putting out a newspaper.

A: Hmm.

4.

A: What's your opinion of the extracurricular activities at the high school? Do you think we have enough?

B: Yes, I guess so.

A: Hmm. Me too.

5.

A: What did you think of the PTA meeting last week?

B: Oh, I didn't go. I think it's a waste of time.

A: Why is that?

B: Oh, I don't know. Nothing important ever happens.

A: Well, next month we're going to discuss the new extracurricular activities. I think it should be interesting.

B: Hmm.

ANSWER KEY:

1. They agree; 2. They disagree; 3. They disagree; 4. They agree; 5. They disagree

Culture Note:
★ Remind students if necessary that *PTA* stands for *Parent Teacher Association,* an organization of parents and teachers who work together to make the school better.

EXPANSION ACTIVITY: Survey

★ Put students in small groups.

★ Have each group create a list of 4 questions about education that they would like to know people's opinions about. Point out that the questions should ask about agreement or disagreement (*Do you agree that single-sex schools are better for students? Why or why not?*).

★ Tell each student to ask 5 people the 4 questions in their survey.

★ Have the groups compile the results.

★ Call on students to share the results with the class.

4. Use the Communication Strategy 🎧, page 62

★ Go over the directions.

★ Have students read the conversation, or read the conversation aloud line by line and have students repeat.

★ Have students practice reading the conversation in pairs.

★ Direct students' attention to the Communication Strategy box. Go over the information in the box.

★ Say each example and have students repeat.

★ Model the conversation with a student. Have the student read B's lines. Demonstrate how to substitute your own ideas. Elicit appropriate responses from the student.

★ Have pairs practice the conversation, substituting their own ideas for the underlined words.

★ Walk around to make sure students understand the activity. Provide help if needed.

BIG PICTURE EXPANSION ACTIVITY: SPEAKING—Agree or Disagree

★ Put the Big Picture color transparency for Unit 4, Lesson 1 on the overhead projector, or have students look at the Big Picture in their books.

★ With input from the students, identify the issues that people are protesting in the picture.

★ Put students in pairs and assign each pair an issue, or let students choose.

★ Have students create conversations about the topic in which they either agree or disagree. Remind them to use the communication strategy in the conversation.

★ Have volunteers perform their conversations for the class. Ask other students if they agree or disagree with the speakers.

★ In a variation, you could set the activity up as a debate. Explain that in a debate, each side will present an argument in support of their position (1 minute), and then each side will have 1 minute to argue against the other side's position. Vary the times and structure as needed.

OBJECTIVE

Learning about Government Agencies

TRY THIS STRATEGY

Understanding Acronyms

VOCABULARY

acronym	federal
consumer	harmful
contact	initial
crime	investigate
disaster	obey
enforce	recall

1. Scan, page 64

★ Have students look at the information on page 64. To set the context, ask questions (*What is this information about?*).

★ Go over the directions. Remind student that when they scan, they are looking quickly for specific information.

★ Read the questions and have students answer them.

★ Put students in pairs to check their answers.

★ Call on students to share their answers with the class.

EXPANSION ACTIVITY: Create Questions

★ Have students write 5 questions that require scanning to answer. Tell students to choose different pages in the book and to note the page with each question.

★ Put students in pairs to exchange and answer the questions.

★ Call on students to ask other classmates a question.

2. Read and Respond, page 64

★ Go over the directions. Read each question aloud.

★ Have students read the information and answer the questions.

★ Have students check their answers with a partner.

★ Go over the answers with the class.

ANSWER KEY:

1. They are government agencies that help people. 2. CPSC and OSHA; 3. EEOC and OSHA; 4. *Answers will vary.*

Grammar Note:

★ You may want to point out that in the information on pages 64–65, a capital letter does not signal the start of a sentence. To read this as complete sentences, students have to read the name of the agency with the information (*EEOC makes sure that people are not discriminated against when they apply for a job and when they are at work.*).

EXPANSION ACTIVITY: Word Forms

★ Elicit or present suffixes that typically identify a certain part of speech. See list below.

Noun	Verb	Adjective	Adverb
-ment	-ate	-ical	-ly
-ency	-ize	-able	
-tion		-ible	
-sion		-y	
-ion		-al	
-ity		-ous	
-er/-or		-ful	

★ Have students work in pairs to find words in the information on pages 64–65 that fit these patterns.

★ Go over the answers with the class.

★ Have students work in pairs to think of words for any suffixes that remain.

ANSWER KEY:

Nouns: management, agency, consumer, employment, commission, opportunity, protection, investigation, administration, government, regulation

Verbs: operate, discriminate, investigate (*industrialize*)

Adjectives: federal, local, natural, hazardous, harmful (*methodical, flammable, edible, tasty*)

Adverb: fairly

3. Predict, page 64

★ Go over the directions.

★ Have students write the initials of the agency next to the information.

★ Call on students to share their answers with the class.

ANSWER KEY:

1. EEOC; 2. FEMA; 3. EPA; 4. CPSC; 5. FEMA; 6. OSHA; 7. FBI; 8. FTC

EXPANSION ACTIVITY: Website Visit

★ Put students in pairs or small groups. Assign each group one of the agencies on pages 64–65 to research.

★ Have the groups visit the website for the agency they are researching by using a search engine and entering the agency's name or initials. They should write 5 things they learn about the agency.

★ Ask each group to present their findings to the class.

★ ★

TRY THIS STRATEGY: Understanding Acronyms, page 64

★ ★

★ Read the strategy aloud.

★ Have students identify the other acronym and the 5 initials in the lesson.

★ Put students in pairs to compare their answers with a partner.

★ Go over the answers with the class.

ANSWER KEY:

Acronyms: FEMA, OSHA
Initials: CPSC, FTC, EEOC, EPA, FBI

OBJECTIVE

Using Active and Passive Verbs

Active and Passive Verb Forms, page 66

★ Have students look at the notes in the box. Read the information and examples aloud.

★ Ask questions to check comprehension (*When do we use the passive? Which is more common, the active or the passive?*).

> **Grammar Notes:**
> ★ You may want to point out that not all verbs have passive forms.
> ★ Only verbs that take an object (*eat* apples) can be made passive because the object is moved into the subject position (*apples are eaten*).

1. Identify, page 66

★ Read the directions aloud.

★ Go over the first sentence. Elicit that *A* should be written on the line.

★ Have students write *A* or *P* next to each sentence.

★ Have students check their answers with a partner.

★ Go over the answers with the class.

ANSWER KEY:

1. A; 2. P; 3. A; 4. P; 5. A; 6. P; 7. P; 8. P; 9. P; 10. A; 11. A

2. Choose the Correct Verb, page 66

★ Read the directions aloud.

★ Go over the first sentence. Elicit that *do* should be written on the line.

★ Have students write the verbs in the blank.

★ Have students compare their answers with a partner.

★ Call on students to share their answers with the class.

ANSWER KEY:

1. do; 2. are given; 3. are required; 4. treats; 5. receive

Forming the Passive, page 67

★ Have students look at the notes in the box. Read the information and examples aloud.

★ Ask questions to check comprehension (*How do you form the simple present passive? The simple past passive?*).

3. Complete the Sentences, page 67

★ Read the directions aloud.

★ Go over the first sentence. Elicit that *is elected* should be written on the line.

★ Have students complete the sentences and compare answers with a partner.

★ Call on students to share their answers with the class.

ANSWER KEY:

1. is elected; 2. was elected; 3. was ruled; 4. was outlawed; 5. is added; 6. was signed; 7. was written; 8. was added; 9. are held; 10. is sent; 11. is based

EXPANSION ACTIVITY: Rewrite

★ Read the first sentence in Activity 1 aloud. Ask students to rewrite it as a passive sentence (*Many of the rights of U.S. citizens are spelled out in the Bill of Rights.*).

★ Have students work in pairs or groups of 3 to rewrite the sentences in Activity 1 where possible. Point out that #3 and #4 cannot be changed.

★ Call on volunteers to write the new sentences on the board.

ANSWER KEY:

1. Many of the rights of U.S. citizens are spelled out in the Bill of Rights.

2. In the U.S., the government does not require citizens to vote.

3. can't be changed

4. The government allows U.S. citizens to follow any or no religion.

5. can't be changed

6. The government does not allow employers to pay employees less than the minimum wage.

7. In most states, the state allows parents to teach their children at home. We call this home schooling.

8. The state decides what children learn at school/are taught at school.

9. Income taxes and property taxes pay for education.

10. Environmental laws are enforced by the EPA.

11. Statistics on crime are collected by the FBI.

4. Interview, page 67

★ Go over the directions.

★ Put students in pairs to take turns asking and answering questions. Remind students to use complete sentences.

★ Call on students to tell the class about their partners.

BIG PICTURE EXPANSION ACTIVITY: GRAMMAR—We aren't paid overtime.

★ Make copies of **Worksheet #8** and distribute them to students.

★ Put the Big Picture color transparency for Unit 4, Lesson 1 on the overhead projector, or have students look at the Big Picture in their books.

★ Instruct students to complete the activities and then check their answers with a partner.

★ Go over the answers with the class.

ANSWER KEY:

A.

1. Some workers aren't/weren't paid overtime.

2. A man was interviewed by a female reporter.

3. The labor protest was scheduled weeks ago.

4. The man in the wheelchair was injured in a car accident.

5. A protester was questioned by the police officer.

B.

1. Overtime pay and equal pay are represented in the protest.

2. The White House and the Washington Monument are pictured.

3. One school bus was sent to pick up the children.

OBJECTIVE

Understanding Workers' Rights

VOCABULARY

accountable
deserve
remedy
say
security
work for a living

WINDOW ON MATH

Understanding Graphs

1. Warm Up, page 68

★ Go over the directions.

★ Read each question aloud. Have students answer the questions and then compare their answers with a partner.

★ Call on students to share their ideas with the class.

EXPANSION ACTIVITY: Identify

★ Write the four information sources in question 1 on the board: *newspaper, book, website, magazine.* Point out that each source has certain characteristics that set it apart from other sources.

★ Have students work in pairs to list as many characteristics as they can that help them identify an information source.

★ Call on students to share their ideas with the class.

2. Read and Respond, page 68

★ Go over the directions.

★ Have students read the article and answer the questions.

★ Put students in pairs to check their answers.

★ Go over the answers with the class.

ANSWER KEY:

Answers will vary.
1. A union is a group of workers who work together to have a voice on the job.
2. To get workers' basic rights on the job.
3. A say in their jobs, safety, security, fair and equal treatment.
4. *Answers will vary.*

EXPANSION ACTIVITY: Personal Profiles

★ For a research project, assign groups of students an important figure in the American labor movement. Individuals might include Cesar Chavez, Mother Jones, Samuel Gompers, Albert Shanker, Walter Reuthers, and Eugene V. Debs.

★ Have each group prepare a 5-minute presentation for the class.

3. Apply, page 69

★ Go over the directions.

★ Read the situations aloud, or have students read the situations. Have students answer the questions and then compare answers with a partner.

★ Call on students to share their answers with the class.

ANSWER KEY:

1. Jobs, Wages, and the Economy; 2. Local Union Movements; 3. Workers' Voices

EXPANSION ACTIVITY: Sort

★ Point out that we can often predict what information can be found on the different links of a website.

★ Photocopy and enlarge the list of topics below. Make enough copies so each pair of students has a set.

★ Put students into pairs.

★ Cut the topics into strips. Give each pair of students a set of slips.

★ Have the students sort the slips into the following categories: *All About Unions; Issues and Politics; Jobs, Wages, and the Economy;* and *About the AFL-CIO.*

★ Go over the answers with the class.

Jobs, Wages, and the Economy
  Overtime Pay
  Minimum Wage
  Today's Economy
  Unemployment Help
  Living Wage
  Safety and Health at Work

Issues and Politics
  Medicare
  Immigrant Workers
  Education
  Social Security
  Civil and Human Rights
  Health Care Policy

All About Unions
  Labor Day
  Form Your Union
  How and Why People Join Unions
  State and Local Union Movements
  Allied Organizations
  Global Unions

About the AFL-CIO
  Leadership of AFL-CIO
  About Us
  Executive Council Actions
  Work in Progress
  Our Culture and History
  Letter from AFL-CIO President

WINDOW ON MATH: Understanding Graphs

A. Read the information, page 69

★ Have students read the information. Ask comprehension questions (*What kind of graph has a vertical and horizontal axis? What kind of graph shows changes over time?*).

B. Look at the bar graph, page 69

★ Go over the directions.

★ Have students answer the questions and then compare their answers with a partner.

★ Go over the answers with the class.

C. Look at the line graph, page 69

★ Go over the directions.

★ Have students answer the questions and then compare their answers with a partner.

★ Go over the answers with the class.

ANSWER KEY:

B.
1. Bachelor's Degree
2. 4
3. $1,269,850.00

C.
1. 1950–2000
2. cases of measles in the U.S. and years
3. 1960–1970

EXPANSION ACTIVITY: Make a Graph

★ Have students work in small groups.

★ Ask each group to decide on a type of information to graph such as age of students in class, number of students in each class in the English program, or some topic of their choice.

★ Tell each group to gather their data and decide which type of graph to use.

★ Have groups share their graphs with the class.

OBJECTIVE

Review and Assessment

1. Listening Review 🎧, page 70

★ Go over the directions for items 1–5 with the class.

★ Read items 1–5 or play the tape or CD and have the students mark their answers in the Answer Sheet box.

★ Walk around to monitor the activity and help students stay on task.

★ Go over the directions for items 6–10, and repeat the procedure.

★ Have students check their answers for 1–10 with a partner.

★ Go over the answers with the class.

LISTENING SCRIPT:

1. Listening Review, page 70

Listen and choose the statement that is closest in meaning to the statement you hear. Use the Answer Sheet.

1. Children are required to go to school.
2. People in the U.S. can follow any religious belief.
3. In public schools in the U.S., girls and boys study together.
4. It is necessary to register before you can vote.
5. People have different opinions about things.

Listen to each conversation and choose the best answer to the question you hear. Use the Answer Sheet.

6.
A: Are you going to vote in the election?
B: Of course.
A: Have you already registered?
B: Yes, I have. I did it last week.

Question: What has the woman already done?

7.
A: Are you going to the school meeting tonight?

B: I don't know. Do you think I should?
A: Yeah. I think it's really important. We need to know what's going on.

Question: What did the woman encourage the man to do?

8.
A: What does the FBI do?
B: The FBI? You know, it investigates crimes.
A: Is it a federal agency?
B: Yes, it is. It's the initials for the Federal Bureau of Investigation.

Question: What does the man ask about?

9.
A: What do you think about protest marches?
B: Well, they bring attention to social problems. So I think they're useful.
A: I do, too.

Question: What do the man and woman agree about?

10.
A: Are you going to pay your taxes?
B: Do I have a choice? I have to pay taxes.

Question: What does the woman say about paying taxes?

ANSWER KEY:

1. b; 2. c; 3. a; 4. a; 5. a; 6. c; 7. b; 8. b; 9. c; 10. a

2. Vocabulary Review, page 71

★ Have students look at the chart. Go over the directions and the example.

★ Have students complete the chart and then compare charts with a partner.

★ Go over the answers with the class.

★ Have students choose 6 words and use them to write 6 questions.

★ Put students in pairs to practice asking and answering the questions.

ANSWER KEY:

Answers are in italics. Additional possible answers are in brackets.

Nouns	Verbs	Adjectives
investigation/ investigator	*investigate*	——
coeducation	——	*coeducational*
constitution	[constitute]	constitutional
consumption/ consumer	consume	*consumed/ consumable*
disaster	——	disastrous
discrimination	discriminate	discriminatory
election	elect	elective
harm	harm	harmful
participation/ participant	*participate*	participatory
peace	——	*peaceful*

LEARNING LOG, page 71

★ Point out the two sections of the Learning Log: *I know these words* and *I practiced these skills, strategies, and grammar points.*

★ Ask students to check the words they know and what they practiced.

★ Walk around to note what students don't know or didn't practice. Use this information to review areas of difficulty.

BIG PICTURE EXPANSION: SPEAKING ASSESSMENT—Talking about the Big Picture

★ You can use the Big Picture as an individual assessment to place new students in classes, to diagnose difficulties, or to measure progress.

★ Work with one student. Show the Big Picture to the student. Ask: *What do you see in the picture?* Or say: *Tell me about the story.* Tell the student to speak for as long as possible. Wait a moment for the student to prepare an answer.

★ If the student has difficulty, you can use prompts (*Who do you see? What are the people doing? Where are they?*).

★ You can use a scoring rubric like the one below to rate speakers.

4	Exhibits confidence; begins speaking without prompting Uses some complex sentences, although may make mistakes with irregular forms Can use several tenses
3	Uses sentences, although form may be incorrect Uses more than one tense Can speak for a sustained length of time Responds to prompts, but doesn't need them to begin speaking
2	Can use nouns and verbs in sentences Uses one tense most of the time Answers informational questions Limited vocabulary
1	Can name objects Uses single words Can answer yes/no questions
0	Cannot say anything independently May be able to point to objects when prompted

★ Review areas of difficulty.

TEACHER NOTES:

Things that students are doing well:

_____

_____

_____

_____

_____

Things students need additional help with:

_____

_____

_____

_____

Ideas for further practice or for the next class:

_____

_____

_____

_____

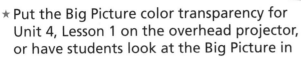

BIG PICTURE EXPANSION ACTIVITY: WRITING—Express Your Opinion

★ Put the Big Picture color transparency for Unit 4, Lesson 1 on the overhead projector, or have students look at the Big Picture in their books.

★ Ask the class: *What activities and issues do you see in the picture? What is your opinion?*

★ Have students brainstorm ideas to prepare to write.

★ Have students write a paragraph to express an opinion about an issue. Remind students to use active and passive verbs in their paragraphs.

★ Put students in pairs to take turns reading their paragraphs to their partners.

OBJECTIVE

Adjusting Your Reading Speed

Adjusting Your Reading Speed, page 72

★ Direct students' attention to the information in the box. Explain the strategy.

★ Go over the ways to read and the 5 common reading goals.

★ Check comprehension by asking questions (*What kind of reading do you do when you want to get the gist of an article? What do you think your goal is when you scan?*).

1. How would you read the following items, page 72

★ Go over the directions.

★ Have students check their answers and then compare their ideas with a partner.

★ Go over the answers with the class.

ANSWER KEY:

Answers will vary.
1. skim; 2. read slowly; 3. scan; 4. read slowly;
5. read quickly; 6. skim or read quickly;
7. scan; 8. read slowly

2. Follow the steps below, page 72

★ Go over the directions.

★ Have students follow each step and write the answers.

★ Have students compare their answers with a partner.

★ Go over the answers with the class.

ANSWER KEY:

Step 1: *Answers will vary.*
Step 2: rights for immigrant workers
Step 3: 78%, 73%, 68%, 65%, 66%, 74%,
         85%, 83%, 86%, 31%, 25%, 31%,
         42%, 51%, 44%, 51%, 60%
Step 4: Immigrant workers are not treated as
         well as other workers.
Step 5: *Answers will vary.*

EXPANSION ACTIVITY: Revision

★ Ask students to brainstorm a list of expressions that we use to express parts of a whole (*most of, a majority of, fractions, a few, many, almost all*).

★ Have students select a paragraph from the article.

★ Ask students to rewrite the selected paragraph using quantifiers other than percents.

★ Put students in pairs to take turns reading their paragraphs.

★ Call on volunteers to read the paragraphs to the class.

3. Use information from the article, page 73

★ Go over the directions.

★ Have students read the article again and use the information to complete the graph.

★ Have students compare their answers with a partner.

★ Go over the answers with the class.

ANSWER KEY:

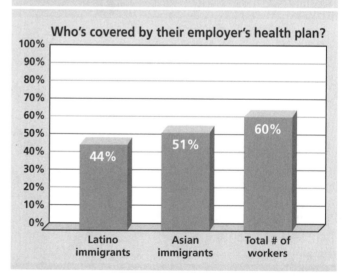

Who's covered by their employer's health plan?

Latino immigrants: 44%
Asian immigrants: 51%
Total # of workers: 60%

OBJECTIVES

Identifying Your Purpose for Writing

Identifying Your Purpose for Writing, page 74

★ Direct students' attention to the information in the box.

★ Go over the strategy and examples.

★ Ask comprehension questions (*When would you write to thank someone? In what kinds of writing do people give opinions?*).

1. Read letters 1 to 3 that follow, page 74

★ Go over the directions.

★ Have students read the letters and identify the writer's purpose.

★ Go over the answers with the class.

ANSWER KEY:

1. give an opinion; 2. ask for help; 3. invite someone to something

2. Identify an issue or problem, page 75

★ Go over the directions.

★ Have students write a letter to the mayor about a local problem. Remind students to offer a solution.

★ Ask volunteers to read their letters to the class.

EXPANSION ACTIVITY: Write Your Own

★ Ask students to identify your state senators and local representatives in congress.

★ Have students write a letter to one of these people expressing an opinion about an issue that is important to them.

★ Put students in pairs to exchange and critique the letters.

★ Have students revise as necessary.

★ Ask volunteers to read their letters to the class.

★ Have students select one or more letters to send to the senator or representative.

EQUIPPED FOR THE FUTURE ROLE

Family

OBJECTIVE

Understanding Tenant and Landlord Rights

A. Whose responsibility is it, Workbook page 72

★ Go over the directions.

★ Read the first question aloud and elicit the answer. Have students check landlord.

★ Have students answer the questions and then check their answers with a partner.

★ Go over the answers with the class.

ANSWER KEY:

1. the landlord; 2. the landlord; 3. the tenant;
4. the landlord; 5. the landlord; 6. the tenant;
7. the tenant

B. Read each person's problem, Workbook page 72

★ Go over the directions.

★ Have students read the information on Workbook page 73 to answer each question.

★ Have students talk about their answers with a partner.

★ Call on students to share their ideas with the class.

ANSWER KEY:

1. Problem: Landlord goes into apartments whenever he wants.
   Solution: Write a letter, make a copy, and send it by certified mail.
2. Problem: Shower doesn't work, and landlord hasn't fixed it.
   Solution: Write a letter, make a copy, and send it by certified mail.
3. Problem: Landlord turns electricity off.
   Solution: Write a letter, make a copy, and send it by certified mail.

4. Problem: Landlord has promised to fix refrigerator but hasn't yet.
   Solution: Write and send a letter reminding the landlord of what he promised to do.

 Take It Online, Workbook page 73

★ Go over the directions.

★ Have students use a search engine to look for the rights of tenants in a state other than Illinois.

★ Have students complete the Venn diagram to compare the two states.

★ Put students in pairs to talk about what they learned.

★ Call on students to share what they learned with the class.

EXPANSION ACTIVITY: Write a Letter

★ Have students use the information on Workbook page 72 as models to write a letter about a housing problem they have or have had. Students can also use the letters in the Writing Strategy on Student Book pages 74 and 75 as models.

★ Collect the letters and redistribute. Have students write responses to the letter.

★ Call on students to read the original letter and their response to the class.

EQUIPPED FOR THE FUTURE ROLE

Community

OBJECTIVE

Interpreting Voter Information

A. Read questions 1 to 5 below, Workbook page 74

★ Go over the directions.

★ Read the questions aloud and have students repeat.

★ Have students answer the questions.

★ Put students in pairs and have them take turns asking and answering the questions.

★ Call on students to share their answers with the class.

ANSWER KEY:

1. 18; 2. yes; 3. Nov. 8; 4. no; 5. Mayela can't vote, Fernando can vote, Lilian can vote

B. Answer these questions, Workbook page 75

★ Go over the directions. Make sure students note how the sections are numbered.

★ Have students circle their answers and then compare answers with a partner.

★ Go over the answers with the class.

ANSWER KEY:

1. 9; 2. 9; 3. 3; 4. 5; 5. 7

 Take It Online, Workbook page 75

★ Go over the directions.

★ Have students list three things they would like to learn about voting in the U.S.

★ Call on students to share their interests with the class.

★ Have students use a search engine to look for the answers and write the information on the line.

★ Put students in pairs to talk about what they learned.

★ Call on students to tell the class something they learned.

EXPANSION ACTIVITY: Interview

★ Brainstorm with students a list of questions they would like to ask one or more American voters. Write the questions on the board.

★ Go over the questions with the class.

★ Have students select 3 questions and interview someone they know who has voted in a U.S. election.

★ Call on students to tell the class what they found out.

Consumer News and Views

UNIT OVERVIEW

LESSON	OBJECTIVE	TEACHER'S EDITION PAGE NUMBER
1. Everything must go.	Interpreting Advertisements	p. 99
2. Are you an impulse buyer?	Understanding Shopping Terms	p. 101
3. Do you have your receipt?	Dealing with Salespeople	p. 103
4. Best Buys	Comparing Price, Quality, and Size	p. 106
5. That's really expensive, isn't it?	Using Tag Questions	p. 108
6. Classified Ads	Using Resources to Find Housing	p. 110
7. What do you know?	Review and Assessment	p. 112
Spotlight: Reading Strategy	Using a Dictionary	p. 115
Spotlight: Writing Strategy	Writing a Letter of Complaint	p. 116

Big Picture Expansion Activities

FOCUS	ACTIVITY	SUGGESTED USE
Speaking	Find It Fast	Lesson 1
Speaking	Who said it?	Lesson 3
Reading	Advertising Strategies	Lesson 4
Grammar	That store has good prices, doesn't it?	Lesson 5
Writing	Describing Ads and Products	Lesson 7
Speaking Assessment	Talking about the Big Picture	Lesson 7

Big Picture Expansion Activity Worksheets

WORKSHEET NUMBER/FOCUS	TITLE	TEACHER'S EDITION PAGE NUMBER
9. Reading	Advertising Strategies	p. 189
10. Grammar	That store has good prices, doesn't it?	p. 190

OBJECTIVE

Interpreting Advertisements

TRY THIS STRATEGY

Setting Goals

1. Warm Up, page 76

★ Put the Big Picture color transparency for Unit 5, Lesson 1 on the overhead projector, or have students look at the Big Picture in their books.

★ To set the context, ask questions about the picture (*What do you see in the picture? Where is this? What's happening?*).

★ As students talk about the Big Picture, write key vocabulary words on the board.

★ Read the questions aloud.

★ Put students in pairs or small groups and have them discuss the questions.

★ Call on students to tell the class about their pair or small group discussion.

Culture/Civics Notes:

★ Your students may notice that advertising is unavoidable in this culture. They will probably have seen ads not only on stores and billboards as in this picture, but on television, radio, in movie theaters, and on the Internet.

★ Although companies are free to advertise their products and services, we do have some laws controlling these practices. For example, companies cannot make untrue claims, and they cannot promise one item and provide another.

★ The consumer can limit the amount of selling that comes into his or her home. A homeowner can refuse to answer the door to solicitors and can sign up for the "do not call" registry so that telephone solicitors cannot call at home.

BIG PICTURE EXPANSION ACTIVITY: SPEAKING—Find It Fast

★ Divide the class into teams.

★ Model the activity. Say: *I want to get my ears pierced.* Elicit from the class where you could do this (*Piercing Parlor*).

★ Have each team create sentences about things they need that one of the businesses in the picture can provide, enough so that each person can say at least one sentence.

★ Call on a member of one team to say a sentence to a member of the other team. Set a time limit for the response (10 or 20 seconds).

★ Continue the activity, alternating teams, until everyone has had a chance to participate.

★ For greater challenge and practice, put students in pairs to create 15 sentences. Then put two pairs together to challenge each other. Remind them to appoint a time-keeper. Walk around to monitor the activity.

2. Analyze, page 76

★ Go over the directions.

★ Put students in pairs or small groups to discuss the questions.

★ Call on students to share their ideas with the class.

ANSWER KEY:

1. There is a final sale; 2. *Answers will vary.*
3. "False advertising" is making a claim that isn't true; the ad for a lawyer is probably false advertising.; 4. *Answers will vary.*

EXPANSION ACTIVITY: Support Your Opinions

★ Say an opinion about something in the picture (*I think Mays would be a good place to shop today*), and give support with evidence from the picture (*It's a final sale, so prices will be low*).

★ Ask if everyone agrees with your opinion. If someone disagrees, ask the student to support that opinion (*There are too many people there today, and it will be difficult to find anything*).

★ Have students write 5 opinion statements about the Big Picture.

★ Put students in pairs to read their opinions and provide support. Their partners should express agreement or disagreement and give a reason.

★ Walk around the room to monitor the activity and provide help if needed.

3. Interview, page 76

★ Go over the directions. Read each question aloud.

★ Put students in pairs and have them take turns asking and answering the questions.

★ Call on students to tell the class about their partner's answers.

EXPANSION ACTIVITY: Payment Pros and Cons

★ Brainstorm methods of payment, and write any new ideas on the board (e.g., debit card).

★ Put students in pairs or small groups.

★ Ask students to list the advantages and disadvantages of each method of payment.

★ Call on students to share their ideas with the class.

TRY THIS STRATEGY: Setting Goals, page 76

★ Read the strategy aloud.

★ Have students number the topics in order of importance.

★ Put students in pairs to compare their ideas with a partner.

★ Call on students to share their ideas with the class.

EXPANSION ACTIVITY: Be Specific

* Have students choose two of the topics listed in the Try This Strategy.

* Ask students to write 3 questions they have about each topic.

* Call on students to share their questions with the class.

* Encourages the class to save their questions to refer to later in the unit.

OBJECTIVE

Understanding Shopping Terms

VOCABULARY

brand	policy
commission	profitable
consignment shop	purchase
cover	quality
end up	rain check
extended warranty	selection
impulse buyer	service contract
in bulk	store credit
increase	suspicious
keep in mind	thrift store
merchandise	time limit
out of stock	yard sale

1. Use Context Clues, page 78

★ Have students look at the pictures, and ask: *What do you see in the photos?*

★ Go over the directions. Review how to use context clues to guess meaning.

★ Have students write definitions next to the words or phrases and then compare answers with a partner.

★ Call on students to share their ideas with the class.

★ Direct students to the glossary at the back of the book to check their definitions.

EXPANSION ACTIVITY: Write Sentences

★ Have students write stories about a shopping experience using at least 4 new words or phrases.

★ Put students in pairs to read their stories.

★ Call on students to read their stories to the class.

2. Read and Respond, page 78

★ Go over the directions.

★ Have students answer the questions in Tips for Consumers and then compare their answers with a partner.

★ Ask students to complete the sentences.

★ Call on students to read their sentences to the class.

Grammar Notes:

★ Students may not have seen these structures before. Explain that *both of us* is a plural subject and that *neither of us* is a singular subject.

★ *Neither* is often used with *nor*, although not in this expression.

ANSWER KEY:

Answers will vary.

EXPANSION ACTIVITY: Venn Diagram

★ Draw a Venn diagram on the board. Write your name above one circle and "My Partner" above the other. Tell students to put things they both answered similarly in the overlapping section of the circles. Tell students to put things they answered differently in the outer parts of the circles.

★ Ask students to draw their own diagrams on a piece of paper.

★ Have students work with their partners to complete the Venn diagram with their answers to the questions in Tips for Consumers.

3. Use the Vocabulary, page 78

★ Go over the directions.

★ Have students stand and walk around the room, asking questions to complete the chart.

★ Call on students to tell the class one thing they found out about a classmate (e.g., *Maria is an impulse buyer. She bought her car on impulse*).

EXPANSION ACTIVITY: Yard Sale

★ Bring in classified ads from the newspaper, or ask students to bring them in.

★ Ask students to list 5 items that they need but don't mind if the item is used instead of new.

★ Put students in pairs to talk about their lists.

★ Have students check the newspaper for ads for yard sales (or garage sales) and see if they can find their items for sale.

★ Call on students to tell the class what they found out.

 EXPANSION ACTIVITY: Publish It

★ Put students in small groups to create a flyer, brochure, or poster of shopping tips.

★ Have students write and illustrate their tips for their publication.

★ Post the projects around the room.

---

4. Write, page 78

★ Go over the direction.

★ Have students write a shopping tip.

★ Call on students to read their tips to the class.

OBJECTIVE

Dealing with Salespeople

TRY THIS STRATEGY

Summarizing

COMMUNICATION STRATEGY

Expressing Doubt

1. Warm Up, page 80

★ Have students look at the pictures on pages 80 and 81. To set the context, ask questions about the pictures (*Who do you see in the pictures? Where are they?*).

★ Read the questions aloud.

★ Put students in pairs or small groups and have them discuss the questions.

★ Call on students to tell the class about their pair or small group discussion.

EXPANSION ACTIVITY: Role Play

★ Put students in pairs. Have them choose a picture and create a conversation for those characters. Tell students that each character must speak at least twice.

★ Walk around and monitor the activity. Provide help as needed.

★ Ask volunteers to perform their conversation for the class. Have the class guess which picture the volunteers are acting out.

---

2. Listen and Match 🎧, page 80

★ Go over the directions.

★ Have students listen and look at the pictures while you read the conversations or play the tape or CD.

★ Have students write the number of the conversation in the circle on the appropriate picture.

★ Have students check their answers with a partner.

★ Read the conversations or play the tape or CD again if necessary.

LISTENING SCRIPT:

2. Listen and Match, page 80

Listen to 5 conversations. Match each conversation to a picture. Write the number of the conversation in the circle next to the picture.

1.

Salesperson:	Can I help you?
Customer:	Yes. I'd like to buy these.
Salesperson:	And how would you like to pay?
Customer:	Do you take personal checks?
Salesperson:	No, I'm sorry we don't. We only accept cash or credit cards.
Customer:	Oh no. Really?
Salesperson:	Yes. That's the store policy.
Customer:	Oh boy. I don't have a credit card, and I don't have enough cash on me.
Salesperson:	Well, there's an ATM machine right over there.
Customer:	Okay, good. I'll be right back.

2.

Salesperson:	Can I help you?
Customer:	Yes, I'd like to return these.
Salesperson:	Do you have your receipt?
Customer:	Yes. Uhm, here it is.
Salesperson:	I'm sorry, but these are nonreturnable.
Customer:	Excuse me?
Salesperson:	You can't return these pants. They were a final sale.
Customer:	Are you sure?
Salesperson:	I think so, but I'm not positive. I can check with the manager.
Customer:	Would you, please? Thank you.

3.

Salesperson: Can I help you?

Customer: Ah, no. No, thank you.

Salesperson: Have you seen our new suits? They just arrived, and they're on sale.

Customer: No, thank you. I don't need a suit.

Salesperson: Are you sure? These won't last long. I've already sold three of them today.

Customer: Ah, no, thank you. I'm just looking. I'll let you know if I need help.

Salesperson: Okay.

4.

A: Can you tell me where the olive oil is?

B: Olive oil. Hmm. I'm pretty sure that it's at the end of Aisle 4, but I'm not absolutely certain. I'm new here.

A: Well, I'll look there. Thanks.

B: You're welcome.

A: Hmm. It's not in Aisle 4. I wonder where it is. Excuse me.

C: Yes?

A: Do you know where the olive oil is?

C: Hmm. It seems to me that I saw it in the next aisle, but I'm not sure.

A: You're not sure?

C: No, sorry. I don't work here.

A: Oh, sorry. I thought you were an employee. Hmm. It's not here either. Maybe they don't sell olive oil.

5.

Salesperson: Can I help you?

Customer: Yes, I'd like some information about computers.

Salesperson: Okay. Do you need a desktop or a laptop?

Customer: Well, it's possible that I'll need to travel with it, but I'm not sure. Right now I just work at home.

Salesperson: Well, we do have this light-weight, high-speed, wirless laptop. It's a great price!

Customer: Hmm. That looks pretty good. What's your return policy on this?

Salesperson: I'd have to check on that.

Customer: Could you, please? I really don't want to buy this if I can't return it.

Salesperson: Sure. I'll check. Just a minute, and I'll be right back.

Customer: Okay. Thanks.

ANSWER KEY:

from left to right, top to bottom
5, 3, 1, 2, 4

EXPANSION ACTIVITY: Main Idea 🎧

★ Review the concept of a main idea with students.

★ Tell students to listen again and write a sentence expressing the main idea of each conversation.

★ Read the conversations or play the tape or CD again as students write the main ideas.

★ Put students in pairs to compare ideas.

★ Call on students to share their ideas with the class.

ANSWER KEY:

Answers will vary.
1. The customer needs to find an ATM in order to pay for his purchase.
2. The customer would like to return some shoes but can't.
3. The salesperson is offering help, but the customer is just looking.
4. The customer asks several people where to find the olive oil.
5. The customer wants a printer but wants to know the return policy.

Culture Note:

★ Some of your students may come from cultures in which it is common to negotiate or bargain when making a purchase. You may want to point out that in this culture, we rarely bargain when purchasing something new, although we still bargain at a yard sale, and when we are buying a car or a home.

3. Listen for Specific Information, page 80

★ Go over the directions.

★ Have students listen and take notes while you read the conversations or play the tape or CD again.

★ Have pairs compare answers.

ANSWER KEY:

1. the location of an ATM
2. to return some shoes
3. doesn't want anything
4. olive oil
5. information about printers.

★ ★

TRY THIS STRATEGY: Summarizing, page 80
★ ★

★ Read the strategy aloud.

★ Have students write a summary of one of the Tips for Consumers on page 79.

★ Put students in pairs to compare their summaries with a partner.

★ Call on students to share their summaries with the class.

4. Use the Communication Strategy 🎧, page 80

★ Go over the directions.

★ Have students read the conversation, or read the conversation aloud line by line and have students repeat.

★ Have students practice reading the conversation in pairs.

★ Direct students' attention to the Communication Strategy box. Go over the information in the box.

★ Say each example and have students repeat.

★ Model the conversation with a student. Have the student read B's lines. Demonstrate how to substitute your own ideas. Elicit appropriate responses from the student.

★ Have students work in pairs to practice the conversation, substituting their own ideas for the underlined words.

★ Walk around to make sure students understand the activity. Provide help if needed.

BIG PICTURE EXPANSION ACTIVITY: SPEAKING—Who said it?

★ Put the Big Picture color transparency for Unit 5, Lesson 1 on the overhead projector, or have students look at the Big Picture in their books.

★ Put students in pairs. Walk around the room and quietly assign each pair of students a pair of characters interacting in the Big Picture.

★ Have students create a conversation for their characters. Remind students to use the communication strategy in the conversation.

★ Have students perform their conversations for the class. Have the class guess who in the picture is speaking.

OBJECTIVE

Comparing Price, Quality, and Size

VOCABULARY

comparison shopper
net weight
ring up
scanner
unit price

1. Warm Up, page 82

★ Have students look at the pictures on pages 82 and 83. To set the context, ask questions about the pictures (*What do you see in the pictures?*).

★ Read the questions aloud.

★ Put students in pairs or small groups and have them discuss the questions.

★ Call on students to tell the class about their pair or small group discussion.

BIG PICTURE EXPANSION ACTIVITY: READING—Advertising Strategies

★ Make copies of **Worksheet #9** and distribute them to students.

★ Put the Big Picture color transparency for Unit 5, Lesson 1 on the overhead projector, or have students look at the Big Picture in their books.

★ Instruct students to complete the activities and then check their answers with a partner.

★ Go over the answers with the class.

ANSWER KEY:

Answers will vary.
Exaggeration: 1-500-LAWYER, Pay Nothing
Small Print: We Make Keys $5.00, Most Cars
Promise of Wealth: Need Cash?

2. Read and Respond, page 82

★ Go over the directions.

★ Have students read the food shopping tips and answer the questions.

★ Have students check their answers with a partner.

★ Go over the answers with the class.

ANSWER KEY:

1. Breakfast Flakes has more ounces for the same price.
2. The Homestyle Rice is cheaper and has more total ounces.
3. Customers are more likely to see and buy that item
4. say something
5. *Answers will vary.*

Grammar Notes:

★ Food lessons provide a good opportunity to review count and noncount nouns, as well as the use of partitives, or quantity words.

★ Review the types of food nouns that are often noncount (liquids, powders, things that are too big or too small to be counted).

EXPANSION ACTIVITY: Count and Noncount Nouns

★ Ask students to look at the two store flyers and list the count and noncount nouns.

★ For each noncount noun, have students identify the quantity words that are used with that food item.

★ Put students in pairs to compare their answers.

★ Go over the answers with the class.

ANSWER KEY:

Count nouns	Quantity words
tissue	roll/square feet
tomatoes	ounces/can
broccoli	bunch/pound
grapes	pound
tortillas	

Noncount nouns	Quantity words
orange juice	ounces
onions	pound/bag
pasta	ounces
milk	gallon
chicken breasts	pound
yogurt	ounces

3. Compare, page 82

★ Go over the directions.

★ Have students check their answers and then compare answers with a partner.

★ Call on students to share their ideas with the class.

ANSWER KEY:

Cheaper at Henry's: cereal, grapes, onions if you buy 1 pound, toilet paper

Cheaper at The Foodbasket: onions, if you want 4 pounds, pasta, orange juice

EXPANSION ACTIVITY: Real Reading

★ Bring in store flyers from at least 2 grocery stores, or have students bring them in.

★ Put students in pairs and give each pair 2 different flyers.

★ Ask the pairs to choose 5 items that are on both flyers to compare prices.

★ Call on students to share what they learned with the class.

4. Write, page 82

★ Go over the directions.

★ Have students choose 4 items and complete the chart.

★ Have students answer the questions.

★ Put students in pairs to talk about what they found out.

★ Call on students to share what they learned with the class.

EXPANSION ACTIVITY: Favorite Recipes

★ Have students bring in or write down a favorite recipe.

★ Ask students to go to their favorite grocery store and price the ingredients for their recipe. Remind them to calculate prices based on the amount actually used in the recipe.

★ Have students write the estimated cost of the dish on the top of the recipe.

★ Collect the recipes. Make enough photocopies so each student has a set.

OBJECTIVE

Using Tag Questions

Asking Tag Questions, page 84

★ Have students look at the notes in the box. Read the information and examples aloud.

1. Complete the Sentences, page 84

★ Read the directions aloud.

★ Go over the first sentence. Elicit that *aren't they* should be written on the line.

★ Have students complete the sentences.

★ Have students check their answers with a partner.

★ Go over the answers with the class.

ANSWER KEY:

1. aren't they; 2. are they; 3. wasn't it; 4. was she; 5. does she; 6. doesn't he; 7. did they; 8. didn't they

EXPANSION ACTIVITY: Tag Challenge

★ Write an opinion on the board (*Gas is too expensive.*). Elicit the appropriate tag question (*Gas is too expensive, isn't it?*).

★ Have students write 4 opinions and then turn the opinions into tag questions.

★ Have volunteers write one of their questions on the board.

ANSWER KEY:

Answers will vary.

Answering Tag Questions, page 85

★ Have students look at the notes in the box. Read the information and examples aloud.

2. Write, page 85

★ Read the directions aloud.

★ Go over the first question and example answer. Elicit other ideas. Have students write their ideas on the line.

★ Have students complete the questions.

★ Have students take turns asking and answering questions with a partner.

★ Call on students to share their answers with the class.

🖼 BIG PICTURE EXPANSION ACTIVITY: GRAMMAR—That store has good prices, doesn't it?

★ Make copies of **Worksheet #10** and distribute them to students.

★ Put the Big Picture color transparency for Unit 5, Lesson 1 on the overhead projector, or have students look at the Big Picture in their books.

★ Instruct students to complete the activities and then check their answers with a partner.

★ Go over the answers with the class.

ANSWER KEY:

A.

1. Dave's Discount Tires have a good warranty, don't they?
2. The breakfast special has a lot of eggs, doesn't it?
3. E-Z Park is the cheapest parking lot, isn't it?
4. May's isn't going out of business, is it?
5. The Elegant Woman is having a sale, isn't it?
6. The used books aren't $.25, are they?
7. I can't get discount coupons if I buy a camera, can I?

B.
1. No, they don't. or Yes, they do.
2. Yes, it does.
3. No, it isn't. or Yes, it is.
4. Yes, it is.
5. Yes, it is.
6. Yes, they are.
7. No, you can't. or Yes, you can.

3. Compare, page 85

★ Read the directions aloud.

★ Read the example sentence. Elicit ideas.

★ Have students write their ideas on the line and then rewrite the sentences as tag questions.

★ Have partners compare their answers.

ANSWER KEY:

Answers will vary.

OBJECTIVE

Using Resources to Find Housing

WINDOW ON PRONUNCIATION

Intonation in Tag Questions

1. Warm Up, page 86

★ Go over the directions.

★ Read each question aloud.

★ Put students in pairs or small groups to answer the questions.

★ Call on students to share their ideas with the class.

EXPANSION ACTIVITY: Your Favorite Home

★ Have students write about or draw the home that they have liked best.

★ Put students in pairs to share their work.

★ Call on students to tell the class what they liked about the home.

2. Read and Respond, page 86

★ Go over the directions.

★ Have students read the ads and answer the questions on page 87.

★ Put students in pairs to check their answers.

★ Go over the answers with the class.

ANSWER KEY:

1. Condominium Rentals; 2. Unfurnished Apartments; 3. 555-3325, 555-0949 or 555-3356; 4. 555-9984 or 555-3657 for pets other than dogs; 5. *Answers will vary.* 6. *Answers will vary.*

Vocabulary Notes:

★ Your students should know most of the vocabulary and abbreviations used in the ads. Review if necessary.

★ Some expressions may be unfamiliar (*dead-end, open concept, stall*). Elicit or explain meanings.

EXPANSION ACTIVITY: Online Options

★ Point out that landlords in most areas also post houses and apartments for rent or sale on websites.

★ Have students conduct an online search, entering the name of your city or town and "apartments" or "houses."

★ Ask students to list similarities and differences between online postings and newspaper ads.

★ Discuss the advantages and disadvantages of the 2 resources.

3. Apply, page 87

★ Go over the directions.

★ Have students write want ads for their own house or apartment.

★ Call on students to read their ads to the class.

ANSWER KEY:

Answers will vary.

EXPANSION ACTIVITY: Rent or Buy?

★ Put students in pairs to brainstorm the advantages and disadvantages of buying a home and of renting a home.

★ Ask students to create a tip sheet to help prospective home buyers decide if they should buy or rent.

★ Call on volunteers to present their ideas to the class.

WINDOW ON PRONUNCIATION: Intonation in Tag Questions

A. Read the information, page 87

★ Have students read the information. Ask comprehension questions (*When do we use tag questions? How is the pronunciation different when we use a tag question to confirm an expected answer vs. when we don't know the answer?*).

B. Listen to the questions 🎧, page 87

★ Go over the directions.

★ Have students look at the questions while you read them or play the tape or CD.

★ Read the tag or play the tape or CD a second time, pausing after each question to have students repeat.

C. Listen to the questions again 🎧, page 87

★ Go over the directions.

★ Have students check the appropriate box while you read the questions or play the tape or CD.

★ Go over the answers with the class.

ANSWER KEY:

1. confirmation; 2. confirmation; 3. yes/no; 4. yes/no; 5. confirmation

D. Write two tag questions, page 87

★ Go over the directions.

★ Have students write 2 tag questions.

★ Put students in pairs to practice asking and answering the questions. Encourage students to vary the intonation pattern in the questions.

★ Walk around to monitor the activity, and help with intonation if necessary.

EXPANSION ACTIVITY: Role Play

★ Put students in pairs to role play a phone call between a prospective renter/buyer and the seller/landlord. They can call about the homes in the ads. Remind students to use tag questions in their role plays.

★ Ask volunteers to perform their role plays for the class.

OBJECTIVE

Review and Assessment

1. Listening Review 🎧, page 88

★ Go over the directions for items 1–5 with the class.

★ Read items 1–5 or play the tape or CD and have the students mark their answers in the Answer Sheet box.

★ Walk around to monitor the activity and help students stay on task.

★ Go over the directions for items 6–10, and repeat the procedure.

★ Have students check their answers for 1–10 with a partner.

★ Go over the answers with the class.

LISTENING SCRIPT:

1. Listening Review, page 88

Listen to each conversation and choose the best answer to the question you hear. Use the Answer Sheet.

1.

A: Excuse me. Can you help me?

B: Sure. What can I do for you?

A: I'd like to return this sweater.

B: No problem. The return counter is straight ahead. They can help you there.

A: Thanks.

Question: What does the man want?

2.

A: Excuse me.

B: Yes. Can I help you?

A: Yes, I'd like to buy one of these computers.

B: Okay. I'll have to get you one from out back. Uhm, do you want to get an extended warranty with that?

A: Well, it says here that it comes with a 1-year warranty.

B: Yes, but for an extra 50 dollars you can buy an extended warranty. It's a good deal. It gives you an extra year of protection.

A: Well, thanks, but I don't think so. I'll just take the computer.

B: Okay.

Question: What does the woman buy?

3.

A: Excuse me.

B: Yes?

A: I think there's a mistake on my receipt.

B: Let me see.

A: On the receipt it says that milk costs 2 dollars a gallon, but the price in the store flier is a dollar forty-nine.

B: Sorry about that. I'll correct that right away.

Question: What was the man's problem?

4.

A: How much is rice this week at the FoodBasket?

B: Hmm. Just a minute. Uhm, it's only $2.99 for a 5-pound bag.

A: That's a great price. Maybe we should get several bags.

B: Good idea.

Question: What are they going to buy in bulk?

5.

A: This is a really nice coat, isn't it?

B: Yeah, it sure is.

A: But it's kind of expensive, isn't it?

B: Well, actually, it's not a bad price.

Question: What do the man and the woman agree on?

Listen and choose the sentence that is closest in meaning to the sentence you hear. Use the Answer Sheet.

6. The warranty is included in the purchase price.
7. Can I get a cash refund if I return this?
8. I think you can return this, but I'm not certain.
9. This is delicious, isn't it?
10. Grapes aren't cheap, are they?

ANSWER KEY:

1. C; 2. B; 3. A; 4. A; 5. A; 6. B; 7. A; 8. B;
9. C; 10. B

2. Dictation 🎧, page 88

★ Go over the directions.

★ Have students write the sentences as you read the sentences or play the tape or CD.

★ Put students in pairs to compare sentences.

★ Go over the sentences with the class.

LISTENING SCRIPT:

2. Dictation, page 88

Listen and write the questions you hear.

1. What's your return policy?
2. Do you have your receipt?
3. Could I have a rain check, please?

3. Vocabulary Review, page 89

★ Direct students' attention to the crossword puzzle.

★ Go over the directions. Make sure students understand how to fill in the crossword. Remind them to use words from the unit.

★ Have students check their answers with a partner.

★ Go over the answers with the class.

ANSWER KEY:

Across:
2. thrift; 5. selection; 9. purchase;
10. profitable; 11. suspicious; 12. check;
13. merchandise

Down:
1. credit; 3. extended; 4. commission; 6. service;
7. brands; 8. bulk

LEARNING LOG, page 89

★ Point out the two sections of the Learning Log: *I know these words* and *I practiced these skills and strategies.*

★ Ask students to check the words they know and what they practiced.

★ Walk around to note what students don't know or didn't practice. Use this information to review areas of difficulty.

BIG PICTURE EXPANSION: SPEAKING ASSESSMENT—Talking about the Big Picture

★ You can use the Big Picture as an individual assessment, to place new students in classes, to diagnose difficulties, or to measure progress.

★ Work with one student. Show the Big Picture to the student. Ask: *What do you see in the picture?* Or say: *Tell me about the picture.* Tell the student to speak for as long as possible. Wait a moment for the student to prepare an answer.

★ If the student has difficulty, you can use prompts (*Who do you see? What are the people doing? Where are they?*).

★ You can use a scoring rubric like the one below to rate speakers.

4	Exhibits confidence; begins speaking without prompting Uses some complex sentences, although may make mistakes with irregular forms Can use several tenses
3	Uses sentences, although form may be incorrect Uses more than one tense Can speak for a sustained length of time Responds to prompts, but doesn't need them to begin speaking
2	Can use nouns and verbs in sentences Uses one tense most of the time Answers informational questions Limited vocabulary
1	Can name objects Uses single words Can answer yes/no questions
0	Cannot say anything independently May be able to point to objects when prompted

★ Review areas of difficulty.

TEACHER NOTES:

Things that students are doing well:

_____

_____

_____

_____

_____

Things students need additional help with:

_____

_____

_____

_____

_____

_____

Ideas for further practice or for the next class:

_____

_____

_____

_____

_____

BIG PICTURE EXPANSION ACTIVITY: WRITING—Describing Ads and Products

★ Put the Big Picture color transparency for Unit 5, Lesson 1 on the overhead projector, or have students look at the Big Picture in their books.

★ Ask the class: _What kind of ads do you see? What products and services are available?_

★ Have students brainstorm ideas to prepare to write.

★ Have students write a paragraph about the ways things are being sold in the picture.

★ Put students in pairs to take turns reading their paragraphs to their partners.

OBJECTIVE

Using a Dictionary

Using a Dictionary, page 90

★ Direct students' attention to the information in the box. Explain the strategy.

★ Go over the examples.

★ Check comprehension by asking questions (*What are 3 things you can learn using a dictionary? Do words usually have just one meaning?*).

1. Read the dictionary definitions, page 90

★ Go over the directions.

★ Have students answer the questions and then check their answers with a partner.

★ Go over the answers with the class.

ANSWER KEY:

a. large size; b. bulkiest; c. something; d. the majority; e. unwieldy

2. Read the dictionary definitions, page 91

★ Go over the directions.

★ Have students read the definitions and usage note and answer the questions.

★ Have students check their answers with a partner.

★ Go over the answers with the class.

ANSWER KEY:

a. a garage sale is in or near a garage, a yard sale is in a yard, can be used interchangeably; b. yes; c. to explain how words are used; d. *Answers will vary.*

3. Read the sentences, page 91

★ Go over the directions.

★ Have students choose the correct definition, circle 1 or 2, and then check their answers with a partner.

★ Go over the answers with the class.

ANSWER KEY:

a. 2; b. 1; c. 1; d. 1; e. 2 and 1

EXPANSION ACTIVITY: Try It Yourself

★ Have students choose a word from this unit to look up in the dictionary. You might suggest *stock, contract, credit, net,* or *brand* because they have multiple meanings.

★ Write these questions on the board: *How many definitions? What part(s) of speech? Any synonyms or antonyms?*

★ Have students look up the word and answer the questions.

★ Call on students to report their findings to the class.

OBJECTIVE

Writing a Letter of Complaint

Writing a Letter of Complaint, page 92

★ Go over the information in the box.

★ Ask comprehension questions: *Should you describe the purchase? Should the letter be long?*

1. Read the complaint letters, page 92

★ Go over the directions.

★ Have students look at the letters. Ask: *Which letter provides the date the letter was written?* Elicit the answer, and have students check both Letter #1 and Letter #2.

★ Have students read the letters and check the information each letter provides.

★ Put students in pairs to compare answers.

★ Call on volunteers to share their answers with the class.

ANSWER KEY:

1. 1 and 2; 2. 1 and 2; 3. 2; 4. 2; 5. 1 and 2;
6. 1 and 2; 7. 2; 8. 2; 9. 1 and 2; 10. 2

EXPANSION ACTIVITY: Revise Letter 1

★ Have students revise Letter 1 to include the missing information. Point out that they can create the information necessary.

★ Put students in pairs to compare revised letters.

★ Call on volunteers to read their revisions to the class.

2. Think of something you have bought, page 93

★ Go over the directions.

★ Have students write a letter of complaint about something they purchased recently.

★ Remind students to include the information recommended in the box on page 92.

★ Put students in pairs to exchange and provide feedback on the letters.

★ Have students revise if necessary.

EXPANSION ACTIVITY: Write Another Letter

★ Have students write a letter saying something positive either about a recent purchase or about the service.

★ Remind students to include the information recommended in the box on page 92.

★ Put students in pairs to exchange and provide feedback on the letters.

★ Have students revise if necessary.

EQUIPPED FOR THE FUTURE ROLE

Work

OBJECTIVE

Locating Merchandise

A. Study the store floor plan, Workbook page 92

★ Direct students' attention to the information and ask questions: Where is the checkout counter? On what aisle can you find the sports equipment.

★ Have students study the floor plan to answer the questions and then check their answers with a partner.

★ Go over the answers with the class.

ANSWER KEY:

1. c; 2. b; 3. b; 4. b; 5. c

B. A customer and a store clerk, Workbook page 93

★ Go over the directions.

★ Have students complete the conversations and then compare answers with a partner.

★ Go over the answers with the class.

★ Put students in pairs to practice the conversations.

ANSWER KEY:

1. sewing supplies; 2. cleaning/plumbing; 3. 4/sports equipment; 4. 6; 5. 7/painting supplies; 6. garden and yard; 7. gift; 8. No, I'm sorry, we don't.

Take It Outside, Workbook page 93

★ Go over the directions.

★ Have students visit a store and draw the floor plan.

★ Put students in pairs to talk about the floor plan.

★ Call on students to share their floor plans with the class.

EXPANSION ACTIVITY: Stocking the Store

★ Put students in pairs. For each category of supply (*painting*) in the floor plan on page 92, have students list 5 items (*paint brush, roller, pan, tape, rags*). Tell students to write each item on a separate card or slip of paper.

★ Have students shuffle the cards or slips and exchange with another pair.

★ Ask students to sort the cards or slips into categories and check their ideas with the other pair.

EQUIPPED FOR THE FUTURE ROLE

Community

OBJECTIVE

Identifying Consumer Protection Resources

A. Use the list of Resources for Consumers, Workbook page 94

★ Go over the directions.

★ Have students read the list of resources to answer the questions and then check their answers with a partner.

★ Go over the answers with the class.

> **Academic Notes:**
> ★ Your less technologically savvy students may not realize that some websites are more reliable than others.
> ★ Point out that URLs ending in *gov* are government websites, those ending in *edu* are educational websites, and those ending in *org* are usually nonprofit organizations. Government and educational websites are usually the most reliable. Websites for nonprofit organizations are often more reliable than commercial websites.
> ★ Websites ending in *com* often want to sell something and are not necessarily reliable.

ANSWER KEY:

1. INSURE.COM; 2. FCC, FTC and HUD; 3. FTC; 4. U.S. Department of Housing and Urban Development; 5. Call 877-FTC-HELP; 6. Call a local office listed in the telephone book

B. Read about each person, Workbook page 95

★ Go over the directions.

★ Have students answer the questions and then check their answers with a partner.

★ Go over the answers with the class.

ANSWER KEY:

1. HUD; 2. BBB; 3. FTC, BBB

C. Choose the correct form, Workbook page 95

★ Go over the directions.

★ Have students choose the correct form to complete the sentences and then compare their answers with a partner.

★ Go over the answers with the class.

ANSWER KEY:

1. complain/complaint; 2. protect; 3. Discrimination; 4. inform; 5. organization

Take It Outside, Workbook page 95

★ Go over the directions.

★ Have students list 3 ways telephone users are protected.

★ Call on volunteers to share the information with the class.

 Take It Online, Workbook page 95

★ Go over the directions.

★ Have students look online, search for one of the resources, and write 3 things they learn.

★ Call on volunteers to share the information with the class.

> **EXPANSION ACTIVITY: Online Scavenger Hunt**
>
> ★ Have students visit the websites for the government and nonprofit organizations on page 94 to find the answers to the following questions or to questions you create.
>
> 1. *How can you join the ACLU?*
> 2. *What is the name of your state's attorney general?*
> 3. *What are 2 types of complaint you can make about identity theft to the BBB?*
> 4. *How many commissioners are on the FCC?*
> 5. *When was the FTC founded?*
> 6. *What resources are available through HUD?*
> 7. *What are the public citizen divisions?*

Rules and Laws

UNIT OVERVIEW

LESSON	OBJECTIVE	TEACHER'S EDITION PAGE NUMBER
1. She has jury duty.	Describing a Court of Law	p. 120
2. It's a felony.	Identifying Infractions and Crimes	p. 122
3. To hear this message again, press 9.	Interpreting Permit and License Requirements	p. 124
4. Traffic Infractions and Misdemeanors	Understanding Driving Laws	p. 127
5. It shows the amount that you must pay.	Using Adjective Clauses	p. 129
6. Neighborhood Watch	Participating in Your Community	p. 131
7. What do you know?	Review and Assessment	p. 133
Spotlight: Reading Strategy	Recognizing Cause and Effect	p. 136
Spotlight: Writing Strategy	Using Graphic Organizers for Writing	p. 137

Big Picture Expansion Activities

FOCUS	ACTIVITY	SUGGESTED USE
Speaking	Who is that?	Lesson 3
Reading	Who's who?	Lesson 2
Grammar	What is a juror?	Lesson 5
Writing	Describing people in the courtroom	Lesson 7
Speaking Assessment	Talking about the Big Picture	Lesson 7

Big Picture Expansion Activity Worksheets

WORKSHEET NUMBER/FOCUS	TITLE	TEACHER'S EDITION PAGE NUMBER
11. Reading	Who's who?	p. 191
12. Grammar	What is a juror?	p. 192

OBJECTIVE

Describing a Court of Law

VOCABULARY

bailiff	innocent
battery	judge
court reporter	jury
criminal	lawyer
defendant	prosecutor
defense attorney	summons
dismiss	testimony
guilty	witness
incite	

1. Warm Up, page 94

★ Put the Big Picture color transparency for Unit 6, Lesson 1 on the overhead projector, or have students look at the Big Picture in their books.

★ To set the context, ask questions about the picture (*Who do you see in the picture? What's happening?*).

★ As students talk about the Big Picture, write key vocabulary words on the board.

★ Read the questions aloud.

★ Put students in pairs or small groups and have them discuss the questions.

★ Call on students to tell the class about their pair or small group discussion.

Culture/Civics Notes:

★ Point out some differences between civil and criminal cases. Although both can involve judges and juries, the state is the plaintiff, or party making a complaint, in a criminal case. In civil cases, the defendant often has to pay money or correct a situation if found guilty. In criminal cases, if the defendant is found guilty, he or she may have to pay a fine or go to prison.

★ Students may not know how juries work in this country. An accused person has the right to be judged by a jury, rather than by a single person. All citizens must report for jury duty if they receive a jury duty notice. If there is a big conflict, a potential jury member may ask to be excused or rescheduled. A person who does not show up for jury duty can be fined or even jailed.

★ Most juries have 12 people, although certain special juries, called grand juries, can have more.

★ Students will learn more about the severity of different crimes in Lesson 2. Not all crimes require a jury trial. Traffic infractions and misdemeanors are usually settled by a judge.

EXPANSION ACTIVITY: Research It

★ Have students go to http://www.abanet.org/publiced/courts/trialsteps.html.

★ Ask students to select a topic or assign each student a topic from the Website. (e.g., Diagram of How a Case Moves Through the Courts, Civil and Criminal Cases, Settling Cases).

★ Have students prepare a 1-minute presentation on the topic to present to the class.

2. Identify, page 94

★ Go over the directions.

★ Have students write their guesses and then check their answers with a partner.

★ Direct students to the glossary at the back of the book to check their answers.

★ Go over the answers with the class.

ANSWER KEY:

1. jury; 2. court reporter; 3. judge; 4. bailiff; 5. defense attorney; 6. prosecutor; 7. witness

EXPANSION ACTIVITY: Dictation

★ Tell students you are going to dictate 5 true-false sentences about the picture.

★ Create 5 sentences or say the sentences below. Repeat twice.
The prosecutor is talking to the jury.
The defendant is male.

There are 12 people on the jury.
The prosecutor and the defendant sit at the same table.
The jury sits behind the judge.

★ Have students compare their sentences with a partner.

★ Ask students to write *true* or *false* next to each sentence.

★ Go over the answers.

3. Put in Sequence, page 94

★ Go over the directions.

★ Have students put the events in order. Remind students to write *1* next to the event that happens first.

★ Put students in pairs to compare their answers.

★ Go over the answers with the class.

★ Ask pairs to take turns telling the story in their own words.

ANSWER KEY:

1. She received a summons for jury duty in her mailbox.
2. She went to court for the first time.
3. A judge and two lawyers interviewed her.
4. She became a member of the jury.
5. She listened to the testimony of many witnesses.
6. The jury went into a special room.
7. The jury made a decision.
8. She received a check from the court.

EXPANSION ACTIVITY: Tell a Story

★ Have students think of a courtroom experience they have had or a story they know about.

★ Instruct students to write at least 5 sentences telling the story in order.

★ Have students read their sentences to a partner.

★ Call on students to read their sentences to the class.

OBJECTIVE

Identifying Infractions and Crimes

VOCABULARY

aggravated assault	murder
assault	offense
burglary	pay a fine
commit	prison
felony	probation
imprisonment	punishable
infraction	rape
jaywalking	violation
misdemeanor	

1. Read a Bar Graph, page 96

★ Have students look at the information. Ask: *What is this lesson about?*

★ Read the questions aloud. Make sure students understand how to read the bar graph.

★ Put students in pairs or small groups and have them discuss the questions.

★ Call on students to tell the class about their pair or small group discussion.

ANSWER KEY:

1. burglary, burglary; 2. burglary, murder, robbery; 3. *Answers will vary.*

EXPANSION ACTIVITY: Convert to Pie Charts

★ Explain that a pie chart shows the relationship of parts to a whole.

★ Draw a circle on the board. Write the numbers on the board for each crime in 1980 (assault: 672,650; burglary: 3,795,200; murder: 23,040; rape: 82,990; robbery: 565,840). With the class, determine the total number for all crimes in these categories (5,139,720), and then create a pie chart to show the share of each. Your circle should be about 3/4 burglary.

★ Have students create pie charts for 1990 and 2000.

★ Ask students what they notice about the changes in the pie charts over time.

2. Use the Vocabulary, page 96

★ Go over the directions.

★ Have students use the chart to answer the questions.

★ Put students in pairs to take turns asking and answering the questions.

★ Go over the answers with the class.

ANSWER KEY:

1. a felony; 2. infraction: littering/jaywalking/minor traffic violations; misdemeanor: petty theft/shoplifting/trespassing/vandalism; felony: arson/burglary/murder/rape/aggravated assault; 3. a misdemeanor; 4. felonies; 5. infraction, pay a fine; 6. burglary

EXPANSION ACTIVITY: Chart Your Own

★ Ask students to think about traffic infractions and violations members of their families have received tickets for.

★ Have students list the types of infractions or violations (*parking in a no parking zone, parking over the time limit, speeding, making an illegal turn, etc.*) and the number of instances of each for their entire family, or have students create such statistics.

★ Have students create bar graphs for their statistics.

★ Put students in pairs to take turns asking questions about their partner's bar graph (*How many tickets were for parking violations? What was the reason for most tickets?*).

3. Expand Your Vocabulary, page 96

★ Go over the directions.

★ Have students complete the chart and then compare answers with a partner.

★ Have students complete the questions and check answers with a partner.

★ Go over the answers with the class.

★ Put students in pairs to take turns asking and answering the questions.

★ Call on students to answer the questions.

ANSWER KEY:

Chart: 1. violation; 2. punish; 3. vandalism;
    4. pay; 5. imprisonment; 6. burglary
Questions: 1. violation; 2. punishment;
        3. vandalism or burglary; 4. pay;
        5. imprisonment; 6. vandalism or
burglary
Answers to questions:
  1. yes; 2. imprisonment for more than a year;
  3. no (for vandalism) or yes (for burglary);
  4. infractions and misdemeanors; 5. yes; 6. no
(for vandalism) or yes (for burglary)

 BIG PICTURE EXPANSION ACTIVITY: READING—Who's who?

★ Make copies of **Worksheet #11** and distribute them to students.

★ Put the Big Picture color transparency for Unit 6, Lesson 1 on the overhead projector, or have students look at the Big Picture in their books.

★ Instruct students to complete the activities and then check their answers with a partner.

★ Go over the answers with the class.

ANSWER KEY:

1. defense attorney; 2. witness; 3. someone on the jury; 4. bailiff; 5. prosecutor

OBJECTIVE

Interpreting Permit and License Requirements

COMMUNICATION STRATEGY

Paraphrasing to Check Understanding

1. Warm Up, page 98

★ Have students look at the pictures on page 98. To set the context, ask questions about the pictures (*What are they doing?*).

★ Read the questions aloud.

★ Put students in pairs or small groups and have them discuss the questions.

★ For Question 2, have students put a check mark next to the things they think you have to do in the *Before Listening* column on page 99.

★ Call on students to share their ideas with the class.

Culture/Civics Notes:

★ You may want to point out that the requirements for obtaining a marriage license vary from state to state. Some require blood tests, and others have waiting periods. The identification required may also vary somewhat.

★ The age at which you can get a driver's license also varies from one state to another. Generally, at about 16 years of age a teenager can get a learner's permit. Frequently, more rural states allow people to drive at a younger age. Many states also have graduated licenses for teen drivers; such licenses may restrict the hours a teen can drive or who he or she can have in the car.

EXPANSION ACTIVITY: State by State

★ For an out-of-class or lab assignment, have students research the marriage license or driver's license requirements for one of the 50 states. Assign each student a different state.

★ Have students report their findings to the class.

2. Listen and Compare 🎧, page 98

★ Go over the directions.

★ Have students listen and check the boxes in the *After Listening* column while you read the recorded messages or play the tape or CD.

★ Have students check their answers with a partner.

★ Read the messages or play the tape or CD again if necessary.

LISTENING SCRIPT:

2. Listen and Compare, page 98

Listen to a recorded message about getting a marriage license. Check the things you have to do in the **After Listening** *column on page 99.*

You have reached the County Clerk's automated information system.
For office hours and location, press 1.
For marriage license information, press 2.
For ceremony information, press 3.
For passport information, press 4.

As of Jan. 1, 1995, a blood test is no longer required to obtain a marriage license. To obtain a public marriage license, the couple must appear together at the county clerk's office with picture identification. You can use a passport, driver's license, naturalization form, resident alien card, or military ID showing your full legal name. If the legal picture ID card does not contain your full legal name, you must also present a certified copy of your birth certificate or Social Security card, showing your full legal name.

If neither party speaks English, someone who can translate must accompany the couple. It usually takes about 30 minutes to issue a marriage license.

You do not need to be a California resident to marry in California. The same requirements apply whether you are a U.S. citizen or a tourist.

If either party has been married before, you will need to know the exact date of when the marriage was finalized. If the marriage was finalized within the last 90 days, we ask that a copy of the final judgment be brought—a certified copy of the divorce, annulment, or a death record.

The fee for a public marriage license is $83.00. It is effective the day it is issued. Your license is only valid for 90 days after it is issued, so a marriage ceremony must take place within 90 days after receiving your certificate.

To order a marriage license information sheet, press 1 now.
If you need additional information, press 2 now.
To hear this message again, press 9 now.

Listen to a recorded message about getting a driver's license. Check the things you have to do in the After Listening column on page 99.

Thank you for calling the Department of Motor Vehicles.

There are 4 frequently asked questions about obtaining a new driver's license. The answer to each question is provided. To skip a question, press 9. To repeat the answer, press pound. To transfer to an agent, press 0.

1. What is the fee to obtain an original CA license?

The fee to obtain a new California license is $24.

2. How do I obtain a new license?

You will need to visit a DMV office. This process cannot be completed by mail or over the telephone. For your convenience, an appointment is recommended. You will need to complete an application for a new license. The application must be signed in person at the DMV office. You may request this form at the end of this message. You will need to provide evidence of your birth date, your valid Social Security card, which will be verified while you're in the DMV office, documents proving your true full name, such as an original certified copy of your birth certificate, an original passport, a military ID, or documents verifying proof of legal presence in the U.S.

3. What is the process that will take place at the DMV office?

You must take a vision and written test. Study the California driver handbook before you take the written exam. There are 36 questions about traffic laws and signs on the test. You have 3 chances to pass. Once you pass the written test, you may schedule an appointment for a behind-the-wheel driving test. You must supply proof of insurance and current registration for the vehicle used.

4. What happens after I pass the written and behind-the-wheel test?

Once all requirements are met and tests passed, you will be issued a 60-day temporary license until your new license is mailed to you. A fingerprint and photograph will be taken.

To hear frequently asked questions again, press 1.
To locate the nearest DMV office or schedule an appointment, press 2.
To request forms, press 3.
To repeat this information, press 4.
To transfer to an agent, press 0.

ANSWER KEY:

1. Check: d, e, i; 2. Check: b, g, h, i, j

3. Listen for Specific Information 🎧, page 98

★ Go over the directions.

★ Direct students' attention to the *Note-Taking Chart* on page 99.

★ Have students take notes in the chart while you say the recorded messages or play the tape or CD again.

★ Say the messages or play the tape or CD again if necessary.

★ Have students work with a partner to take turns asking and answering the questions.

★ Go over the answers with the class.

ANSWER KEY:

Marriage license questions: 1. a passport, driver's license, naturalization form, resident alien card, or military ID showing your full legal name; 2. $83; 3. about 30 minutes

Driver's License Questions: 4. an original certified copy of your birth certificate, an original passport, a military ID, or docs verifying proof of legal presence in the U.S, and a valid Social Security card; 5. $24; 6. 36

EXPANSION ACTIVITY:
Write Your Own 🎧

★ Have students listen to the messages again and create 3 new questions about the information.

★ Put students in pairs to exchange questions.

★ Have students answer the new questions while you say the messages or play the tape or CD again.

★ Call on students to ask and answer questions.

4. Use the Communication Strategy 🎧, page 98

★ Go over the directions.

★ Have students read the conversation, or read the conversation aloud line by line and have students repeat.

★ Have students practice reading the conversation in pairs.

★ Direct students' attention to the Communication Strategy box. Go over the information in the box.

★ Model the conversation with a student. Have the student play B's role. Demonstrate how to ask different questions, using paraphrasing. Elicit appropriate responses from the student.

★ Have students work in pairs to practice asking questions and paraphrasing to check for understanding.

★ Walk around to make sure they understand the activity, and provide help if needed.

ANSWER KEY:

Answers will vary.

BIG PICTURE EXPANSION ACTIVITY: SPEAKING—Who is that?

★ Put the Big Picture color transparency for Unit 6, Lesson 1 on the overhead projector, or have students look at the Big Picture in their books.

★ Model the activity. Call on a student and ask about someone in the picture (*What does the bailiff do?*). Elicit the answer from the student (*He keeps peace in the courtroom*), and paraphrase to confirm (*So the bailiff makes sure that everything is calm and orderly?*).

★ Put students in pairs. Have students take turns asking questions about the people in the courtroom. Remind them to use the communication strategy in the conversation.

★ Call on students to ask and answer questions about the people in the courtroom.

OBJECTIVE

Understanding Driving Laws

TRY THIS STRATEGY

Asking Questions

1. Warm Up, page 100

★ Have students look at the pictures and information on pages 100 and 101. To set the context, ask questions (*What do you see in the pictures?*).

★ Read the questions aloud.

★ Put students in pairs or small groups and have them discuss the questions.

★ Call on students to tell the class about their pair or small group discussion.

ANSWER KEY:

1. *Answers will vary.*
2. Illegal Parking
3. *Answers will vary.*
4. 1. pedestrian crossing;
    2. no crossing/jaywalking;
    3. do not enter;
    4. yield;
    5. handicapped zone/wheelchair crossing;
    6. no parking;
    7. one way traffic;
    8. detour;
    9. slippery road;
    10. divided highway ends

EXPANSION ACTIVITY: Traffic Signs

★ Review the use of modals and modal-like expressions to express obligation and advisability (*must, should, have to, ought to, had better*).

★ Have students write a sentence for each sign using a modal or modal-like expression.

★ Call on students to read a sentence to the class.

2. Read and Take Notes, page 100

★ Go over the directions.

★ Have students read the information and take notes in the chart.

★ Have students compare notes with a partner.

★ Go over the answers with the class.

Academic Notes:

★ You may want to discuss note-taking strategies at this time. Elicit or present key points: write legibly, be concise, use your own words, and only write what is important.

★ The chart is set with key terms or concepts in a column on the left and room for important details, examples, and explanations on the right. Point out that students can use this same style whenever they take notes.

ANSWER KEY:

Topic	Important details
Parking tickets	• You don't have to go to court • Cost is on the ticket • Contact agency if problem • Amount can go up if don't pay • If don't pay, can't renew registration
Infraction tickets	• From police • For things like driving too fast • Go to court • Need proof of car insurance or infraction
Misdemeanor tickets	• More serious • Go to court • Sign ticket, doesn't mean you're guilty • If alcohol or drugs, you could be arrested
What happens	• Police ask for driver's license, car registration, and proof of insurance • May get ticket to sign • Get copy of ticket

EXPANSION ACTIVITY: Note-Taking Practice

★ Brainstorm a list of legal topics that your students have questions about, and write their ideas on the board.

★ Have students choose a topic and research it online or at the library. Remind them to use note-taking skills.

★ Put students in pairs to talk about their notes.

★ Call on students to tell the class what they learned.

3. Summarize, page 100

★ Go over the directions.

★ Have students write summaries of the information and then compare summaries with a partner.

★ Call on students to share their ideas with the class.

EXPANSION ACTIVITY: Flashcard Quiz

★ Give students 3 index cards.

★ Have students write one word on each card: *parking, infraction, misdemeanor.*

★ Tell students you will ask a question, and they should hold up one or more cards in response.

★ Keep the activity fast-paced. Create questions, or use the ones below.
Which ones are not filed with the court?
Which ones require a court visit?
Which one do you get if you are drinking and driving?
Which one is for parking too long at a meter?
What kind of ticket will you get for going through a red light?

★ In a variation, have students write 5 questions based on the information on page 101. Collect the questions and use them for the flashcard quiz.

★★★★★★★★★★★★★★★★★★★★★★★★★★★★★★★★★★★★★★

TRY THIS STRATEGY: Asking Questions, page 100
★★★★★★★★★★★★★★★★★★★★★★★★★★★★★★★★★★★★★★

★ Go over the strategy.

★ Have students answer the questions about the article.

★ Call on students to share their ideas with the class.

OBJECTIVE

Using Adjective Clauses

Adjective Clauses, Part 1, page 102

★ Have students look at the notes in the box. Read the information and examples aloud.

★ Direct students' attention to the tip box. Make sure they understand how *who, which,* and *that* are used.

Grammar Notes:

★ Although it is not part of this lesson, students may wonder about usage differences among the pronouns *who, which,* and *that.* Because *that* can be used for people or things, students sometimes want to use that as the default option for all adjective clauses.

★ You might want to mention that some adjectives clauses are essential in identifying who we are talking about (*She is the woman who witnessed the accident.*), whereas others are not (*The police talked to Mary Martin, who witnessed the accident.*). Point out that the comma is a clue.

★ When an adjective clause is necessary for identification, we do not use commas. When it merely adds additional information, we do use commas.

★ We do not use *that* in adjective clauses that are not necessary in identifying things (*We're leaving on April 10th, which is my birthday.*). We usually use *that* in the necessary clauses.

1. Match, page 102

★ Read the directions aloud.

★ Go over the first main clause. Elicit that *that lasted for several months* completes the sentence, so *c* should be written on the line.

★ Have students write the letters of the adjective clauses next to the appropriate main clause.

★ Have students check their answers with a partner.

★ Go over the answers with the class.

ANSWER KEY:

1. c; 2. h; 3. g; 4. d; 5. e; 6. a; 7. b; 8. f

2. Write, page 102

★ Read the directions aloud.

★ Go over the first sentence. Elicit ideas to complete the sentence.

★ Have students complete the adjective clauses.

★ Have students compare their answers with a partner.

★ Call on students to share their answers with the class.

ANSWER KEY:

Answers will vary.

Adjective Clauses, Part 2, page 103

★ Have students look at the notes in the box. Read the information and examples aloud.

3. Identify and Rewrite, page 103

★ Read the directions aloud.

★ Go over the first sentence and ask students if *who* is the subject or object in the clause *who is in jail.* Elicit that it is the subject. Have students write *subject* on the line.

★ Have students write *subject* or *object* to identify the function of the pronoun in the adjective clauses and then check their answers with a partner.

★ Have students rewrite the 5 sentences with an object pronoun, omitting the pronoun.

★ Call on students to read their sentences to the class.

ANSWER KEY:

A.
1. subject; 2. object; 3. subject; 4. object;
5. object; 6. object; 7. subject; 8. object

B.

1. He got a parking ticket he didn't deserve.
2. The officer I was telling you about is on the phone.
3. He paid the ticket he got for speeding.
4. The stop sign I drove through was taken down.
5. My husband opened the summons I received in the mail yesterday.

4. Write, page 103

★ Go over the directions.
★ Have students complete the adjective clauses.
★ Call on students to read their sentences to the class.

BIG PICTURE EXPANSION ACTIVITY: GRAMMAR—What is a juror?

★ Make copies of **Worksheet #12** and distribute them to students.
★ Put the Big Picture color transparency for Unit 6, Lesson 1 on the overhead projector, or have students look at the Big Picture in their books.
★ Instruct students to complete the activities and then check their answers with a partner.
★ Go over the answers with the class.

ANSWER KEY:

Possible answers include:

A.
1. He is the one who is talking to the jury.
2. He is the man who is sitting at the table on the left.
3. She is the person who sits at the big desk in the center of the room.
4. A witness is someone who gives testimony at a trial.
5. The prosecutor is the lawyer who is charging the defendant with a crime.

B.
Answers will vary.

C.
A juror is a person who sits on a jury.
A verdict is the decision that says if the defendant is guilty or innocent.

OBJECTIVE

Participating in Your Community

WINDOW ON PRONUNCIATION

Changing stress with *that*

1. Warm Up, page 104

★ Go over the directions.

★ Read each question aloud.

★ Put students in pairs or small groups to answer the questions.

★ Call on students to share their ideas with the class.

EXPANSION ACTIVITY: Go Online

★ For an out-of-class or lab activity, have students go online and enter the words "crime prevention" and the name of your city or state.

★ Have students write down 3 things they learn.

★ Call on students to tell the class what they learned.

2. Read and Respond, page 104

★ Go over the directions.

★ Have students read the article and answer the questions.

★ Put students in pairs to check their answers.

★ Go over the answers with the class.

ANSWER KEY:

Answers will vary.
1. The streets were filled with muggers, drug addicts, and other dangerous people.
2. He worked with police and other community leaders. They formed groups to watch for trouble.
3. It's a special place with stores and restaurants.
4. *Answers will vary.*

EXPANSION ACTIVITY: Sequence It

★ Photocopy the story, enough so there is one copy for each pair.

★ Cut the story into separate paragraphs.

★ With books closed, have students reorder the paragraphs.

★ For a greater challenge, complete this activity *before* Activity 2 on page 104. Then students can check their ordering as they read the story.

3. Apply, page 105

★ Go over the directions.

★ Read the options aloud. Have students choose one option and follow the directions.

★ Call on students to share what they learned with the class.

EXPANSION ACTIVITY: Practice the Grammar

★ Have students go online to find out about neighborhood watches and other crime prevention strategies (as in the Expansion Activity for Activity 1 and in Activity 3).

★ Have students write down 3 websites where they found interesting information.

★ Ask students to write a description of each website using an adjective clause (*Neighborhood Watch is an organization that helps neighbors work together to make their communities safer.*).

WINDOW ON PRONUNCIATION: Changing Stress with *that*

A. Read the information, page 105

★ Have students read the information. Ask comprehension questions (*When do we stress the word* that?).

B. Listen to the sentences, page 105

★ Go over the directions.

★ Have students look at the sentences and questions while you read them or play the tape or CD.

★ Read the sentences or play the tape or CD a second time, pausing after each sentence to have students repeat.

C. Listen to the sentences, page 105

★ Go over the directions.

★ Have students circle the stressed *that* in each item as you read the sentences or questions or play the tape or CD again.

★ Have students check their answers with a partner. Go over the answers with the class.

ANSWER KEY:

1. <u>That's</u> the man that was on TV.
2. Remember the movie that I told you about? It's at <u>that</u> theater over there.
3. Did you meet the girl that Matt likes? <u>That's</u> her.
4. Not <u>that</u> book. I want the one that I gave you last week.
5. The neighbor that had an accident last week lives in <u>that</u> house.

D. Work with a partner, page 105

★ Go over the directions.

★ Put students in pairs to practice asking and answering the questions.

★ Walk around the room to monitor the activity and provide help if needed.

★ Call on students to answer the questions.

OBJECTIVE

Review and Assessment

1. Listening Review 🎧, page 106

★ Go over the directions for items 1–5 with the class.

★ Read the items 1–5 or play the tape or CD and have the students mark their answers in the Answer Sheet box.

★ Walk around to monitor the activity and help students stay on task.

★ Go over the directions for items 6–10, and repeat the procedure.

★ Have students check their answers for 1–10 with a partner.

★ Go over the answers with the class.

LISTENING SCRIPT

1. Listening Review, page 106

Listen and choose the sentence that is closest in meaning to the sentence you hear. Use the Answer Sheet.

1. A misdemeanor is more serious than an infraction.
2. If you commit an infraction, you will probably have to pay a fine.
3. A blood test is no longer required to obtain a marriage license.
4. You have 3 chances to pass the written test.
5. The defendant was accused of assault and burglary.

Listen to each conversation and choose the best answer to the question you hear. Use the Answer Sheet.

6.
A: Did anyone witness the crime?
B: Yes. I did.

Question: What did the woman do?

7.
A: Do you have a picture ID with you?
B: No, I don't. Do I need one?
A: Yes, you do.

Question: What does the man need?

8.
A: Do I need a blood test to get a marriage license?
B: No, but you do have to fill out an application.
A: Can I get one here?
B: Sure. Just a minute and I'll get it for you.

Question: What does the man get from the woman?

9.
A: Did you really get a traffic ticket?
B: Yes. Can you believe it?
A: What did you do?
B: I went through a red light. Well, I thought it was yellow.

Question: What kind of traffic ticket did the woman get?

10.
A: Did you see the book that was just here on the chair?
B: No, I didn't. But there's a book on the dining room table.
A: No. That's not the one I'm looking for.

Question: What is the woman looking for?

ANSWER KEY:

1. A; 2. C; 3. C; 4. A; 5. B; 6. B; 7. A; 8. C; 9. B; 10. A

2. Vocabulary Review, page 107

★ Have students look at the chart. Go over the directions and the example.

★ Have students complete the chart, and then compare charts with a partner.

★ Go over the answers with the class.

★ Have students choose 6 words and use them to write 6 questions.

★ Put students in pairs to practice asking and answering the questions.

ANSWER KEY:

Noun	Verb	Adjective
commitment	commit	
defender/defense	defend	———
fatality	———	*fatal*
guilt	———	*guilty*
innocence	———	*innocent*
jaywalker	*jaywalk*	———
judgment/judge	*judge*	———
punishment/punisher	punish	*punishable*
violation	*violate*	———

LEARNING LOG, page 107

★ Point out the two sections of the Learning Log: *I know these words* and *I practiced these skills, strategies, and grammar points.*

★ Ask students to check the words they know and what they practiced.

★ Walk around to note what students don't know or didn't practice. Use this information to review areas of difficulty.

BIG PICTURE EXPANSION: SPEAKING ASSESSMENT—Talking about the Big Picture

★ You can use the Big Picture as an individual assessment, to place new students in classes, to diagnose difficulties, or to measure progress.

★ Work with one student. Show the Big Picture to the student. Ask: *What do you see in the picture?* Or say: *Tell me about the picture.* Tell the student to speak for as long as possible. Wait a moment for the student to prepare an answer.

★ If the student has difficulty, you can use prompts (*Who do you see? What are the people doing? Where are they?*).

★ You can use a scoring rubric like the one below to rate speakers.

4	Exhibits confidence; begins speaking without prompting Uses some complex sentences, although may make mistakes with irregular forms Can use several tenses
3	Uses sentences, although form may be incorrect Uses more than one tense Can speak for a sustained length of time Responds to prompts, but doesn't need them to begin speaking
2	Can use nouns and verbs in sentences Uses one tense most of the time Answers informational questions Limited vocabulary
1	Can name objects Uses single words Can answer yes/no questions
0	Cannot say anything independently May be able to point to objects when prompted

★ Review areas of difficulty.

TEACHER NOTES:

Things that students are doing well:

_____

_____

_____

_____

Things students need additional help with:

_____

_____

_____

_____

Ideas for further practice or for the next class:

_____

_____

_____

_____

BIG PICTURE EXPANSION ACTIVITY: WRITING—Describing People in the Courtroom

★ Put the Big Picture color transparency for Unit 6, Lesson 1 on the overhead projector, or have students look at the Big Picture in their books.

★ Ask the class: *Who do you see? What does each person do?*

★ Have students brainstorm ideas to prepare to write.

★ Have students write a paragraph about the different people and their roles in the courtroom. Remind students to use adjective clauses.

★ Put students in pairs to take turns reading their paragraphs to their partners.

OBJECTIVE

Recognizing Cause and Effect

Recognizing Cause and Effect, page 108

★ Direct students' attention to the information in the box. Explain the strategy.

★ Go over the examples.

★ Check comprehension by asking questions (*What are some words that signal a cause and effect relationship?*).

Grammar Note:
★ Your students will probably remember that *if* signals a condition. They have used if clauses with result clauses before. Point out that a conditional clause is one type of cause and effect relationship, one that describes an effect when a certain condition is met.

1. Read the paragraph, page 108

★ Go over the directions.

★ Have students read the paragraph and then take notes in the chart.

★ Have students check their answers with a partner.

★ Go over the answers with the class.

ANSWER KEY:

Effects: cost of insurance can go up, price increase can last for 5 years, can cause an accident, can cause a death

2. Read the paragraph, page 108

★ Go over the directions.

★ Have students read the paragraph and complete the chart.

★ Have students check their answers with a partner.

★ Go over the answers with the class.

ANSWER KEY:

Cause: drunk driving or drinking and driving
Effects: fatal car accidents, could hurt yourself, could injure or kill another person, lose your license

3. Read the article, page 109

★ Go over the directions.

★ Have students read the article and take notes in the chart.

★ Then have students compare ideas with a partner.

★ Have students write summaries of the article.

★ Call on students to read their summaries to the class.

ANSWER KEY:

Effects: you may think violence is more common and less serious than it is, you may think bad guys are everywhere and that you will have to use violence to defend yourself

EXPANSION ACTIVITY: Find 3 More

★ Have students find 3 more possible causes in the reading.

★ Put students in pairs to exchange causes and list effects.

★ Call on students to tell the class about a cause and effect relationship they found in the article.

OBJECTIVE

Using Graphic Organizers for Writing

Using Graphic Organizers for Writing, page 110

★ Direct students' attention to the information in the box. Go over the graphic organizers and how they are useful.

★ Ask comprehension questions (*What kind of chart is useful when you want to compare or contrast two things?*).

1. Use a graphic organizer ▢, page 110

★ Go over the directions. Point out that there are 3 questions and 3 types of graphic organizers.

★ Have students complete each diagram in answer to the questions.

★ Put students in pairs to share ideas.

★ Have students write paragraphs using the ideas in the diagrams.

★ Call on volunteers to read their paragraphs to the class.

ANSWER KEY:

Answers will vary.

EXPANSION ACTIVITY: Real Articles

★ Bring in articles from newspapers or magazines, or have students bring them in.

★ Give each student an article to read.

★ Have students create a graphic organizer for their articles.

★ Put students in pairs to exchange articles and create organizers for the new article.

★ Have pairs compare graphic organizers.

★ Call on students to tell the class about their organizers.

EQUIPPED FOR THE FUTURE ROLE

Family

OBJECTIVE

Evaluating Discipline Practices

A. Read questions 1 to 3, Workbook page 112

★ Go over the directions

★ Have students read the information.

★ Have students answer the questions and then check their answers with a partner.

★ Go over the answers with the class.

ANSWER KEY:

1. He missed school and stayed out late;
2. They locked him in his room for two days;
3. His teacher reported it.

B. Read the sentences, Workbook page 113

★ Go over the directions.

★ Read the first sentence and elicit if it is true or false. Have students check *False*.

★ Have students read the sentences and check *True* or *False*.

★ Go over the answers with the class.

ANSWER KEY:

1. False; 2. False; 3. True; 4. True; 5. True

C. There are many forms, Workbook page 113

★ Go over the directions. Make sure students understand the examples.

★ Have students write the examples in the appropriate place on the chart and then compare answers with a partner.

★ Go over the answers with the class.

ANSWER KEY:

Physical	Emotional	Neglect
burning kicking shaking slapping	shaming name calling	failing to send to school failing to take to the doctor not feeding properly not using a child seat for a baby in the car

Take It Outside, Workbook page 113

★ Read each question aloud and have students repeat.

★ If you do this in class, students can interview classmates. If they do this as an out-of-class assignment, they can interview family members, friends, or coworkers.

★ Call on volunteers to share the information with the class.

 Take It Online, Workbook page 113

★ Have students use a search engine and enter "laws about child neglect." Tell students to write down three websites that give information on this topic.

★ Call on volunteers to share the information with the class.

EXPANSION ACTIVITY: Compare and Contrast

★ Have students create a Venn diagram to compare and contrast laws regarding child abuse in the U.S. and in another country.

★ Have students write a paragraph using the information in the Venn diagram.

★ Call on students to read their paragraphs to the class.

EQUIPPED FOR THE FUTURE ROLE

Work

OBJECTIVE

Interpreting Work-Related Laws

A. Read the questions in the chart below, Workbook page 114

★ Go over the directions.

★ Have students read the situations and write their guesses in response to the questions (in column 2).

★ Put students in pairs to talk about their guesses.

ANSWER KEY:

Answers will vary.

B. Read the information, Workbook page 115

★ Go over the directions.

★ Have students read the information on Workbook page 115 and write the answers in column 3 on Workbook page 114.

★ Put students in pairs to compare answers.

★ Go over the answers with the class.

ANSWER KEY:

a. Yes. Her boss can ask her to do things not in her job description.
b. No. Employers do not have to pay extra for weekend work.
c. $475
d. She could deliver newspapers, work in a family business, baby-sit, or do chores in a private home. She could also make wreaths.
e. Andy can do all the things Jesse can do and more.

 Take It Online, Workbook page 115

★ Go over the directions.

★ Have students look for state requirements online and summarize what they learn.

★ Call on volunteers to share the information with the class.

EXPANSION ACTIVITY: Take It Outside

★ Write 3 questions about work-related laws on the board (*What work-related law do you think is most important? How are labor laws in the U.S. different from those in your home country? Are there any work-related laws that you don't agree with?*).

★ For an out-of-class assignment, have students interview a family member, friend, or coworker who is currently employed. If you do this activity in class, put students in pairs to take turns asking and answering questions.

★ Call on students to tell the class what they found out.

Career Paths

UNIT OVERVIEW

LESSON	OBJECTIVE	TEACHER'S EDITION PAGE NUMBER
1. Who's in charge?	Solving Problems	p. 141
2. Experience is preferred.	Identifying Job Responsibilities	p. 143
3. He spoke very clearly.	Understanding Job Applications	p. 145
4. Performance Evaluations	Analyzing Performance Evaluations	p. 149
5. If I had known . . .	Using the Past Perfect	p. 151
6. Family-Friendly Companies	Exploring Job Benefits	p. 153
7. What do you know?	Review and Assessment	p. 155
Spotlight: Reading Strategy	Identifying a Sequence of Events	p. 158
Spotlight: Writing Strategy	Understanding the Writing Process	p. 159

Big Picture Expansion Activities

FOCUS	ACTIVITY	SUGGESTED USE
Speaking	Who needs a new job?	Lesson 3
Reading	Workplace Disciplinary Action	Lesson 4
Grammar	If he hadn't done that, . . .	Lesson 5
Writing	Describing Job Performance	Lesson 7
Speaking Assessment	Talking about the Big Picture	Lesson 7

Big Picture Expansion Activity Worksheets

WORKSHEET NUMBER/FOCUS	TITLE	TEACHER'S EDITION PAGE NUMBER
13. Reading	Workplace Disciplinary Action	p. 193
14. Grammar	If he hadn't done that, . . .	p. 194

OBJECTIVE

Solving Problems

VOCABULARY

absenteeism	ignore
disciplinary	loaf
dismissal	reprimand
disorderly	unacceptable
excessive	violate

TRY THIS STRATEGY

Understanding Prefixes

1. Warm Up, page 112

★ Put the Big Picture color transparency for Unit 7, Lesson 1 on the overhead projector, or have students look at the Big Picture in their books.

★ To set the context, ask questions about the picture (*Who do you see in the picture? What's happening?*).

★ As students talk about the Big Picture, write key vocabulary words on the board.

★ Read the questions aloud.

★ Put students in pairs or small groups and have them discuss the questions.

★ Call on students to tell the class about their pair or small group discussion.

Culture/Civics Notes:

★ Students may be surprised by how many rules regulate workplace safety and behavior. You may want to remind students that OSHA regulates workplace safety, and EEOC regulates workplace discrimination practices.

★ Point out that most workplaces have employee handbooks that spell out rules and that many rules are posted in prominent places in the workplace.

EXPANSION ACTIVITY: Vote with Your Feet

★ Write *Agree* on one side of the board and *Disagree* on the other.

★ Have a group of volunteers come to the front of the class.

★ Tell students that you will read a statement and the volunteers should move to the word that best expresses their opinion regarding the statement.

★ Say, *The best job is one where I don't have to work very hard.* Remind the volunteers to stand next to the appropriate word. Ask students to explain their opinions.

★ Continue with other statements. Create your own or use the ideas below. After 2 or 3 statements, continue with a new group of volunteers.
The best job is one where I can work independently.
A good job is exciting.
I'd prefer a job where every day is different from the one before.
The best job is one where you have to interact with people all the time.
A good job involves little if any stress.

2. Analyze, page 112

★ Go over the directions. Read the questions aloud.

★ Direct students' attention to the picture. Put students in pairs to answer the questions.

★ Call on students to share their answers with the class.

ANSWER KEY:

1. *Answers will vary.*

2. *Answers will vary.*

3. *Possible answers include:* horseplay, arguing, riding on cart, standing/sitting on shoulders, watching TV

4. The guy in the tie because he is talking to the workers who are arguing and he's wearing a tie

EXPANSION ACTIVITY: Review from A to Z

★ Put students in pairs or small groups.

★ Set a time limit of 3 minutes. Tell students to list things they see in the picture, with a goal of naming one thing that begins with each letter of the alphabet.

★ After 3 minutes, go through the letters of the alphabet, eliciting examples from the class.

3. Solve Problems, page 112

★ Go over the directions. Read each situation aloud.

★ Put students in pairs to discuss the situations.

★ Call on students to share their ideas with the class

ANSWER KEY:

Answers will vary.

EXPANSION ACTIVITY: Dear Advice Doctor

★ Have students write a letter asking advice about a problem they have had at work or a work problem they know about.

★ Put students in pairs to exchange letters and write responses giving advice.

★ Call on students to read the letters and responses to the class.

TRY THIS STRATEGY: Understanding Prefixes, page 112

★ Read the strategy aloud.

★ Have students find 3 more examples of these prefixes in the work rules.

★ Put students in pairs to compare their ideas with a partner.

★ Call on students to share their ideas with the class.

ANSWER KEY:

Words with an asterisk are in this lesson; possible answers include: improper*, unacceptable*, unexcused*, disorderly

Vocabulary Notes:

★ You may want to point out that *il-* is used before words beginning with *l* and *im-* is used before words beginning with *m* or *p.*

★ Make sure students are aware that not all words that begin with these combinations of letters have prefixes (*including, disciplinary*).

OBJECTIVE

Identifying Job Responsibilities

VOCABULARY

assist	prepare
courteous	previous
ensure	process
handle	recruitment
oversee	retail
possess	shipment
prefer	

1. Scan, page 114

★ Have students look at the job postings, and ask: *Where would you find this information?*

★ Read the questions aloud.

★ Put students in pairs or small groups and have them discuss the questions.

★ Call on students to tell the class about their pair or small group discussion.

Grammar Note:
★ You may want to point out that job postings often use the passive voice. Elicit examples of the passive in the postings.

EXPANSION ACTIVITY: Online Job Search

★ For an out-of-class or lab activity, have students choose a company that they know about.

★ Ask students to go online and search for the name of the company and "jobs." Have students write down at least one position they find posted.

★ Call on students to tell the class what they found.

2. Use the Vocabulary, page 114

★ Go over the directions.

★ Have students write the missing verbs and check their answers with a partner.

★ Then have students check *SS* or *SM* to indicate who is responsible for each task.

★ Go over the answers with the class.

ANSWER KEY:

1. provides/SS; 2. handles/SS; 3. resolves/SS;
4. oversees/SM; 5. orders/SM; 6. balances/SS;
7. reviews/SM; 8. oversees/SM; 9. uses/SS;
10. does/SM; 11. ensures/SM; 12. prepares/SS

EXPANSION ACTIVITY: Ball Toss

★ Remind students that it is easier to remember new vocabulary if they remember collocations, or how a word is used with other words.

★ Brainstorm examples of objects for each verb in the lesson, and write the ideas on the board.

★ Give students 3 minutes to review the verbs and associated objects (*provides customer service*).

★ Tell students that you will call on them and toss a ball or beanbag as you say a verb. They should respond with an appropriate object. Remind students that there may be many correct answers.

★ Call on a student as you toss a beanbag and say *count*. Elicit *money*. Point out that other answers may be correct.

★ Continue until everyone has had a chance to respond.

3. Expand Your Vocabulary, page 114

★ Go over the directions.

★ Have students complete the chart and compare answers with a partner.

★ Have students write a sentence using each word they added to the chart.

★ Call on students to read their sentences to the class.

ANSWER KEY:

Answers are in italics.

Noun	Verb	Adjective
supervisor	*supervise*	*supervisory*
recruitment, recruiter	recruit	----
preparation	*prepare*	preparatory
applicant/ application	apply	applicable
preference	*prefer*	preferable

Pronunciation Note:

★ Remind students that some suffixes cause a change in the stress pattern. Point out that the primary stress shifts for the word families for *supervise, prepare, apply,* and *prefer.*

EXPANSION ACTIVITY: Marking Stress

★ Tell students that you are going to read the first job description aloud and that students should mark the primary stress in all words of more than two syllables. Have students underline the stressed syllable.

★ Have students mark the stress as you read.

★ Put students in pairs to compare their ideas.

ANSWER KEY:

supervisor, **fol**lowing, respon**si**bilities, ad**di**tion, **oth**er, **du**ties, as**signed**, pro**vides**, **ex**cellent, **cus**tomer, **ser**vice, **re**gister, com**plete**, trans**ac**tions, **han**dles, re**funds**, ex**chang**es, as**sists**, **shop**ping, re**solves**, com**plaints**, **bal**ances, **mon**ey, pre**pares**, de**pos**its, en**sures**, **ship**ments, cor**rect**ly, **pro**cessed, ap**pear**ance, **pleas**ing

4. Write, page 114

★ Go over the directions.

★ Have students write job descriptions and then share their ideas with a partner.

★ Call on students to read their job descriptions to the class.

OBJECTIVE

Understanding Job Applications

COMMUNICATION STRATEGY

Expanding Your Answers

1. Warm Up, page 116

★ Have students look at the pictures on page 116. To set the context, ask questions (*Where are they? What do you think the people are doing?*).

★ Read the questions aloud.

★ Put students in pairs or small groups and have them discuss the questions.

★ Call on students to tell the class about their pair or small group discussion.

2. Listen for Specific Information 🎧, page 116

★ Go over the directions.

★ Have students listen and add the missing information to the job application on page 117 while you read the conversations or play the tape or CD.

★ Have students check their answers with a partner.

★ Read the conversation or play the tape or CD again if necessary.

LISTENING SCRIPT:

2. Listen for Specific Information, page 116

Listen to Roberta's interview and add the missing information to her job application on page 117.

A: Can I help you?

B: Yes. I have an appointment to see Mr. Harrison.

A: And your name, please?

B: Roberta Madera.

A: Just a moment, Ms. Madera. I'll tell him you're here. He'll be with you in just a minute, Ms. Madera. Won't you have a seat?

B: Thanks.

C: Ms. Madera?

B: Yes.

C: Hello. I'm Mr. Harrison.

B: Hello, Mr. Harrison. It's nice to meet you.

C: Please come in.

B: Thank you.

C: Have a seat.

B: Thank you.

C: I have your application here, and I see here that you are applying for the assistant manager's position.

B: Yes, that's right. I was very excited to find a job opening at Sayer's.

C: And you'd be able to start on June 1st?

B: Yes, that's right.

C: I see that you went to Northeast Community College.

B: Yes, I've completed two years of work so far, and I hope to continue taking courses part time so I can get my degree.

C: Yes, I see that your major is business administration.

B: Yes. It's a good way to combine math and interpersonal skills.

C: That's true. But tell me, do you find it difficult to work full time and take courses at the same time?

B: It's challenging, but I just have to manage my time carefully.

C: Yes, I see. Let's see, now, why don't you tell me a little about your last job? It says that you worked at Floormart until last April. That's when the store moved out of state, isn't it?

B: Yes, that's right. They offered me a job if I was willing to move, but my family is here, so I decided against moving.

C: What was it like working at Floormart?

B: Well, as the assistant manager, I was able to do a lot of different things, from working with customers to financial planning. I like that. And I had an excellent boss. He was always willing to teach me new things and give me more responsibility.

C: Yes, I see. And, uh, what about your job at Reiko's?

B: Yes. That was my first full-time job. I was a clerk, then a supervisor. I think it was that job that made me realize that I liked being in charge. I mean, I liked being responsible for the store and making decisions. And I enjoyed working with and training the salespeople. I would have stayed there, but the job at Floormart came up, and I couldn't refuse it.

C: Yes, of course.

ANSWER KEY:

Start date: June 1; Years completed: 2; Major: Business Administration; Most recent job title: assistant manager; Reason for leaving: company moved and family is here; Reason for leaving: offered job at Floormart

EXPANSION ACTIVITY:
Was that a question? 🎧

★ Point out that sometimes we make statements that are really questions. In the interview, the man makes 3 statements to which the job applicant responds as if they were questions.

★ Read the conversations or play the tape or CD, and have the students write the three statements.

★ Then have pairs practice reading the statements as questions.

ANSWER KEY:

I see here that you are applying for the assistant manager's position.
I see that you went to Northeast Community College.
I see that your major is business administration.

3. Listen and Evaluate 🎧, page 116

★ Go over the directions.

★ Ask the first question. Direct students' attention to the first photo on page 116, and elicit the answer. Have them check *Yes, very.*

★ Have students listen and check their answers while you read the first interview or play the tape or CD again.

★ Have students compare their answers with a partner.

★ Read the interview or play the tape or CD again if necessary.

★ Go over the directions for the interview with Richard Smith.

★ Have students answer the questions while you read the interview or play the tape or CD.

★ Have students compare answers with a partner.

★ Call on students to share their answers with the class.

⌐ LISTENING SCRIPT ¬

3. Listen and Evaluate, page 116

Now listen to Richard's interview. On another piece of paper, answer questions 1–7 about him. Then compare each interview.

A: Can I help you?

B: Yeah. I want to see Ms. Michaels.

A: Do you have an appointment?

B: Yeah.

A: And your name, please?

B: Richard.

A: Uh, and your last name?

B: Smith. Richard Smith.

A: Just a moment, Mr. Smith. I'll tell her you're here. She'll be with you in just a minute, Mr. Smith. Why don't you have a seat?

B: Okay.

C: Mr. Smith?

B: Yeah, that's me.

C: Why don't you come in? Have a seat.

B: Yeah, okay.

C: I have your application here, and I see that you worked for a travel agent for several years.

B: Yeah. It was so boring. And my boss was really mean. If I was even 10 minutes late in the morning, he'd yell at me. I was so glad when that place went out of business.

C: I see. Well, Mr. Smith. Thank you for coming in.

B: Is that all?

C: Yes.

ANSWER KEY:

Answers may vary, but students should answer *yes* for Roberta and *no* for Richard.

Culture Notes:

★ Depending on your students' backgrounds, you may want to point out that it is common for both men and women to interview job applicants and that the guidelines for appropriate applicant behavior are the same in either case.

★ Your students may not know that certain questions are not legal in a job interview: those that ask about age, religion, or pregnancy plans.

★ Review with students appropriate attire for an interview, Make sure students know that both men and women usually wear business attire (e.g., a suit) to an interview.

Vocabulary Note:

★ Point out or elicit that we use more formal language in interviews, and we don't use slang or words such as *yeah.*

 EXPANSION ACTIVITY: Online Research

★ Have students go online and enter the words "job interview tips." Have students print or copy the tips they think are the most helpful.

★ Put students in pairs or small groups to talk about what they found out.

★ Call on representatives to share a tip with the class.

EXPANSION ACTIVITY: Role Play

★ Put students in pairs to role play job interviews. Ask them to include at least one mistake the applicant makes.

★ Have students perform their role plays for the class. Elicit the mistake that the applicant makes.

★ In a variation, have students prepare role plays in which the applicant is terrible. Have the class note the mistakes as they watch.

Use the Communication Strategy 🎧, page 116

★ Direct students' attention to the Communication Strategy box. Go over the information in the box.

★ Go over the directions.

★ Model the conversation with a student. Have the student ask you a question. Demonstrate how to answer the question and then expand on the answer.

★ Have students work in pairs to ask and answer the questions, using their own ideas to expand.

★ Walk around to make sure they understand the activity and provide help if needed.

BIG PICTURE EXPANSION ACTIVITY: SPEAKING—Who needs a new job?

★ Put the Big Picture color transparency for Unit 7, Lesson 1 on the overhead projector, or have students look at the Big Picture in their books.

★ Point to an employee in the picture. Brainstorm things the employee might say on his or her next job interview. Encourage students to use information from the picture (*He might say he enjoys using the equipment.*). You may want to suggest students include inappropriate job interview comments as well, if they are in keeping with the character's personality.

★ Put students in pairs. Walk around the room and quietly assign each pair of students an employee in the Big Picture.

★ Have students create a conversation between that employee and an interviewer. The employee is applying for a job at another store. Remind them to use the communication strategy as well as information from the picture in the conversation.

★ Have students perform their conversations for the class. Have the class guess which employee in the picture is applying for a job.

OBJECTIVE

Analyzing Performance Evaluations

VOCABULARY

attendance
creativity
deliver
independence
initiative
performance

1. Warm Up, page 118

★ Have students look at the employee evaluation on page 119. To set the context, ask questions (*What kind of form is this? Have you ever had a performance evaluation? What kind of information is usually on them?*).

★ Read the questions aloud.

★ Put students in pairs or small groups and have them discuss the questions.

★ Call on students to tell the class about their pair or small group discussion.

EXPANSION ACTIVITY: Compare and Contrast

★ Have students draw Venn diagrams to compare and contrast the characteristics of an ideal employee with the characteristics of an ideal student.

★ Put students in pairs to talk about their diagrams.

★ Call on students to share their ideas with the class.

2. Read and Respond, page 118

★ Go over the directions.

★ Have students read the employee evaluation. Ask comprehension questions (*What qualities are evaluated on this form? Who is being evaluated? What is her job?*).

★ Have students answer the questions and then check their answers with a partner.

★ Go over the answers with the class.

ANSWER KEY:

1. *Answers will vary.* 2. She's creative and takes initiative; 3. She's not very dependable or reliable because she is often late; 4. *Possible answers include:* come on time, arrange better transportation, work more quickly

EXPANSION ACTIVITY: Online Search

★ Have students use a search engine and enter the words "employee performance evaluation." Ask students to find a copy of an evaluation form and print it, or they can take notes on the behaviors and characteristics being evaluated as well as the type of workplace.

★ Put students in pairs or small groups to compare what they found.

★ Call on students to tell the class what differences they found.

3. Make Inferences, page 118

★ Go over the directions and the example.

★ Read the first comment, and point out that 3 answers are possible.

★ Have students match the comments and inferences.

★ Go over the answers with the class.

ANSWER KEY:

Answers may vary; possible inferences include:
1. c, e, h; 2. c, h, i; 3. c, d, g, i; 4. f, g, h, c; 5. j; 6. c, e, f, h; 7. b, g; 8. e, g, h; 9. a

**BIG PICTURE EXPANSION ACTIVITY:
READING—Workplace Disciplinary
Action**

★ Make copies of **Worksheet #13** and
distribute them to students.

★ Put the Big Picture color transparency for
Unit 7, Lesson 1 on the overhead projector,
or have students look at the Big Picture in
their books.

★ Instruct students to complete the activities
and then check their answers with a
partner.

★ Go over the answers with the class.

ANSWER KEY:

Answers will vary.
A.
  Verbal warnings: guy watching TV
  Referrals to EAP: employees arguing
  Written reprimands: worker on box, worker
   riding on cart, worker on shoulders
  Suspension without pay: maybe arguing
   workers or worker standing on the box

B.
  1. Verbal warnings; 2. Referral to EAP

OBJECTIVE

Exploring Job Benefits

VOCABULARY

discount
flooded
interfere with
quarterly
substantial

WINDOW ON MATH

Computing Averages

1. Warm Up, page 122

★ Go over the directions.

★ Read each question aloud.

★ Put students in pairs or small groups to answer the questions.

★ Call on students to share their ideas with the class.

** EXPANSION ACTIVITY: Online Research**

★ Have students go online to research "family-friendly companies."

★ Have students find out what makes one company family friendly.

★ Call on students to tell the class what they found out.

Culture/Civics Notes:

★ Your students may come from countries where work policies are more family-friendly. You may want to point out that Congress passed a family leave law just a few years ago that guarantees workers 12 weeks of unpaid time off to take care of family emergencies and special circumstances.

★ Many companies in the U.S. are not really family-friendly. Family-oriented and career magazines often provide information on the companies that are most friendly to families.

Vocabulary Note:

★ Review the meaning of *telecommuting* and *flextime* if students have forgotten these words from *All-Star Book 3*. Telecommuting is working from home, using computer, telephone, and fax machine. Flextime is choosing one's own work hours.

2. Read and Respond, page 122

★ Go over the directions.

★ Have students read the article and answer the questions.

★ Put students in pairs to check their answers.

★ Go over the answers with the class.

ANSWER KEY:

1. They like it. 2. quarterly bonuses, opportunity to purchase material at discounts, flexible schedules; 3. *Answers will vary.*
4. Possible answers include: provide on-site day care, extra family leave time, job-sharing, telecommuting

---

EXPANSION ACTIVITY: Interview

★ Put students in pairs to take turns asking and answering questions about a workplace they have worked in or know about. Tell students to focus on the aspects of the workplace that make it family-friendly or family-unfriendly.

★ Have students write a summary of the workplace their partners talked about.

★ Call on students to read their summaries to the class.

---

3. Apply, page 123

★ Go over the directions.

★ Have students number the family-friendly job benefits in order of importance to them and then compare their ideas with a partner.

★ Call on students to share their answers with the class.

ANSWER KEY:

Answers will vary.

EXPANSION ACTIVITY: Timeline

★ Have students create a timeline of the important events in their family lives.

★ Ask students to write the job benefit that was or would have been most important to them at each point on the timeline.

★ Put students in pairs to share their ideas.

WINDOW ON MATH: Computing Averages

A. Read the information, page 123

★ Have students read the information. Ask comprehension questions (*What is another word for average? What do you divide by to find the average?*).

B. Compute the average, page 123

★ Have students compute the averages and then check their answers with a partner.

★ Go over the answers with the class.

ANSWER KEY:

1. $12.50; 2. 4.25

EXPANSION ACTIVITY: Group Averages

★ Put students in small groups.

★ Have students choose 4 characteristics that the group shares that can be expressed numerically (e.g., age, number of children, number of years of schooling, number of days sick last year).

★ Ask each small group to compute the averages for the 4 things they selected.

★ Call on students to tell the class about their group averages.

OBJECTIVE

Review and Assessment

1. Listening Review 🎧, page 124

★ Go over the directions for items 1–5 with the class.

★ Read items 1–5 or play the tape or CD and have the students mark their answers in the Answer Sheet box.

★ Walk around to monitor the activity and help students stay on task.

★ Go over the directions for items 6–10, and repeat the procedure.

★ Have students check their answers for 1–10 with a partner.

★ Go over the answers with the class.

LISTENING SCRIPT

1. Listening Review, page 124

Listen to each conversation and choose the best answer to the question you hear. Use the Answer Sheet.

1.

Woman: Sam, there are several customers waiting at the checkout.

Man: Oh, okay. I didn't see them.

Woman: Sam, I don't want to find you loafing back here again. I don't want to have to tell you again.

Man: Okay.

Question: What work rule did Sam break?

2.

Man: Excuse me. Do you work here?

Woman: Yeah. What do you want?

Man: Uhm, I'd like to pay for this.

Woman: Okay, okay. I'll be with you in a minute.

Question: How would you describe the salesclerk?

3.

Woman: Come in.

Man: Am I interrupting?

Woman: No, come on in Tom.

Man: I finished the report. You said you needed it by tomorrow, right?

Woman: Yes. Oh great. I knew I could count on you.

Question: How could you describe Tom?

4.

Man: Ms. Smith?

Woman: Yes.

Man: Please come in.

Woman: Thanks.

Man: Have a seat.

Woman: Thank you.

Man: I see on your résumé that you worked at Sayer's Department Store for 2 years.

Woman: Yes, that's right.

Man: Could you tell my why you left the company?

Woman: Yes, of course. I enjoyed the job, but I wanted a job with more responsibility. At the time, there weren't any openings at Sayer's.

Man: I see.

Woman: When a better job came up at Reiko, I decided to apply for it. I didn't want to leave Sayer's, but my supervisor there gave me a great recommendation, and she understood why I wanted to leave.

Question: Why did the woman leave her job at Sayer's Department Store?

5.

Woman: You look happy.

Man: I am. I had my performance evaluation today.

Woman: So it went well?

Man: Yes. He said my interpersonal skills are great. I work well with others.

Question: What is one of the man's strengths on the job?

Listen and choose the statement that is closest in meaning to the sentence you hear. Use the Answer Sheet.

6. Joshua is responsible for ordering merchandise.
7. Jill has two years of supervisory experience.
8. Bob can handle customer refunds and exchanges.
9. Tito had a good reason for leaving the job.
10. Noah is very cooperative, and he works well with others.

ANSWER KEY:

1. A; 2. B; 3. C; 4. C; 5. C; 6. B; 7. C; 8. A; 9. A; 10. C

2. Vocabulary Review, page 124

★ Have students look at the chart. Go over the directions and the example.

★ Have students complete the chart, and then compare charts with a partner.

★ Go over the answers with the class.

★ Have students choose 6 words and use them to write 6 questions.

★ Put students in pairs to practice asking and answering the questions.

ANSWER KEY:

Answers are in italics. Additional possible answers are in brackets.

Nouns	Verbs	Adjectives
absenteeism	----	absent
acceptance	*accept*	*acceptable*
assistant/ *assistance*	*assist*	[*assisted*]
courtesy	----	*courteous*
delivery	deliver	*deliverable*
discipline	discipline	*disciplinary*, [*disciplined*]
excess	[*exceed*]	*excessive*
possession	*possess*	possessive
preference	*prefer*	*preferable*, [*preferential*]
resolution	*resolve*	----

LEARNING LOG, page 125

★ Point out the two sections of the Learning Log: *I know these words* and *I practiced these skills, strategies, and grammar points.*

★ Ask students to check the words they know and what they practiced.

★ Walk around to note what students don't know or didn't practice. Use this information to review areas of difficulty.

3. Write, page 125

★ Go over the directions with the class.

★ Have partners exchange job descriptions and decide if they would like such a job.

★ Ask students to share their descriptions with the class.

🖼 BIG PICTURE EXPANSION: SPEAKING ASSESSMENT—Talking about the Big Picture

★ You can use the Big Picture as an individual assessment, to place new students in classes, to diagnose difficulties, or to measure progress.

★ Work with one student. Show the Big Picture to the student. Ask: *What do you see in the picture?* Or say: *Tell me about the picture.* Tell the student to speak for as long as possible. Wait a moment for the student to prepare an answer.

★ If the student has difficulty, you can use prompts (*Who do you see? What are the people doing? Where are they?*).

★ You can use a scoring rubric like the one below to rate speakers.

4	Exhibits confidence; begins speaking without prompting Uses some complex sentences, although may make mistakes with irregular forms Can use several tenses
3	Uses sentences, although form may be incorrect Uses more than one tense Can speak for a sustained length of time Responds to prompts, but doesn't need them to begin speaking
2	Can use nouns and verbs in sentences Uses one tense most of the time Answers informational questions Limited vocabulary
1	Can name objects Uses single words Can answer yes/no questions
0	Cannot say anything independently May be able to point to objects when prompted

★ Review areas of difficulty.

TEACHER NOTES:

Things that students are doing well:

Things students need additional help with:

Ideas for further practice or for the next class:

BIG PICTURE EXPANSION ACTIVITY: WRITING—Describing Job Performance

★ Put the Big Picture color transparency for Unit 7, Lesson 1 on the overhead projector, or have students look at the Big Picture in their books.

★ Ask the class: *What activities do you see? What are the employees doing right? Wrong?*

★ Have students brainstorm ideas to prepare to write.

★ Have students write a paragraph about how the employees were doing their jobs at the time of the picture. Ask students to use the past perfect and past unreal conditionals at least twice in the paragraph.

★ Put students in pairs to take turns reading their paragraphs to their partners.

OBJECTIVE

Identifying a Sequence of Events

Identifying a Sequence of Events, page 126

★ Direct students' attention to the information in the box. Explain the strategy.

1. Read the paragraph below, page 126

★ Go over the directions.

★ Have students read the article and circle the words that help them follow the sequence of events. Have students check their answers with a partner.

★ Go over the answers with the class.

ANSWER KEY:

Working part-time can be a good way to get your foot in the door, says Nancy Lin. Her (first) job was as a part-time sales associate with Lowe's Hardware at their store in Springvale. (Meanwhile) she continued studying full time to get her degree. (Immediately after) graduating, she began working full time at the store. (Soon after that) she became an assistant store manager, and (today) she is a successful general manager of the Lowe's store in San Bernardo. Who knows what's next, but (before) she started college, Nancy wasn't quite sure what kind of job she would have. She's happy with the outcome.

2. Read about Franklin Chang-Diaz, page 126

★ Go over the directions. Write a timeline on the board.

★ Have students read the biographical information individually, or read it aloud.

★ Have students take notes on the timeline.

★ Have students compare their timelines with a partner.

★ Have volunteers complete the timeline on the board.

ANSWER KEY:

possible answers from left to right on the timeline

Grew up in Costa Rica
Dreamt about exploring outer space
Finished high school
Got a job as a bank teller
8 months later, moved to Hartford
Enrolled in high school to improve English
Got a scholarship to UConn
Graduated
Got a scholarship for PhD program at MIT
Completed PhD
Applied to NASA and was rejected
Received citizenship (1980)
Applied again and was accepted
Began astronaut training (1981)
Went up in space (1986)
Went into space again numerous times

EXPANSION ACTIVITY: Your Timeline

★ Have students create a timeline for their own lives. They can refer to the timeline they created in the Expansion Activity for Activity 3 in Lesson 6.

★ Then have students create a 3-paragraph narrative of their own lives, using the timeline and sequencing words.

★ Have students exchange narratives and provide feedback.

★ Ask students to revise if necessary.

3. Use your notes, page 126

★ Have students use their notes to write a summary.

★ Have partners compare their summaries.

OBJECTIVE

Understanding the Writing Process

Understanding the Writing Process, page 128

★ Direct students' attention to the information in the box.

★ Go over the writing process.

★ Ask comprehension questions: *What should you do first? What should you do after you write a first draft?*

1. Follow the steps below, page 128

★ Go over the directions.

★ Read the first step aloud. Go over the example.

★ Set a time limit of 5 minutes. Have students quickwrite about the person they have chosen.

★ Read Step 2 aloud. Put students in pairs to talk about their subjects.

★ Read Step 3 aloud.

★ Have students map their ideas about the person.

★ Read Step 4 aloud.

★ Have students write a first draft.

★ Read Step 5 aloud.

★ Have students read their own drafts.

★ Put students in pairs to take turns reading their drafts and providing feedback.

★ Read Step 6 aloud.

★ Have students rewrite their drafts, incorporating new ideas and responding to feedback.

EXPANSION ACTIVITY: Describe a Process

★ Point out that students can use the words that help them understand a sequence of events to describe not only a life, but also a process.

★ Have students use sequencing words to describe the writing process, or have them select another process to describe. If needed, brainstorm some things that involve a process (*making tea, brushing one's teeth, using an ATM*).

★ Call on students to read their process descriptions to the class.

EQUIPPED FOR THE FUTURE ROLE

Work

OBJECTIVE

Interpreting Information about the U.S. Workforce

A. Study the charts, Workbook page 132

★ Direct students' attention to the charts and ask questions: *Which occupation shows the greatest increase in jobs? The greatest decrease?*

★ Read the first sentence and elicit if it is true or false. Have students check *True*.

★ Have students look at the charts and check *True* or *False* for each sentence.

★ Have students answer the questions and then check their answers with a partner.

★ Go over the answers with the class.

ANSWER KEY:

1. True; 2. False; 3. True; 4. False; 5. True

B. Use the charts, Workbook page 133

★ Go over the directions.

★ Have students circle their answers and then compare answers with a partner.

★ Go over the answers with the class.

ANSWER KEY:

1. b; 2. c; 3. a; 4. c

C. What advice would you give? Workbook page 133

★ Go over the directions.

★ Have students read the situations and give advice.

★ Put students in pairs to compare their answers.

★ Call on students to share their ideas with the class.

ANSWER KEY:

1. Answers may vary but should include the advice that nursing is expected to grow, whereas computer operators is expected to decrease.

2. Answers may vary but might include that retail sales and wholesale and manufacturing sales positions are expected to increase, while telemarketing and door-to-door sales are expected to decrease.

 Take It Online, Workbook page 133

★ Go over the directions.

★ Have students use a search engine to find the U.S. Department of Labor, Bureau of Labor Statistics.

★ Tell students to find a chart that is interesting to them and write down 3 interesting things they learn from the chart.

★ Call on volunteers to share the information with the class.

EXPANSION ACTIVITY: Role Play

★ Put students in pairs. Have students select or suggest a scenario in which one person is thinking about future career plans and the other is giving advice.

★ Have students create conversations and perform them for the class.

EQUIPPED FOR THE FUTURE ROLE

Community

OBJECTIVE

Exploring Continuing Education

A. Read the questions in the chart, Workbook page 134

★ Go over the directions.

★ Read the questions aloud.

★ Have students answer the questions, using the middle column, and compare answers with a partner.

★ Call on students to share their ideas with the class.

★ Have students read the information and write their answers in the column on the right.

★ Go over the answers with the class. Ask students if they had correctly guessed the answers to the questions before reading.

ANSWER KEY:

1. someone who continues to learn, even after becoming an adult; 2. a General Educational Development certificate, an alternative to a high school diploma; 3. in the phone book under "adult education" or from the local school district; 4. for work-related reasons

B. Study the ad, Workbook page 135

★ Go over the directions.

★ Have students study the ad and then check True or False after each statement.

★ Have students compare their answers with a partner.

★ Go over the answers with the class.

ANSWER KEY:

1. True; 2. False; 3. True; 4. True; 5. False; 6. True

Take It Outside, Workbook page 135

★ Go over the directions.

★ If you do this in class, students can interview classmates. If students do this as an out-of-class assignment, they can interview family members, friends, or coworkers.

★ Call on volunteers to share the information with the class.

 Take It Online, Workbook page 135

★ Go over the directions.

★ Call on volunteers to share the information with the class.

EXPANSION ACTIVITY: Set Goals

★ Elicit ideas from students for goals they hope to accomplish in the future. Write the ideas on the board.

★ Point to one goal on the board and elicit several ideas for how the goal could be reached. For example, if the goal is *be my own boss,* ideas might include: *take business classes, start saving money, ask for more responsibility at work, look into small business opportunities.*

★ Put students in pairs or small groups. Have them generate ideas to help reach each group member's goal.

★ Call on students to tell the class one idea they might try to reach their goal.

Money Matters

UNIT OVERVIEW

LESSON	OBJECTIVE	TEACHER'S EDITION PAGE NUMBER
1. It's not in the budget.	Budget Planning	p. 163
2. FAQs about Money	Understanding Financial Terms	p. 165
3. Does this account earn interest?	Comparing Banking Services	p. 167
4. Credit Card Fraud	Interpreting Information	p. 170
5. She said it was a good deal.	Using Quoted Speech and Reported Speech	p. 171
6. Deductions from a Paycheck	Interpreting Pay Stubs	p. 173
7. What do you know?	Review and Assessment	p. 175
Spotlight: Reading Strategy	Comparing and Contrasting	p. 178
Spotlight: Writing Strategy	Using Transition Words and Phrases	p. 179

Big Picture Expansion Activities

FOCUS	ACTIVITY	SUGGESTED USE
Speaking	Role Play	Lesson 3
Reading	Dear Financial Guru	Lesson 2
Grammar	How much did we spend on groceries?	Lesson 5
Writing	Evaluating a Budget	Lesson 7
Speaking Assessment	Talking about the Big Picture	Lesson 7

Big Picture Expansion Activity Worksheets

WORKSHEET NUMBER/FOCUS	TITLE	TEACHER'S EDITION PAGE NUMBER
15. Reading	Dear Financial Guru	p. 195
16. Grammar	How much did we spend on groceries?	p. 196

OBJECTIVE

Budget Planning

TRY THIS STRATEGY

Classifying

1. Warm Up, page 130

★ Put the Big Picture color transparency for Unit 8, Lesson 1 on the overhead projector, or have students look at the Big Picture in their books.

★ To set the context, ask questions about the picture (*What do you see in the picture? What's happening?*).

★ As students talk about the Big Picture, write key vocabulary words on the board.

★ Read the questions aloud.

★ Put students in pairs or small groups and have them discuss the questions.

★ Call on students to tell the class about their pair or small group discussion.

Grammar Notes:
★ Students learned about gerunds in *All Star 3*. You may want to review continuous verbs (*I am eating dinner now*) and gerunds (*They spend 20% of their income on housing*). In this lesson, spending is a gerund that functions as a modifier (e.g., *dinner* plan).

★ Participial adjectives are a third *-ing* form. You could point out examples (*interesting idea, exciting movie*).

EXPANSION ACTIVITY: Family Budget

★ Put students in groups of four.

★ Tell students that each small group is a family with a monthly income of $2,500. Ask them to decide on a monthly budget.

★ Call on students to share their ideas with the class.

2. Evaluate, page 130

★ Go over the directions. Read the questions aloud.

★ Direct students' attention to the picture. Put students in pairs to answer the questions.

★ Call on students to share their answers with the class.

ANSWER KEY:

1. Housing = 30%, Transportation = 15%, Food = 15%; 2. *Answers will vary.* 3. housing, clothing, entertainment, utilities; 4. *Possible answers include:* reduce food costs by using coupons and comparison shopping, walk more

EXPANSION ACTIVITY: Anticipation

★ Put students in pairs to list factors that may cause budget items to increase or decrease over a certain time period. Ask students to consider factors for a family living in California, Illinois, Florida, and New Jersey.

★ Ask the pairs to estimate an amount that a family like the Lees would need to budget for these fluctuations in each geographical area.

★ Call on students to share their ideas with the class.

3. Plan, page 130

★ Go over the directions.

★ Have students list their budget goals and how they can meet them.

★ Put students in pairs to talk about their budgets.

★ Call on students to share their ideas with the class

ANSWER KEY:

Answers will vary.

EXPANSION ACTIVITY: Sort it out.

★ Ask each student to write the name of something specific he or she spent money on last month. Tell students they should not write a general category word such as *housing* or *transportation* but should instead write something specific such as *bus fare to the basketball game.*

★ Collect the slips, and redistribute them.

★ Have students stand and walk around the room to find classmates who have an expense in the same category. You do not need to tell students the categories beforehand—they can create their own system.

★ This activity prepares students for the Try This Strategy.

★★★★★★★★★★★★★★★★★★★★★★★★★★★★★★★★★★★★★★★

TRY THIS STRATEGY: Classifying, page 130

★★★★★★★★★★★★★★★★★★★★★★★★★★★★★★★★★★★★★★★

★ Read the strategy aloud.

★ Have students add 5 items to each of the groups.

★ Put students in pairs to compare their ideas with a partner.

★ Call on students to share their ideas with the class.

ANSWER KEY:

Answers will vary.

OBJECTIVE

Understanding Financial Terms

VOCABULARY

budget
budget deficit
CD
certificate of deposit
fee
fixed
individual retirement account
inflation
invest
IRA
max out
minimum monthly payment
penalty fee
perk
set back
share (of stock)
specific
stock
vary

1. Warm Up, page 132

★ Have students look at the information and pictures, and ask: *What are FAQs? What do these questions have in common?*

★ Read the questions aloud.

★ Put students in pairs or small groups and have them discuss the questions.

★ Call on students to tell the class about their pair or small group discussion.

 EXPANSION ACTIVITY: Go Online

★ Have students visit a bank in person or online to find out about credit card interest rates, or bring in mail offers.

★ Put students in pairs to compare the offers.

★ Call on students to tell the class about the rates.

Vocabulary Notes:

★ Point out that vocabulary constantly changes. Elicit some ideas for the sources for new words (e.g., other languages, slang from young people).

★ Explain that some words are formed by shortening other words. There are two examples in this lesson (*max out* from *maximum/maximize, perk* from *perquisite*). Other examples include *perm, fax,* and *rehab.* Have students work in pairs or small groups to look up the longer form of those words. (*permanent, facsimile, rehabilitate*)

2. Summarize, page 132

★ Go over the directions and the example.

★ Put students in pairs to take turns asking and answering the questions.

★ Call on students to answer the questions.

ANSWER KEY:

Answers will vary but should reflect the content on pages 132 and 133.

EXPANSION ACTIVITY: Phrase It as a Question

★ Tell students that you will call on a student and give an answer to one of the FAQs (e.g., *No, they have different perks, annual fees, and interest rates*). Elicit the question (*Are all credit cards the same?*).

★ Have students review the FAQs and then close their books.

★ Call on a student and give an answer. Elicit the question. Continue with other answers and questions.

---

3. Use the Vocabulary, page 132

★ Go over the directions.

★ Have students stand and walk around the room, asking questions of classmates to complete the chart.

★ When students are finished, call on volunteers to tell the class about one of their classmates.

**EXPANSION ACTIVITY:
Pair Interview**

★ Brainstorm a list of questions students can ask about unpleasant credit experiences (*Have you ever lost a card? Did you ever have a card stolen? Was it hard to replace your card? Do you know anyone who has been a victim of identity theft?*). Write the questions on the board.

★ Put students in pairs to take turns asking and answering the questions.

★ For additional writing experience, have students write a paragraph about the interview.

★ Call on students to read their paragraphs to the class.

4. Evaluate, page 132

★ Go over the directions.

★ Read the situations aloud and have students answer the questions.

★ Put students in pairs to compare answers.

★ Call on students to share their ideas with the class.

ANSWER KEY:

1. She should go with the 18% interest card because she never carries a balance, so she won't pay any interest.
2. a savings account or a short-term CD because you're not supposed to take money out of an IRA until you retire

 **EXPANSION ACTIVITY:
Dear Money Matters**

★ Have students write letters seeking advice on a money situation.

★ Put students in pairs to exchange and respond to the letters.

★ Call on students to share their ideas with the class.

 **BIG PICTURE EXPANSION ACTIVITY:
READING—Dear Financial Guru**

★ Make copies of **Worksheet #15** and distribute them to students.

★ Put the Big Picture color transparency for Unit 8, Lesson 1 on the overhead projector, or have students look at the Big Picture in their books.

★ Instruct students to complete the activities and then check their answers with a partner.

★ Go over the answers with the class.

ANSWER KEY:

A.
1. no; 2. yes; 3. yes; 4. yes; 5. no

B.
1. food, miscellaneous, clothing; 2. housing; 3. personal care

OBJECTIVE

Comparing Banking Services

COMMUNICATION STRATEGY

Repeating to Confirm

1. Warm Up, page 134

★ Have students look at the pictures on page 134.

★ Read the questions aloud.

★ Put students in pairs or small groups and have them discuss the questions.

★ Call on students to tell the class about their pair or small group discussion.

EXPANSION ACTIVITY: Bank Visit

★ For an out-of-class activity, have students visit a local bank and pick up a brochure describing the bank's services.

★ Put students in pairs to compare bank services. Match partners who visited different banks.

★ Call on students to tell the class what they learned.

---

2. Listen and Check 🎧, page 134

★ Go over the directions.

★ Have students listen and look at the pictures while you read the conversations or play the tape or CD.

★ Have students check 3 questions the customer asks.

★ Have students check their answers with a partner.

★ Read the conversation or play the tape or CD again if necessary.

LISTENING SCRIPT:

2. Listen and Check, page 134

Read questions 1 to 9 on page 135. Then listen to a conversation between a bank officer and a customer. Check 4 questions the customer asks.

A: Can I help you?

B: Yes. I'd like to speak to someone about opening a new checking account.

A: Can you have a seat, and I'll see if Ms. Jeffries is available.

B: Sure. Thank you.

C: Hi. I'm Ms. Jeffries.

B: Hi, Ms. Jeffries. I'm Sylvia Taylor.

C: Nice to meet you, Ms. Taylor. Why don't you come over to my desk and have a seat?

B: Thank you.

C: How can I help you today?

B: I just wanted to get some information about opening a checking account.

C: Sure. Which kind of account are you interested in?

B: Well, uhm, actually I'm not sure. I really don't know what your bank has to offer.

C: Well, we have 3 types of checking accounts. There's the Circle Checking Account, the Green Checking Account, and the Basic Checking Account.

B: I see. And, ah, how are they different?

C: Well, the Circle Account is the only one that earns interest.

B: That's nice.

C: And the Circle Account is the only one that *doesn't* charge a fee when you use an ATM at other banks.

B: I see.

C: Yes. And the Circle Account is the only one that gives you free checks. You don't have to pay for *any* of your checks.

B: That's great. So, uhm, how much money do you need to open a checking account?

C: Well, for the circle account, you need $50 and for the other two you just need $25.

B: That was 50 for the Circle Account and 25 for the Green Account and the Basic Account?

C: That's right.

B: And how much is the monthly maintenance fee?

C: Well, for the Circle Account it's fifteen dollars. But if you keep $5,000 in your account, you don't have to pay the monthly fee.

B: Not much chance of that.

C: Excuse me.

B: Oh, nothing.

C: And the Green Account is special because it's for online banking only, so there is no monthly maintenance fee. And the Basic Account has a $2.50 monthly fee.

B: Does this account provide free online banking?

C: Yes, it does. In fact, all three types of accounts provide free online banking. Each account also provides an ATM and debit card at no additional charge.

B: I see. And I can pay my bills online free of charge?

C: Absolutely.

B: Well, I think that gives me the information I need. I thank you for your time.

B: Well, if there is anything else I can do for you, let me know. Here's my card.

B: Thanks.

C: Good bye.

B: Good bye.

ANSWER KEY:

check: 1, 5, 8, 9

3. Listen and Take Notes 🎧, page 134

★ Go over the directions.

★ Have students listen and add the missing information to the chart on page 135 while you read the conversations or play the tape or CD.

★ Have students check their answers with a partner.

★ Read the conversation or play the tape or CD again if necessary.

ANSWER KEY:

Answers are in italics.

Seattle Banking	Circle Checking Account	Green Checking Account	Basic Checking Account
1. ☐ How much money do I need to open a checking account?	*$50*	*$25*	*$25*
2. ☐ Does this account earn interest?	*yes*	*no*	*no*
3. ☐ Will I be charged to use the ATM at other banks?	*no*	*yes*	*yes*
4. ☐ Does this account provide free checks?	*yes*	*N/A*	*no*
5. ☐ How much is the monthly maintenance fee?	*$15.00*	*$0*	*$2.50*
6. ☐ How much do I have to keep in my account to avoid a monthly maintenance fee?	*$5,000*	*N/A*	*N/A*
7. ☐ Does a free ATM or debit card come with this account?	*yes*	*yes*	*yes*
8. ☐ Does this account provide free online banking?	*yes*	*yes*	*yes*
9. ☐ Can I pay my bills online?	*yes*	*yes*	*yes*

Grammar Note:

★ You may want to mention that some adverbs are focus adverbs. They give special attention to certain words and help to explain how much/many or how few/little. Examples include: *only, just, merely, almost, nearly, even, simply, really.*

 EXPANSION ACTIVITY: Listen for Focus Adverbs

★ Read the conversations or play the tape or CD again.

★ Have students note which focus adverbs are used and how.

4. Write, page 134

★ Go over the directions.

★ Have students complete the sentences and then compare answers with a partner.

★ Call on students to read their sentences to the class.

ANSWER KEY:

1. earns interest/allows free use of another bank's ATMs
2. have a monthly maintenance fee
3. requires a smaller initial deposit/earns no interest/charges for use of another bank's ATMs/has no monthly maintenance fee
4. require $25 to open an account/earn no interest/charge for use of another bank's ATMs
5. come with a free ATM or debit card/provide free online banking/allow you to pay bills online

Grammar Note:

★ *Both* takes a plural form of the verb, whereas *neither* takes the singular form.

EXPANSION ACTIVITY: More Practice

★ Have students write sentences using *both, neither/nor,* and *unlike* to describe the two banks in the Expansion Activity for the Warm Up.

5. Use the Communication Strategy 🎧, page 134

★ Go over the directions.

★ Have students read the conversation, or you read the conversation aloud line by line and have students repeat.

★ Have students practice reading the conversation in pairs.

★ Direct students' attention to the Communication Strategy box. Go over the information in the box.

★ Say each example and have students repeat.

★ Model the conversation with a student. Have the student read A's lines. Demonstrate how to substitute your own ideas. Elicit appropriate responses from the student.

★ Have students work in pairs to practice the conversation, substituting their own ideas for the underlined words.

★ Walk around to make sure they understand the activity. Provide help if needed.

BIG PICTURE EXPANSION ACTIVITY: SPEAKING—Role Play

★ Tell students they are going to role play a conversation between Mr. or Mrs. Lee and a financial advisor. The advisor is a little hard of hearing.

★ Put the Big Picture color transparency for Unit 8, Lesson 1 on the overhead projector, or have students look at the Big Picture in their books.

★ Ask students what questions an advisor might ask a client based on the information in the Big Picture. Point out that the advisor is merely gathering information at this point. Elicit ideas such as *How much did you actually spend on entertainment in March?* Write a few examples on the board.

★ Put students in pairs to create 10 questions about information in the picture.

★ Have the pairs create conversations between the advisor and one of the Lees. Remind students to use the communication strategy.

★ Walk around to monitor the activity and provide help if needed.

OBJECTIVE

Interpreting Information

VOCABULARY

activate	guard
black market	secure
bogus	tear up
crook	telemarketer
fortunately	

1. Warm Up, page 136

★ Have students look at the pictures on page 136. To set the context, ask questions about the pictures (*What do you see in the pictures?*).

★ Read the questions.

★ Put students in pairs or small groups, and have them discuss the questions and complete the chart.

★ Call on students to tell the class about their pair or small group discussion.

EXPANSION ACTIVITY: Brainstorm

★ Put students in small groups.

★ Have students brainstorm ways they can protect their credit card information.

★ Call on representatives from each group to tell the class one idea.

2. Read and Respond, page 136

★ Go over the directions.

★ Have students read the article and answer the questions.

★ Have students check their answers with a partner.

★ Go over the answers with the class.

ANSWER KEY:

Possible answers include:

1. We all do, through higher credit card charges.
2. a fake, or not real, credit card
3. refuse to give it

4. People become victims of credit card fraud when a wallet is stolen or a sales slip with credit card numbers is taken.

5. (*any 3*) write down toll-free numbers to report a stolen card, always check that you got your card back, tear up all credit card receipts, keep billing statements in a safe place, use secure websites

EXPANSION ACTIVITY: Outline

★ Remind students that charts and other graphic organizers can help them remember information. Review what an outline includes.

★ Have students create an outline of the article. To help students learn to write down only what is important, set a word limit for the outline (e.g., 30 words).

★ Put students in pairs to compare outlines.

★ Call on volunteers to put an outline on the board.

3. Give Advice, page 136

★ Go over the directions.

★ Read each situation aloud. Put students in small groups to discuss what the person should or shouldn't have done and what they should do next.

★ Call on students to share their ideas with the class.

EXPANSION ACTIVITY: Online Research

★ Have students go online and search for "consumer protection tips."

★ Ask students to write down 3 new tips they find on the Internet.

★ Put students in small groups to create a tip sheet based on their research.

★ Call on representatives of each group to present their tips to the class.

OBJECTIVE

Using Quoted Speech and Reported Speech

Quoted Speech, page 138

★ Have students look at the notes in the box. Read the information and examples aloud.

★ Review correct punctuation for quoted speech, including placement of quotation marks, commas, and closing punctuation.

1. Write the Quotation Marks, page 138

★ Read the directions aloud.

★ Write the first sentence on the board. Elicit where quotation marks should be inserted.

★ Have students add quotation marks to the sentences.

★ Have students check their answers with a partner.

★ Have volunteers write the sentences on the board.

ANSWER KEY:

1. "Stay out of debt," his father said.
2. Laura said happily, "I cut up all my credit cards last night."
3. "I always pay my credit card bills in full," Jane said.
4. Jane asked, "Did you have to pay a late fee?"
5. Rob said, "I decided to put money in an IRA."
6. "The interest rate is 18%," Joel answered.
7. "How did you max out your credit card?" Fernando asked.
8. His accountant asked, "Do you own any stocks?"
9. "How much money can I put in my IRA?" Lisa asked her accountant.
10. "You need to pay off your credit card bill first," Janet said.

2. Interview and Write, page 138

★ Read the directions aloud. Go over the first example.

★ Put students in pairs to take turns asking and answering the questions. Remind students to write their partner's answers as quoted speech.

★ Call on students to read their sentences to the class.

ANSWER KEY:

Answers will vary.

Reported Speech, page 139

★ Have students look at the notes in the box. Read the information and examples aloud, or call on students to read them.

EXPANSION ACTIVITY: Write the Rule

★ Put students in pairs to write rules that describe how the tense changes from quoted to reported speech.

★ Call on students to share their rules with the class.

---

3. Complete the Sentences, page 139

★ Read the directions aloud.

★ Have students answer the questions.

★ Put students in groups of 3 to practice the conversations.

ANSWER KEY:

1. wanted; 2. has; 3. was

BIG PICTURE EXPANSION ACTIVITY: GRAMMAR—How much did we spend on groceries?

★ Make copies of **Worksheet #16** and distribute them to students.

★ Put the Big Picture color transparency for Unit 8, Lesson 1 on the overhead projector, or have students look at the Big Picture in their books.

★ Instruct students to complete the activities and then check their answers with a partner.

★ Go over the answers with the class.

ANSWER KEY:

A. *Answers may vary but should include this information:*
1. We spent $450.
2. We spent $150 more than we planned.
3. No, you can't. That's more than we can spend on entertainment.
4. No. We wanted to save $150, and we only saved $100.
5. No. It's too expensive.
6. Our greatest expense is housing.

B. *Answers depend on answers in A.*
1. She asked him how much more they had spent on transportation than they had planned.
2. Mr. Lee said that they had spent $150 more than they had planned.
3. Sam asked if he could go to the beach.
4. She said they had spent $450.
5. Annie told him there was a dress she really wanted to buy.
6. Mr. Lee said their greatest expense was housing.

OBJECTIVE

Interpreting Pay Stubs

WINDOW ON MATH

Understanding Rates

1. Warm Up, page 140

★ Go over the directions.

★ Read each question aloud.

★ Put students in pairs or small groups to answer the questions.

★ Call on students to share their ideas with the class.

2. Read and Respond, page 140

★ Go over the directions.

★ Have students read the pay stub and answer the questions.

★ Put students in pairs to practice asking and answering the questions.

★ Go over the answers with the class.

ANSWER KEY:

1. $1,103.78; 2. $496.22; 3. twice a month/ every two weeks; 4. $6,400; 5. $1,040

EXPANSION ACTIVITY: Interview

★ Have students interview 3 people (in class or out) who are currently working and receive a pay stub. Ask students to find out what other deductions are made from their paychecks.

★ Call on students to share what they learned with the class.

3. Apply, page 141

★ Go over the directions.

★ Call on students to share their answers with the class.

ANSWER KEY:

$800/$8,800/$800/$8,800/$968/$265.21/ $248.11/$551.89

EXPANSION ACTIVITY: Voluntary Deductions

★ Point out that many employers provide for voluntary deductions.

★ Have students go online and search for "voluntary deductions." Ask students to list 3 voluntary deductions.

★ Call on students to share what they learned with the class.

WINDOW ON MATH: Understanding Rates

A. Read the Information, page 141

★ Have students read the information. Ask comprehension questions (*If I got paid $15 for 2 hours babysitting, how much did I earn an hour?*).

B. Change the following rates to unit rates, page 141

★ Have students calculate the amounts and then check their answers with a partner.

★ Go over the answers with the class.

ANSWER KEY:

1. $2.50; 2. 1 day; 3. $5; 4. $3

C. Solve the following, page 141

★ Go over the directions.

★ Have students solve the problems and compare answers with a partner.

★ Go over the answers with the class.

ANSWER KEY:

1. the new job; 2. 25 miles per gallon

EXPANSION ACTIVITY: Your Rates

★ Model the activity. Tell students some information about yourself using rates (*I drink 3 cups of coffee a day, I run 10 miles a week, I want to lose 20 pounds in 6 months*).

★ Ask questions about the information (*How many cups do I drink in a week? How many miles do I average a day? How much weight should I lose each month to meet my goal?*).

★ Ask students to write 5 sentences about themselves using rates.

★ Ask students to write a question about each sentence that requires calculation.

★ Put students in pairs to exchange and answer questions.

★ Call on students to tell the class something about their partner.

OBJECTIVE

Review and Assessment

1. Listening Review 🎧, page 142

★ Go over the directions for items 1–5 with the class.

★ Read items 1–5 or play the tape or CD and have the students mark their answers in the Answer Sheet box.

★ Walk around to monitor the activity and help students stay on task.

★ Go over the directions for items 6–10, and repeat the procedure.

★ Have students check their answers for 1–10 with a partner.

★ Go over the answers with the class.

⌐LISTENING SCRIPT:⌐

1. Listening Review, page 142

Listen and choose the sentence that is closest in meaning to the sentence you hear. Use the Answer Sheet.

1. They spend 30 percent of their income on housing.
2. She pays an annual fee for her credit card.
3. John owns stock in a company that makes medicines.
4. Sue puts money in her IRA every year.
5. Carlos had to pay a penalty fee because he forgot to pay his credit card bill on time.

Listen to each conversation and choose the best answer to the question you hear. Use the Answer Sheet.

6.
A: What are you going to do with your money?
B: I think I'll buy a CD.
A: Are you sure you don't want to put it in your savings account?
B: No. I think a CD is better.

Question: What is the man going to do with his money?

7.
A: Does this account come with free checks?
B: No, it doesn't, but it does come with a free ATM card.
A: Well, I'm not really interested in that.

Question: What does the man want?

8.
A: How much money do I need to open a savings account?
B: A savings account?
A: Mmm-hm.
B: Fifty dollars.
A: Is that all?
B: Yes.

Question: What does the woman need to open a savings account?

9.
A: Hello?
B: Hello. May I speak to Mr. Delmotto, please?
A: This is Mr. Delmotto.
B: Well, congratulations, Mr. Delmotto. You have won a new TV set.
A: Really?
B: Yes. And I'm going to send it right out to you today.
A: Oh?
B: Yes. All I need is your credit card number. That's just for the shipping. So, what credit card do you want to put it on?
A: I'm not interested. Goodbye.

Question: What did the man refuse to do?

10.
A: What's the interest rate on a 6-month CD these days?
B: I think it's about 2.5 percent.
A: Did you say 2.5?
B: Mmm-hm, yes.
A: That's not much.

Question What did the woman want to know?

ANSWER KEY:

1. B; 2. C; 3. B; 4. A; 5. B; 6. B; 7. C; 8. A;
9. C; 10. A

2. Vocabulary Review, page 143

★ Direct students' attention to the crossword.

★ Go over the directions. Make sure students understand how to fill in the crossword. Remind them to use words from the unit.

★ Have students check their answers with a partner.

★ Go over the answers with the class.

ANSWER KEY:

Across:
    2. specific; 5. fortunately; 9. fixed;
    10. telemarketers; 11. retirement

Down:
    1. budget; 3. certificate; 4. deficit; 5. fee;
    6. crook; 7. perks; 8. inflation

LEARNING LOG, page 143

★ Point out the two sections of the Learning Log: *I know these words* and *I practiced these skills, strategies, and grammer points.*

★ Ask students to check the words they know and what they practiced.

★ Walk around to note what students don't know or didn't practice. Use this information to review areas of difficulty.

BIG PICTURE EXPANSION: SPEAKING ASSESSMENT—Talking about the Big Picture

★ You can use the Big Picture as an individual assessment, to place new students in classes, to diagnose difficulties, or to measure progress.

★ Work with one student. Show the Big Picture to the student. Ask: *What do you see in the picture?* Or say: *Tell me about the picture.* Tell the student to speak for as long as possible. Wait a moment for the student to prepare an answer.

★ If the student has difficulty, you can use prompts (*Who do you see? What are the people doing? Where are they?*).

★ You can use a scoring rubric like the one below to rate speakers.

4	Exhibits confidence; begins speaking without prompting Uses some complex sentences, although may make mistakes with irregular forms Can use several tenses
3	Uses sentences, although form may be incorrect Uses more than one tense Can speak for a sustained length of time Responds to prompts, but doesn't need them to begin speaking
2	Can use nouns and verbs in sentences Uses one tense most of the time Answers informational questions Limited vocabulary
1	Can name objects Uses single words Can answer yes/no questions
0	Cannot say anything independently May be able to point to objects when prompted

★ Review areas of difficulty.

TEACHER NOTES:

Things that students are doing well:

Things students need additional help with:

Ideas for further practice or for the next class:

BIG PICTURE EXPANSION ACTIVITY: WRITING—Evaluating a Budget

★ Put the Big Picture color transparency for Unit 8, Lesson 1 on the overhead projector, or have students look at the Big Picture in their books.

★ Ask the class: *What does the family spend money on? Are they following their budget? What advice would you give the Lee family?*

★ Have students brainstorm ideas to prepare to write.

★ Have students write a paragraph in which they evaluate the Lees' budget.

★ Put students in pairs to take turns reading their paragraphs to their partners.

OBJECTIVE

Comparing and Contrasting

Comparing and Contrasting, page 144

★ Direct students' attention to the information in the box. Explain the strategy.

★ Go over the examples.

★ Check comprehension by asking questions (*What are some words we use when we are comparing two things? What words show contrast?*).

1. Follow the steps below, page 144

★ Go over the directions.

★ Read Step 1 aloud and discuss.

★ Read Step 2 and elicit ideas.

★ Read Step 3. Have students find and circle the words that show a comparison (*as rich as a king, like you, also, both, no difference*).

★ Have students check their answers with a partner.

★ Go over the answers with the class.

★ Read Step 4. Have students complete the chart and then compare charts with a partner.

ANSWER KEY:

The king	The boy
not cheerful	hardworking
not in good humor	cheerful
powerful	good humor
rich	no parents
	poor
	grateful

★ Read Step 5. Have students reread the story and complete the diagram.

★ Have students compare diagrams with a partner.

★ Call on students to share their ideas with the class.

ANSWER KEY:

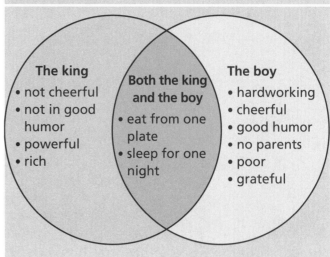

The king
- not cheerful
- not in good humor
- powerful
- rich

Both the king and the boy
- eat from one plate
- sleep for one night

The boy
- hardworking
- cheerful
- good humor
- no parents
- poor
- grateful

EXPANSION ACTIVITY: Tell a Tale

★ Have students bring in, write, or tell a folktale from their culture. If they want they can look online (e.g., http://www.darsie.net/talesofwonder) for folktales. Ask students to choose a folktale that has 2 main characters.

★ Ask students to plan how they will present the folktale to the class. Remind them to focus on words that compare and/or contrast the 2 characters as they tell the story.

★ Call on students to tell their tale to the class. After each story, ask the class questions (*What do the characters have in common? How are they different?*).

★ If your students need more writing practice, have them write the story in their own words. Collect for their portfolios.

OBJECTIVE

Using Transition Words and Phrases

Using Transition Words and Phrases, page 146

★ Direct students' attention to the information in the box. Go over the examples.

★ Ask comprehension questions (*What word can I use to show I'm adding information? To show the result of something?*).

1. Circle the transition words, page 146

★ Go over the directions.

★ Have students read the paragraphs and circle the transition words. Remind students to write the purpose of the transition to the right.

★ Have students compare their answers with a partner.

★ Go over the answers with the class.

ANSWER KEY:

1. *and*, to add information; *for example*, to give an example; *on the other hand*, to show contrast

2. *first*, to show order in time; *however*, to show contrast; *for instance*, to give an example

3. *because*, to show cause and effect; *for this reason*, to show cause and effect

4. *the most important*, to give order of importance; *despite*, to show a contrast; *also*, to add information; *if*, to show cause and effect

5. *even though*, to show contrast; *due to*, to show cause and effect; *such as*, to give an example; *instead*, to show contrast

2. Complete the sentences, page 147

★ Go over the directions.

★ Elicit ideas to complete the first sentence (e.g., *the second most important thing*).

★ Have students complete the sentences and then compare ideas with a partner.

★ Call on students to read their sentences to the class.

ANSWER KEY:

Possible answers include:

1. The second most important thing; 2. but; 3. In addition, 4. due to; 5. however; 6. as a result; 7. Instead of; 8. so

3. Describe your spending habits 📁, page 147

★ Go over the directions.

★ Remind students to use the writing process they learned about in Unit 7.

★ Have students write about their spending habits.

★ Put students in pairs to exchange papers and provide feedback.

★ After students have revised their drafts, ask volunteers to read their papers to the class.

EXPANSION ACTIVITY: Real World Reading

★ Bring in articles from magazines or newspapers or have students bring some in.

★ Ask students to identify transition words and explain the purpose of each.

★ Call on students to read sentences from the article to the class, and elicit the transition word and purpose.

EQUIPPED FOR THE FUTURE ROLE

Family

OBJECTIVE

Managing Money

A. Read the story and answer the questions, Workbook page 152

★ Go over the directions.

★ Have students read the questions and then read the article to find the answers.

★ Go over the answers with the class.

ANSWER KEY:

1. to be frugal, to live within her means, to have good credit, and stay out of debt; 2. by example; 3. they never bought what they couldn't afford, they rarely bought fast food, they took turns getting new shoes, they lived in housing projects; 4. she worked; 5. to stay out of debt; 6. she gave her a fixed amount of money to spend.

B. Answer the questions below, Workbook page 153

★ Go over the directions.

★ Have students answer the questions about themselves.

★ Put students in pairs to take turns asking and answering the questions.

★ Call on students to answer the questions.

ANSWER KEY:

Answers will vary.

C. Match the proverbs with their meanings, Workbook page 153

★ Go over the directions.

★ Have students match the proverbs with their meanings and then check their answers with a partner.

★ Go over the answers with the class.

ANSWER KEY:

1. d; 2. e; 3. a; 4. b; 5. f; 6. c

Take It Outside, Workbook page 153

★ Go over the directions.

★ If you do this in class, students can interview classmates. If they do this as an out-of-class assignment, they can interview family members, friends, or coworkers.

★ Call on volunteers to share the information with the class.

 Take It Online, Workbook page 153

★ Have students use a search engine to look for parenting magazines.

★ Tell students to look for 2 articles with ideas for teaching children about money and to write the 2 titles down.

★ Call on volunteers to share the information with the class.

EXPANSION ACTIVITY: Tell a Tale

★ Have students recall a story or folktale they have heard about money or wealth (e.g., *Rumpelstiltskin, King Midas, The Goose that Laid the Golden Egg*).

★ Put students in pairs or small groups to share their stories.

★ Call on students to tell a story to the class.

EQUIPPED FOR THE FUTURE ROLE

Community

OBJECTIVE

Interpreting Economic Information

A. What do you think? Workbook page 154

★ Go over the directions.

★ Have students read the statements and indicate their predictions in Column 2.

★ Call on students to share their ideas with the class.

ANSWER KEY:

Answers will vary.

B. Read the information below, Workbook page 154

★ Direct students' attention to the information, and ask them what they see.

★ Have students read the information, look at the charts, and check *True* or *False* in Column 3.

★ Go over the answers with the class.

ANSWER KEY:

1. True; 2. False; 3. True; 4. True; 5. False

C. Answer the questions, Workbook page 155

★ Go over the directions.

★ Have students answer the questions and then compare their answers with a partner.

★ Go over the answers with the class.

★ Have students take turns asking and answering the questions with a partner.

ANSWER KEY:

1. deficit; 2. 200 billion; 3. $4,500; 4. *Possible answers include:* that the national debt is increasing, that it was fairly level from 1950 to 1980, that it went down in 2000, that in 1945 it went up because of WWII

 Take It Online, Workbook page 155

★ Go over the directions.

★ Have students go online to search for the U.S. National Debt Clock and write the current amount in the box.

★ Call on a volunteer to tell the class the amount.

**EXPANSION ACTIVITY:
Country Comparison**

★ Have students select a country other than the U.S.

★ Ask students to go online and find out about their selected country's national debt, and then compare that country to the U.S.

★ Call on students to share the information with the class.

Name: _____   Date: _____

Grammar: Do you know?

A. Look at the Big Picture. Write indirect questions for each answer below.

1. A: _____?

   B: Yes, I do. It's just one week.

2. A: _____?

   B: Yes, I can. It's in room 302.

3. A: _____?

   B: Of course, I can. I'm the teacher. It's $75.

4. A: _____?

   B: Yes, it has. It started at 6:45. But there's still an hour and a half left.

5. A: _____?

   B: No, I'm sorry I don't. I think most classes run for less than 12, but I don't know about the writing classes.

6. A: _____?

   B: Yes, you will. According to the course description, all students make at least one pot.

7. A: _____?

   B: Yes, I can. Let me look. Yes, we have one class, Stress Management, that starts at that time.

8. A: _____?

   B: Sure. It's between small engine repair and the pottery class, across from the office.

B. Create indirect questions about these things in the Big Picture.

1. (the location of the pottery class)

   _____

2. (the time of the small engine repair class)

   _____

3. (the number of weeks of the photography course)

   _____

Name: _____   Date: _____

Reading: Course Catalog

A. Look at the Big Picture. Read the course descriptions in the catalog. Write the name of the course on the line above the description.

1. _____

   In this class, students will learn the basics of operating a camera, film development, and composition. The instructor will cover techniques such as cropping, editing, and special effects.

2. _____

   In this course, students will learn how to work with clay and operate a wheel to create beautiful cups, bowls, plates, and vases. No previous art experience is necessary, but students should be prepared to work hard and get messy.

3. _____

   Students will learn how to create competent compositions, beginning with the paragraph, then moving on to essays and short stories. The instructor will focus on mechanics such as punctuation, capitalization, grammar, and spelling. Students will develop drafts and take them through a thorough revision process.

4. _____

   Learn to relax through an ancient Chinese form of martial arts. Students will increase strength and balance as they learn to manage stress. No previous experience is necessary, but students should consult a physician before taking this course.

5. _____

   Students will learn to prepare meals from soup to nuts, and Rome to Venice. The instructor will focus on basic techniques, such as making pasta and preparing sauces. This course is intended for the casual cook who would like to be more adventurous in the kitchen.

6. _____

   This course will help students become more comfortable with presentations, introductions, formal speeches, and interacting in social situations. Students will learn to write and revise material, as well as to speak to groups on the spur of the moment.

B. Look at the jobs below. Write the number of the course in A next to the appropriate job.

_____ sales and marketing assistant   _____ stay-at-home dad

_____ newsletter photographer   _____ secretary

Name: _____   Date: _____

Reading: Safe Driving Tips

A. Look at the Big Picture. Read the tips and answer the questions.

Safe Driving Tips

Many factors can affect your safety when you are driving a vehicle. If you follow these safety tips, you may be able to avoid some hazards and minimize others.

CELL PHONE USAGE AND OTHER DISTRACTIONS: Using a hand-held cell phone is illegal in some states and is distracting to the driver. If you do use a cell phone, make calls when you are stopped or have someone else dial. Keep the phone in easy reach. Use the speaker phone or a hands-free device. Don't use the phone in bad weather or congested traffic. Other behaviors can also distract the driver, such as adjusting the radio, reading a map, and eating or drinking.

DRIVING ON AN EXPRESSWAY: When entering an expressway, signal and wait for an opening. Make sure your speed is equal to that of the traffic already on the highway. When you exit, make sure you know if the exit is on the right or left and get in the correct lane. Check mirrors often, and use signals when changing lanes. Don't follow too closely. Pass in the left lane; the right lane is for slower traffic. If you need to stop, pull onto the shoulder and turn on your flashers. Do not leave your car.

AGGRESSIVE DRIVING: Aggressive driving can make a bad situation worse. Aggressive driving can include speeding, tailgating, passing on the shoulder, cutting off another car, yelling, honking, and making rude gestures. Don't be aggressive, and avoid other aggressive drivers.

---

1. Is Takeshi driving safely? Why or why not?

_____

2. What should Andy and Tom do?

_____

3. Would you describe Tito's behavior as safe? Why or why not?

_____

4. What is one tip you would add based on a behavior you see in the picture?

_____

Name: _____   Date: _____

Grammar: He could have watched the news.

A. Look at the Big Picture. Use the cues and *should have* or *shouldn't have* to answer the questions.

1. What did Tom do wrong?

   _____ (drive so fast)

2. What advice would you give the man who is fishing?

   _____ (pick a quieter spot)

3. What mistake did Sue make?

   _____ (wear a helmet)

4. Leo was arrested. How could he have avoided arrest?

   _____ (hitch-hike on the highway)

5. What advice would you give the man with the trees in his truck?

   _____ (tie the trees down)

B. Look at the Big Picture. Answer the questions using *could have* or *couldn't have*.

1. Tom's accident was at 8:45 A.M. By the time Jack left for work at 9, the highway was backed up for 3 miles. How could Jack have avoided the traffic problems?

   _____

2. Steve got a ticket. What could he have done to avoid the ticket?

   _____

3. Do you think Tom had a good day? Why or why not?

   _____

4. Kyle got wet on the way to work. What could he have done?

   _____

5. How do you think Maria got her job?

   _____

6. How do you think Marco lost his dog?

   _____

Name: _____   Date: _____

Grammar: What did he do when he saw the bill?

A. Look at the Big Picture. Match the adverb clause to the main clause.

1. While the nurse was taking Oscar's pulse, _____
2. As soon as he saw the bill, _____
3. A nurse took Oscar out in a wheelchair _____
4. Oscar and Rita were playing cards _____
5. They were listening to music _____
6. Oscar recovered _____
7. The ambulance came _____
8. Because Oscar fell to the floor, _____
9. Whenever bills come to their house, _____
10. Before Oscar had the first heart attack, _____

a. he had another heart attack.
b. because he was still weak.
c. although his problems were serious.
d. he felt just fine.
e. someone brought his lunch.
f. after Rita called 911.
g. when he felt a pain in his chest.
h. Rita knew it was an emergency.
i. Rita should open them first.
j. while they were playing cards.

B. Look at the Big Picture. Answer the questions. Use a main clause and an adverb clause in your answer.

1. How did Rita feel when Oscar had his first heart attack?

_____

2. What happened after Oscar got to the hospital?

_____

3. Why did Oscar and Rita yell when they got the bill from the hospital?

_____

4. What advice would you give Oscar?

_____

© McGraw-Hill

Name: _____ . Date: _____

Reading: FAQs about Heart Attacks

A. Look at the Big Picture. Read the FAQs and write the number(s) of the appropriate picture after each one.

A. What should you do if you think you or someone else is having a heart attack?

Call 911 immediately. Don't delay seeking medical help. Quick treatment can reduce the damage caused by the heart attack. _____

B. Should you go to the doctor's office or the emergency room?

You should call 911 and have emergency personnel come as quickly as possible. Emergency personnel are usually trained to give medications and other treatments that may save your life. _____

C. What are the symptoms of a heart attack?

The symptoms of a heart attack can vary. Many people feel a tightness or heaviness in the chest or chest pain. Others feel tingling or numbness in their left arm. Women sometimes have different symptoms, often complaining of nausea and trouble breathing. _____

D. Are heart attacks mostly a problem for men?

No, women have heart attacks too, but they don't always recognize the symptoms. _____

E. How are heart attacks treated?

If you get to the hospital within a few hours of the heart attack, you can be treated with medicines that dissolve blood clots. Such medications can help you avoid surgery to repair the damage and can restore blood flow. _____

F. How can I prevent a heart attack?

The best way to avoid future heart attacks is to eat foods low in fat, exercise, and avoid stress. _____

B. Circle *True* or *False*.

1. Heart attacks don't really affect women.	True	False
2. Once you have the heart attack the damage is done.	True	False
3. You should call your doctor if you have a heart attack.	True	False
4. The primary symptom of a heart attack is chest pain.	True	False
5. You shouldn't call 911 unless you are sure it's a heart attack.	True	False

Name: _____ Date: _____

Reading: Peaceful Protests

A. Look at the Big Picture. Read the information and circle *True* or *False*.

> The Constitution of the United States protects certain rights, including the right of free expression. You have the right to express your opinion in speech or writing, even if it is unpleasant and discriminatory, as long as your ideas do not cause harm. The written or oral expression of ideas is not protected if it threatens violence, libels someone, or is pornographic. You cannot yell "Fire" in a crowded theater because people might get killed in the rush to get outside.
>
> To carry out a peaceful, lawful protest, you should follow these guidelines.
> - You have the right to assemble and protest peacefully. Many communities require permits for marches.
> - You should observe all local ordinances and state laws. Law enforcement personnel may ask you to move or follow other directions for safety reasons.
> - Remind participants that speech advocating violence or any threat to others is not protected and may be prosecuted.

1. Someone is advocating violence in the protest.	True	False
2. Workers have a right to say treatment is un-American.	True	False
3. The signs are protected under the Constitution.	True	False
4. All signs would be protected under the Constitution.	True	False
5. The police officers are going to arrest someone.	True	False
6. The people had to get a permit for the protest.	True	False

B. Answer the questions.

1. What document guarantees your right to free speech?

_____

2. What types of opinions are protected?

_____

3. What types of "speech" are not allowed?

_____

© McGraw-Hill

Name: _____   Date: _____

Grammar: We aren't paid overtime.

A. Look at the Big Picture. Write sentences using the passive and the cues. Use the past tense.

1. some workers/not/pay/overtime

_____

2. a man/interview/a female reporter

_____

3. the labor protest/schedule/weeks ago

_____

4. the man in the wheelchair/injure/a car accident

_____

5. a protester/question/by the police officer

_____

B. Look at the Big Picture. Answer the questions with complete sentences using the passive.

1. What issues are represented in the protest?

_____

2. What buildings are pictured?

_____

3. How many buses did the school send to pick up the children? (challenge)

_____

Name: _____ Date: _____

Reading: Advertising Strategies

A. Read the information about advertising strategies and write the number of the strategy next to the ad.

ADVERTISING STRATEGIES

Businesses use many types of advertising to sell their products and services: television and radio commercials, print ads, flyers, and billboards. Although the form of the advertisement may vary, the strategies used are often similar.

1. Make it funny.
2. Make it sexy.
3. Promise that the consumer will be rich or have high status.
4. Appeal to tradition ("We've been good at this for 100 years.").
5. Appeal to the normal ("If you like good, plain things, you'll like this.").
6. Make the consumer want to join the crowd, not be excluded.
7. Appeal to emotions.
8. Exaggerate.
9. Use an authority or suggest that the consumer will be just like some important person.
10. Use small print disclaimers ("Actual size is smaller than in photo.").

_____ Oatmeal: "It's a family tradition that warms you all over."
_____ Car: "Our distinguished leather-bound edition."
_____ Shoe polish: "Shoes make the man. Shoddy shoes make the man a lonely bachelor."
_____ Software: "187 million users are better protected by our technology. Shouldn't you be too?"
_____ Cereal: "The smallest big breakfast you'll ever have."
_____ Cleaner: "Someone used the toilet and didn't wash his hands."

B. Look at the Big Picture. Find an example of each of the following.

Exaggeration: _____

Small print disclaimer: _____

Promise of wealth: _____

Name: _____   Date: _____

Grammar: That store has good prices, doesn't it?

A. Look at the Big Picture. Create tag questions using the cues.

1. (Dave's Discount Tires/have/a good warranty)

   _____

2. (the breakfast special/not/have/a lot of eggs)

   _____

3. (E-Z Park/be/the cheapest parking lot)

   _____

4. (May's/not/go/out of business)

   _____

5. (The Elegant Woman/have/a sale)

   _____

6. (the used books/not/be/$.25)

   _____

7. (I/can/not/get/discount coupons/if I buy a camera)

   _____

B. Look at the Big Picture. Write answers to each question.

1. _____

2. _____

3. _____

4. _____

5. _____

6. _____

7. _____

Name: _____ Date: _____

Reading: Who's who?

A. Look at the Big Picture. Read each person's statement and identify who is talking.

1. "The trial went well today for our side. I think we were able to question the credibility of the state's chief witness. It was a rough day for my client, however. It hurt him to hear all the details of the situation again. One good thing—the jury could see him as sympathetic."

   _____

2. "I was terrified up there. I thought I was prepared, but some of the questions were really confusing. I know exactly what I saw that night, but I think I sounded confused. I tried to do the right thing, but it was harder than I thought."

   _____

3. "Nobody told me how boring and exciting trials could be. Sometimes, the testimony we are hearing is really interesting, but when the witness is describing something really technical, I find my mind drifting away. I have to concentrate really hard on listening and remembering because, difficult though it sometimes is, I know this job is important. Someone's future may depend on what we decide."

   _____

4. "I had some excitement in court today. One of the spectators stood up and started yelling at a witness. I had to escort him out. It took a few minutes to settle everyone down again."

   _____

5. "Well, we made some progress today but not as much as I would have liked. The first two witnesses were pretty damaging for the defendant, but our last witness was a little shaky on cross-examination. I think we established that the defendant was there that night at least."

   _____

B. Reread the statements. Write a statement from someone else in the courtroom that day.

   _____

   _____

   _____

   _____

Name: _____   Date: _____

Grammar: What is a juror?

A. Look at the Big Picture. Write sentences with adjective clauses to complete the conversation between two spectators in the courtroom.

1. A: Where is the defense attorney?

   B: _____

2. A: Which one is the defendant?

   B: _____

3. A: Who is the judge?

   B: _____

4. A: What is a witness?

   B: _____

5. A: What is the relationship between a defendant and the prosecutor?

   B: _____

B. Write definitions for each of the following, using complete sentences with adjective clauses.

1. A prosecutor is a lawyer who _____.

2. A defense attorney _____.

3. The bailiff _____.

4. A court reporter _____.

5. A jury _____.

C. Read the sentence. Write a definition for the underlined word, using an adjective clause.

There are usually 12 jurors in each criminal trial.

Juror: _____

At the end of the trial, the jury must give a verdict on the defendant's guilt or innocence.

Verdict: _____

Name: _____   Date: _____

Reading: Workplace Disciplinary Action

A. Look at the Big Picture. Read the information on Workplace Disciplinary Action. Write an example of a behavior in the Big Picture next to each type of discipline.

WORKPLACE DISCIPLINARY ACTION

Price Place uses different types of disciplinary action, depending on the nature of the employee's offense.

Verbal warnings are given when an employee is not fulfilling job duties during his or her work hours. Such behaviors might include taking excessively long breaks, sitting down on the job, or general inattentiveness. A supervisor will speak to the employee to warn that this behavior is not acceptable.

Possible Example: _____

Referrals to the Employee Assistance Program (EAP) will be made when employees are experiencing personal problems such as alcohol or drug abuse, depression, and/or problems with anger management.

Possible Example: _____

Written reprimands are formal letters that are included in the employee's personnel file. Because safety is of utmost importance to the company, supervisors can give reprimands for any behavior that the supervisor thinks may result in injury to an employee or to a customer. This includes willful violation of health and safety rules.

Possible Example: _____

Suspension without pay is used when other actions have not resulted in improved employee performance or if the offense is particularly serious, such as workplace violence or drunkenness.

Possible Example: _____

B. Answer the questions.

1. Which type of disciplinary action is the least serious?

_____

2. If an employee comes to work late every day because he was out drinking alcohol the night before, what action do you think his supervisor should take?

_____

Name: _____   Date: _____

Grammar: If he hadn't done that, . . .

A. Look at the Big Picture. Complete the sentences with your ideas. Use the past perfect.

1. He got sick because _____.

2. The manager was angry because John _____.

3. Ricky broke his leg because _____.

4. Tony brought out a mop and bucket because _____.

5. The supervisor had to counsel 2 employees because _____.

B. Read the example. Rewrite the sentences as past unreal conditionals.

> EXAMPLE: Mark was fired because he hit someone at work.
>
> *Mark wouldn't have been fired if he hadn't hit someone at work.*

1. Lydia didn't buy pillows because they weren't on sale.

_____

2. Hugo didn't get a good evaluation because he loafed during work hours.

_____

3. Three employees received salary increases because they improved their job performance.

_____

4. Sam injured his shoulder because he acted in an unsafe way.

_____

C. Look at the Big Picture. Write a sentence using the past unreal conditional to describe something in the picture.

_____

_____

© McGraw-Hill

Name: _____   Date: _____

Reading: Dear Financial Guru

A. Look at the Big Picture. Read the letters and check *yes* or *no*.

Dear Financial Guru,

    My husband and I are trying to save for a house. Now we live in an apartment with our two children. We have a budget and try to save 5 percent of our monthly income. Lately we've had some unexpected medical expenses, and it has set us back. What would you advise to help us reach our goal of owning a house as quickly as possible?

Mrs. Lee

Dear Mrs. Lee,

    Great question. The first thing I recommend is a more realistic spending plan. Although you didn't mention any specifics, it sounds like you didn't budget for those medical expenses. I use these guidelines: 20% of your income for housing and utilities (since you are renting), 10% on transportation, about 15% on personal care (including childcare, doctors, dentists, and insurance), 30% on home living expenses (including food, clothing), 5% on recreation/entertainment, and not more than 15% on paying off debt. If you have no debt, you can increase the percentages in each category by 2 to 3%. This plan will leave you with 5% to put in savings. Once you have a realistic spending plan, you should be able to meet your savings goals.

Financial Guru

Are the Lees within the Financial Guru's guidelines for

1. housing?	yes	no
2. home living expenses?	yes	no
3. transportation?	yes	no
4. recreation/entertainment?	yes	no
5. personal care?	yes	no

B. Look at the Big Picture. Answer the questions.

1. What items in the Big Picture are home living expenses?

_____

2. In what categories are the Lees overspending according to the Financial Guru?

_____

3. What category do the Lees need to add to their budget? _____

Name: _____   Date: _____

Grammar: How much did we spend on groceries?

A. Look at the Big Picture. Complete the conversations.

1. Mr. Lee: How much did we spend on groceries in March?

   Mrs. Lee: _____

2. Mrs. Lee: How much more did we spend on transportation than we planned?

   Mr. Lee: _____

3. Sam Lee: Mom, can I go to the beach with the Outdoors Club? It'll cost $200.

   Mrs. Lee: _____

4. Mr. Lee: Did we save as much as we wanted to?

   Mrs. Lee: _____

5. Annie Lee: There's a dress I really want. It costs $175. Can I get it?

   Mr. Lee: _____

6. Advisor: What is your greatest expense?

   Mr. Lee: _____

B. Answer the questions.

1. What did Mrs. Lee ask Mr. Lee?

   _____

2. What did Mr. Lee answer?

   _____

3. What did Sam ask his mother?

   _____

4. What did Mrs. Lee say about the groceries?

   _____

5. What did Annie tell her father?

   _____

6. What did Mr. Lee tell the advisor?

   _____

Unit 1

Lesson 1, pages 2–3

A.

1. When does the keyboarding class meet?
   Answer: It meets from 7 to 8.
2. When does the computer repair class begin?
   Answer: It begins at 6:30.
3. Which course is the cheapest?
   Answer: The defensive driving course is the cheapest.
4. Which two courses are the most expensive?
   Answer: The interviewing skills and small engine repair classes are the most expensive.
5. How many weeks does the writing course last?
   Answer: It lasts for ten weeks.
6. How much would it cost to take writing II and keyboarding?
   Answer: It would cost $244.
7. In which courses do students probably use computers?
   Answer: Students probably use computers in the basic computer skills, careers in banking, computer repair, keyboarding, and writing II courses.
8. Which courses might help you improve your health?
   Answer: The stress management and Tai Chi courses might help you improve your health.

B.

1. Italian cooking and pottery I
2. basic computer skills, careers in banking, computer repair, keyboarding, and photography
3. Italian cooking
4. photography
5. Italian cooking
6. auto body repair, Italian cooking, pottery I, and small engine repair

C.

Answers will vary.

D.

Answers will vary.

Lesson 2, pages 4–5

A.

Chart

1. essential
2. clearly
3. concisely
4. proficient
5. responsible
6. cooperative
7. differently
8. well
9. possible
10. easy

Questions

1. essential
2. clear
3. concisely
4. proficient
5. responsible
6. cooperatively
7. different
8. well
9. possible
10. easy

Answers to formed questions will vary.

B.

1. h	6. g
2. i	7. c
3. e	8. b
4. a	9. d
5. f	

C.

1. share
2. left out
3. distracted
4. behavior
5. interact
6. proficient
7. resolved
8. affect
9. interpersonal
10. come up with
11. encourage
12. focused

D.

Answers will vary.

Lesson 3, pages 6–7

A.

Conversation A

1. Henry's Market. How can I help you?
2. I'm just calling to find out when you close tonight.
3. We're open until ten tonight.
4. That was ten o'clock?
5. Yes, that's right.
6. Thank you.
7. You're welcome.

Conversation B

1. Hello.
2. Hi. Is Arun there?
3. I'm sorry, but he's not here right now. Can I take a message?
4. Sure. Could you just tell him that Jeff called?
5. Do you want me to have him call you back?
6. Yes, if he could call me back tonight, that would be great.
7. How late can he call?
8. Anytime before 9 would be fine.
9. Okay. I'll give him the message.
10. Great. Thanks.

Conversation C

1. Dr. Sayers' office. Can I help you?
2. Yes. This is Rebecca West. I'm returning Dr. Sayers' call.
3. I'm sorry, but Dr. Sayers just left the office.
4. Can you tell her I called?
5. Yes, of course. Your name again, please?
6. It's Dr. Rebecca West.
7. And your telephone number?
8. It's 555-2345. And tell her I'll be at home this evening.
9. I'll give her the message, Dr. West.
10. Thank you.

Conversation D

1. Metro Supply. This is Joe speaking.
2. Hi. I'd like to speak to Maria Azula, please.
3. I'm sorry, but she's not here right now. Can I take a message?
4. Yes, could you tell her Barbara Abrams from Easy Construction called?
5. Could you spell your last name for me, please?
6. Yes, it's A-b-r-a-m-s. And my number is 555-3994.
7. Okay. I'll tell her you called.
8. Thank you very much.
9. You're welcome.

B.

Conversation C

WHILE YOU WERE OUT	
FOR: Dr. Sayers	
DATE: 1/23	TIME: 10:30 a.m.
FROM: Dr. Rebecca West	
OF:	
PHONE: 555-2345	
EMAIL:	
☐ Telephoned	☐ Will Call Again
☑ Returned Call	☐ Please See Me
☐ Please Call	☐ Important
MESSAGE: Dr. West will be at home this evening	

Conversation D

> **WHILE YOU WERE OUT**
>
> FOR: _Maria Azula_
> DATE: _2/18_   TIME: _10:30 a.m._
> FROM: _Barbara Abrams_
> OF: _Easy Construction_
> PHONE: _555-3994_
> EMAIL: _____
>
> ☑ Telephoned   ☐ Will Call Again
> ☐ Returned Call ☐ Please See Me
> ☐ Please Call   ☐ Important
>
> MESSAGE: _____
> _____
> _____
> _____
> _____

C.

1. You <u>should</u> speak clearly when you talk on the telephone.
2. You <u>shouldn't</u> use words such as "you know" and "you guys" on the telephone at work.
3. You <u>shouldn't</u> talk on your cell phone in a restaurant.
4. You <u>shouldn't</u> leave long messages on a telephone answering machine.
5. You <u>should</u> speak softly on a cell phone when you are on a bus or train.
6. You <u>should</u> identify yourself when you leave a message on an answering machine.
7. You <u>shouldn't</u> put someone on hold for a long time.
8. You <u>should</u> always say "Goodbye" before you hang up the phone.

D.
Answers will vary.

Lesson 4, pages 8–9

A.

1. Are you <u>up</u> to climbing five flights of stairs?
2. <u>According to</u> you, what is the most important skill for all employees to have?
3. How do employers decide who to <u>promote</u>?
4. Why has the <u>demand</u> for people with good writing skills increased?
5. Why do newspaper reporters often <u>quote</u> other people in their articles?
6. Is your watch <u>accurate</u>?
7. How do employers <u>decide</u> who to hire?
8. Which is more important in writing—accuracy or <u>clarity</u>?
9. Do you enjoy filling out <u>complex</u> forms?
10. How can you <u>assess</u> your progress in learning English?
11. What can you do to <u>improve</u> your writing skills?
12. What might you <u>scan</u> rather than read carefully?

Answers to formed questions will vary.

B.

1. *Meating* should be *Meeting*
2. *Woud* should be *Would*
3. *nekt* should be *next*

C.

Top Left: Line Cook
Top Right: Staff Supervisor
Bottom Left: Bilingual Receptionist
Bottom Right: Carpenter Helper

D.

	Line Cook	Staff Supervisor	Bilingual Receptionist	Carpenter Helper
1. Which job requires a college degree?	☐	☑	☑	☐
2. Which job is full time?	☑	☑	☑	☑
3. Which job requires good team skills?	☑	☐	☐	☑
4. Which job provides health insurance?	☑	☑	☑	☐
5. Which job requires good writing skills?	☐	☑	☑	☐
6. Which job requires good communication skills?	☑	☑	☐	☐

Lesson 5, pages 10–11

A.

1. Do you know if she <u>goes</u> to class every day?
2. Do you know if the president <u>speaks</u> Spanish?
3. Can you tell me if this sentence <u>is</u> clear?
4. Do you know if she <u>got</u> her promotion yesterday?
5. Do you know if anyone here <u>went</u> to class yesterday?
6. Do you know if the stores <u>are</u> open now?
7. Do you remember if we <u>had</u> homework yesterday?
8. Can you tell me if I <u>filled out</u> this form accurately?
9. Do you know if she <u>is</u> still sick?
10. Do you know if she <u>passed</u> her driving test yesterday?

B.

Wording of answers will vary.
1. Do you know if/Can you tell me if he is a good problem solver?
2. Do you know if/Can you tell me if she is taking a computer course?
3. Do you know if/Can you tell me if she is a good doctor?
4. Do you know if/Can you tell me if he is a proficient writer?
5. Do you know if/Can you tell me if he was born here?
6. Do you know if/Can you tell me if she was late to class?

7. Do you know if/Can you tell me if the speech was clear?
8. Do you know if/Can you tell me if she speaks more than one language?
9. Do you know if/Can you tell me if they did their share of work?
10. Do you know if/Can you tell me if Jane came up with the solution?

C.

1. d	5. f
2. e	6. b
3. c	7. h
4. a	8. g

D.

Wording of answers will vary.
1. Do you know what the capital of Canada is?
   Answer: Yes, it's Ottawa.
2. Can you tell me what the minimum voting age is in the Unites States?
   Answer: Yes, it's 18.
3. Do you know what the colors of the U.S. flag are?
   Answer: Yes, they are red, white, and blue.
4. Can you tell me who the vice president of the Unites States is today?
   Answer: Answer should be the current vice president.
5. Do you know who the governor of our state is now?
   Answer: Answers will vary.

Application Lesson: Family, pages 12–13

A.

Answers will vary.

B.

Answers will vary.

C.

Wording of answers will vary.
1. She provides resources at home for learning.
2. She set a good example.
3. They encourage her to do her best, and they value education.
4. She is involved with her children's school.
5. He called teachers right away when there was a problem.

D.

1. What <u>involvement</u> should grandparents have in their grandchildren's education?
2. What is the secret to being a <u>successful</u> parent?
3. Why are some children more <u>active</u> than others?
4. Do you think going to the library is <u>enjoyable</u>?
5. How can you <u>encourage</u> children to do their homework?
6. How important is it to get a good <u>education</u>?
7. Who gave you a lot of <u>support</u> when you were a child?
8. In the U.S., what are unacceptable ways to <u>discipline</u> a child?

Take It Online

Answers will vary.

Application Lesson: Community, pages 14–15

A.

1. Wording of answers will vary but should include these facts: someone told Dr. Gomez she could be a doctor; she heads a health clinic; she goes back to the second grade as a volunteer for three hours a week.
2. Wording of answers will vary but should include four of these facts: the program helps people like Dr. Gomez get connected with children in a school; it orients volunteers to the schools; it places them with a school that is convenient for them; it follows up to make sure volunteer placements are successful; it places 2,000 volunteers annually; volunteers listen to children read; volunteers use beads or cubes to reinforce math concepts; volunteers assist in the computer lab; 98% of teachers who have a volunteer say they want one again next year; requests for volunteers continue to grow; there is an urgent need for volunteers for the fall, particularly Spanish and Chinese speakers; all it takes to participate is two to three hours a week during the school year.

B.

Wording of answers will vary but should include these facts:

1. Maria Gomez is a doctor who heads a health clinic.
2. The Community Volunteers in Schools Program helps volunteers get connected with schoolchildren.
3. Volunteers do everything from listening to a child read to using beads or cubes to reinforce math concepts to assisting in the computer lab.

C.

Answers will vary.

Take It Outside

Answers will vary.

Take It Online

Answers will vary.

Review, pages 16–17

1. d	6. b
2. a	7. c
3. c	8. c
4. c	9. a
5. c	10. d

Spotlight: Reading, pages 18–19

A.

1. Ted isn't lazy.
2. Julia is an accurate writer.
3. Daniela is a good employee.
4. Manuel has a lot of friends.
5. Paul didn't do well on the test.
6. Akiko is polite.

B.

Answers will vary. Possible facts: Al is cleaning; Tim is hiding; Don is eating grapes; Bob is looking at a magazine. Possible inferences: Somebody dropped or knocked over the fruit; Tim is going to play a trick on his mother; Don is hungry.

C.

Wording of answers will vary.

1. She is fluent in Spanish.

2 & 3. As the country becomes more diverse, businesses have more customers and employees who don't speak English. Customers feel more comfortable with people who can speak their language. Because of this, knowing another language can help employees be more successful in their jobs.

4. He teaches introductory Spanish at a Montgomery, Alabama technical college.

5. The following boxes should be checked:
   • A number of Spanish-speaking people live in Montgomery County, Alabama.
   • Vazquez is bilingual.
   • Walt Hines speaks some Spanish.

Spotlight: Writing, pages 20–21

A.

1. The word "Sincerely" is a common <u>closing</u> for a business letter.

2. The sender's address is included in the <u>heading</u>.

3. You should handwrite your <u>signature</u> rather than typing or printing it.

4. The <u>body</u> of a letter is the main part.

5. The date is part of the <u>heading</u>.

6. The receiver's address is in the <u>inside address</u>.

7. "Dear Sir / Madam" is an example of a <u>salutation</u>.

B.

Above date, add sender's address:
   245 Harvey Street
   Cincinnati, OH 45201

Below date, add receiver's address:
   Mr. Ian Talbot
   Service Manager
   Cablex, Inc.
   3459 Andrews Street
   Cincinnati, OH 45203

After Dear, add receiver's name:
   Mr. Talbot, / Mr. Talbot:

Below signature, add sender's name, typed/printed:
   Ray Jones

C.

Date: Any date may be used, but it should follow the month, date, year format, and be placed after the sender's address.

Salutation: "Dear Mr. Darcy, / : " between the receiver's address and the body of the letter

Closing: "Sincerely," or another appropriate closing, between the body and signature

D.

Wording of answers will vary.

1. Elizabeth Bennett is the writer of the letter.

2. She wants to exchange the pots and pans she received for the binoculars she ordered.

3. She got pots and pans.

4. She included her telephone number so that the company could contact her by phone.

5. Answers will vary.

6. Answers will vary.

Unit 2

Lesson 1, pages 22–23

A.

Wording of answers will vary.

1. **Indirect question:** Do you know what caused the accident?
   Answer: No, I don't know what caused the accident.

2. **Indirect question:** Do you know what time of day the accident happened?
   Answer: Yes, the accident happened at night.

3. **Indirect question:** Do you know if the car was damaged?
   Answer: No, I don't know if the car was damaged.

4. **Indirect question:** Do you know if anyone got hurt?
   Answer: Yes, someone got hurt.

5. **Indirect question:** Do you know if an ambulance came?
   Answer: Yes, an ambulance came.

6. **Indirect question:** Do you know how many people were in the car?
   Answer: No, I don't know how many people were in the car.

B.

Answers will vary.

C.

Answers will vary.

Take It Outside

Answers will vary.

Lesson 2, pages 24–25

A.

1. g	6. d
2. a	7. c
3. j	8. e
4. b	9. f
5. i	

B.

Chart

1. collision
2. pay
3. insurance
4. agree
5. depreciate
6. cover
7. injure

Questions

1. What might cause two cars to <u>collide</u>?
2. What monthly <u>payment</u> do you make?
3. Do you have health <u>insurance</u>?
4. What are you and your friends usually in <u>agreement</u> about?
5. Why do cars in cold climates <u>depreciate</u> faster than cars in warm climates?
6. Does your insurance <u>cover</u> your personal possessions?
7. What can people do to reduce their chance of <u>injury</u> in a car accident?

Answers to formed questions will vary.

C.

1. The <u>premium</u> is the amount of money you pay for your insurance.
2. The contract between the driver and the insurance company is called a <u>policy</u>.
3. If you hit a wall or some other object, your <u>collision</u> coverage will pay for the damage to your car.
4. If your car is stolen, your <u>comprehensive</u> coverage will pay for the loss.
5. It's important to have <u>liability</u> insurance if you injure someone else in a car accident.
6. <u>Medical</u> insurance helps to pay medical expenses for the driver of the policy holder's car and any passengers.
7. If you want to collect insurance money after an accident, you have to file a <u>claim</u>.
8. If your car is hit by someone without car insurance, <u>uninsured motorist</u> insurance will help to pay for injuries to the people in your car.

D.

1. collision
2. medical
3. uninsured motorist

Take It Online

Answers will vary.

Lesson 3, pages 26–27

A.

Conversation A

1. Next, please.
2. A ticket to Andover, please.
3. Round trip or one way?
4. Round trip, please. And could you tell me when the next bus is?
5. Hmm, let's see. The next bus leaves in thirty-five minutes.
6. What gate does it leave from?
7. Gate 12. And that will be $56.00.
8. Do you take credit cards?
9. We sure do.

Conversation B

1. What can I do for you?
2. I need a one-way ticket to Frankville.
3. Did you say Frankville?
4. Yes, that's right.
5. Okay. That comes to $15.75.
6. Do you have change for a fifty?
7. Sure.
8. Thanks.

B.

1. False	5. True
2. False	6. False
3. True	7. True
4. True	8. False

C.

1. Flights 544 and 299
2. Flight 488
3. Flight 321
4. Flight 488
5. Flight 488 is the best deal because it is both the cheapest and the fastest.

D.

Wording of answers will vary.
1. Yes. It leaves New York at 2:22 P.M.
2. Yes. It arrives in Miami at 12:11 P.M.
3. Yes. It's three hours and three minutes long.
4. Yes. It's one hour and two minutes long.

Lesson 4, pages 28–29

A.

1. four
2. 9:00 A.M.
3. 11:00 P.M.
4. 5:00 P.M.
5. midnight/12:00 A.M.
6. 3:00 P.M. in Los Angeles, 6:00 P.M. in New York
7. five hours long
8. 9:00 P.M.

B.

1. c	4. c
2. b	5. c
3. a	6. b

C.

1. east
2. north
3. north
4. west; south
5. south; east

Lesson 5, pages 30–31

A.

1. should have
2. should have
3. shouldn't have; should have
4. should have
5. should have
6. shouldn't have

B.

Wording of answers will vary.
1. He should have stopped.
2. He should have slowed down.
3. He should have stopped the car completely.
4. He should have stopped to wait for the pedestrians.
5. He should have moved his car over.

C.

1. Possible answers include: she could have waited to eat until she was out of her car, she could have used a napkin.
2. Answers will vary.
3. Possible answers include: he could have brought an umbrella, he could have taken a taxi.
4. Answers will vary.

Application Lesson: Family, pages 32–33

A.

Answers will vary.

B.

1. eight
2. two
3. six
4. $19.00
5. Answers will vary.

C.

Friday: Schoolhouse Rock, Live; The King and I; Lapsit; Books at Bedtime

Saturday: Wayne from Maine family concert; Youth Symphony Orchestra; Schoolhouse Rock, Live; The Tamborines; Storytime; The Masked Bandit

Sunday: Circle Comedy Clowns; An Afternoon of Humor with Sandra Hale; Summer Insects

Take It Outside

Answers will vary.

Take It Online

Answers will vary.

Application Lesson: Work, pages 34–35

A.

1. c   4. a
2. c   5. c
3. a   6. c

B.

1. Go <u>north</u> on Route 1. When you get to S. Broad St. Turn <u>right</u>. The store is on the <u>left</u> side of S. Broad Street.

2. Get onto Route 295 going <u>south.</u> Continue on 295 until you get to <u>Route 29.</u> Go <u>west.</u> After <u>Route 1</u> look for the exit for Sullivan Way. The office is about a mile up on the right side of Sullivan Way.

3. You want to get on Route 13 going <u>north.</u> When you get to Route <u>1,</u> go north. Stay on this road until you get to Route 29 where you want to go <u>east.</u> After Route 29 crosses Route 295, it becomes Route <u>195.</u> Stay on this road until you see the sign for White Horse Avenue. Go <u>north</u> on White Horse until you come to Trenton Gardens. The company is on the right on White Horse Avenue.

C.

Wording of answers will vary.

Go north on White Horse Avenue. Go west on Route 195. After Route 195 crosses Route 295, it becomes Route 29. Go west/northwest on Route 29 until you get to Route 1. Go north on Route 1. Weber Park is on the left.

Take It Outside

Answers will vary.

Take It Online

Answers will vary.

Review, pages 36–37

1. c   6. c
2. c   7. b
3. b   8. a
4. c   9. d
5. b   10. d

Spotlight: Reading, pages 38–39

A.

Wording of answers will vary.

1. **Topic:** my trip to Italy
   Main idea: My trip to Italy was pretty awful.

2. **Topic:** my experiences with bad/distracted drivers
   Main idea: People will do stupid things while they are driving.

3. **Topic:** different ways to get around in the United States
   Main Idea: Public transportation is an inexpensive way to get around.

4. **Topic:** the costs of car ownership
   Main Idea: It's important to think of all the costs before you decide to buy a car/owning a car is convenient, but it's also expensive.

B.

Wording of answers will vary.

1. **Topic:** saving money on gasoline
   Main idea: You can spend less money if you follow a few simple rules.

2. **Topic:** saving money by changing the way you drive
   Main idea: One of the easiest ways to save money on gasoline is to change the way you drive.

3. **Topic:** saving money by checking your tire pressure
   Main Idea: Checking your tire pressure regularly will save you money on gasoline.

4. **Topic:** saving money with regular tune-ups
   Main Idea: Keeping your car in good condition with regular tune-ups can help you save money on gasoline.

5. **Topic:** saving money with good aerodynamics
   Main Idea: Improving the aerodynamics of your car will save you money on gasoline.

6. **Topic:** saving money by filling your gas tank more often
   Main Idea: You might get better gas mileage if you refill the gas tank when it still has a quarter of a tank of gas.

Spotlight: Writing, pages 40–41

A.

Wording of answers will vary.

1. Cars have to have a windshield <u>and bumpers</u>.

2. You can get a traffic ticket for parking illegally <u>and for speeding</u>.

3. Police officers help in emergencies <u>and direct traffic</u>.

4. You should drive extra carefully in fog <u>and snow</u>.

5. It's important to have collision <u>and liability</u> coverage.

6. You should obey all traffic laws <u>and signals</u>.

7. Pull over to the side of the road if a police car <u>or an ambulance</u> wants to pass you.

8. You must take a vision test <u>and a driving test</u> before you can get a driver's license.

9. If you own a car, you have to pay to insure <u>and register</u> it.

10. Your insurance card <u>and your driver's license</u> must be with you whenever you drive.

B.

Wording of answers will vary.

1. Karla doesn't have a driver's license yet, but she is taking driving lessons now.

2. Joel can afford to buy a car, but he can't afford to pay for car insurance.

3. You should change the oil in your car regularly and [you should] keep your tires properly inflated.

4. You should obey the speed limit and [you should] always wear your seatbelt.

5. You can rent a car instead of buying one, but it's expensive [to rent a car].

6. You can get a cheap flight if you are willing to make several stops, but it can take a long time to get to your destination.

7. It's convenient to own a car, but it's expensive [to own a car].

8. You can buy a new car, but a new car depreciates quickly.

C.

Dear Sam,

   I want you to know that I feel terrible about the damage done to your car, and I want to take full responsibility for repairing it.

   It was very thoughtful of you to say it was minor damage, but I won't feel good until it is fixed. I hope you won't mind that I called Dan's Garage and asked them to look at the damage and give an estimate.

   Please accept my apologies, and I hope this will not affect our friendship.

My best,

Josh

Unit 3

Lesson 1, pages 42–43

A.

1. took
2. felt
3. fell
4. arrived
5. rode
6. gave
7. ran
8. passed out
9. brought
10. saw
11. said
12. got

B.

1. Oscar was at home when he got sick, and his wife was there too.
2. Oscar tried to stand up, but he fell to the floor.
3. Oscar's wife ran to the phone and quickly called 911.
4. An ambulance rushed to Oscar's house, but Oscar didn't want to go to the hospital.
5. The EMTs put Oscar in the ambulance and put an oxygen mask on his face.
6. Oscar rode to the hospital in the back of the ambulance, and his wife followed in their car.
7. A doctor gave Oscar some medicine, and a nurse took his vital signs.
8. Oscar wanted to leave the hospital, but the doctor said he should stay there for several days.
9. There was plenty of food to eat at the hospital, but Oscar wasn't very hungry.
10. After a week, Oscar felt much better, and the doctors said he could go home.

C.

Wording of answers will vary.

1. Ted's symptoms were a squeezing pain in the center of his chest, which then spread to his shoulders, neck, and arms.
2. Nancy should have called 911 and gotten Ted to the hospital right away.
3. A triage nurse assesses the patient's condition to determine how serious it is.
4. Patients need to provide information about their medical history, drug allergies, medications, and health insurance coverage.

Lesson 2, pages 44–45

A.

1. optometrist
2. dental hygienist
3. dermatologist
4. nutritionist
5. general practitioner; cardiologist
6. pediatrician
7. psychiatrist
8. obstetrician

B.

Wording of answers will vary.

Dieticians Only: may work in nursing care facilities; must have a bachelor's degree; average expected employment growth

Physical Therapists Only: must graduate from an accredited program and pass a licensure exam; above-average expected employment growth

Both: work in hospitals or private offices; employment growth is expected

C.

Answers will vary but should include some of these facts:

1. organize and evaluate patient medical records for completeness and accuracy

   make sure patients' initial medical charts are complete

   ensure that all forms are completed and properly identified and signed

   ensure that all necessary information is in the computer

   regularly communicate with physicians or other health care professionals to clarify diagnoses or to obtain additional information

2. organizational skills, communication skills, and attention to detail

3. Health information technicians need to have good communication skills because they communicate regularly with physicians and other health care professionals.

4. Answers will vary.

Take It Online

Answers will vary.

Lesson 3, pages 46–47

A.

Conversation A

1. Dr. Ray's Office. How can I help you?
2. I'm calling to set up an appointment.
3. Have you been here before?
4. Yes, I have.
5. Your name, please?
6. It's James. Beverly James.
7. Could you come in at noon on the 15th, Ms. James?
8. Yes, the fifth would work fine.
9. I'm sorry, that was the 15th, not the 5th.
10. The 15th? Oh, that's fine too. You said noon?
11. Yes, that's right. Can I have your phone number, please?
12. Yes. It's 555-9904.

Conversation B

1. Dr. Ray's office.
2. Yes, this is Chris Ma calling. I need to change an appointment I have with Dr. Ray.
3. And when is your appointment?
4. It's this coming Friday at nine.
5. And when would you like to come in?
6. Does she have any openings next week?
7. Let me see. Yes, she has an opening on the 12th at 2. Would you like that?
8. No, that won't work. I can only come in the morning.
9. Okay. Let me look for a morning appointment. What about the 15th at 8:30?
10. That would be perfect.
11. And your telephone number is 555-8847?
12. Yes, that's correct.

Conversation C

1. Dr. Ray's office. Can I help you?
2. Yes, this in Juanita Perez calling. I need to cancel an appointment.
3. What day was your appointment?
4. It was on the 15th.
5. And the time?
6. I think it was 11 o'clock.
7. Yes, I see it now. Do you want to reschedule that?
8. Not right now, thank you. I'll call back later.

B.

1. four
2. 10:30 A.M.
3. follow-up
4. half an hour
5. 12:30 P.M.

C.

1. Dr. Grinel
2. January 23, 2006
3. the top part
4. $0.00
5. yes
6. 555-2596

Lesson 4, pages 48–49

A.

1. True
2. False
3. True
4. False
5. False

B.

1. one
2. reduced fat milk
3. reduced fat milk
4. reduced fat milk
5. four

Lesson 5, pages 50–51

A.

Answers to formed questions will vary.

1. How do you feel after you eat a big meal? / After you eat a big meal, how do you feel?
2. What should you do when you have a fever? / When you have a fever, what should you do?
3. Do you usually fall asleep as soon as you go to bed?
4. Do you open your bills as soon as they arrive in the mail?
5. How hungry are you when you get up in the morning? / When you get up in the morning, how hungry are you?
6. What did you do after you ate breakfast yesterday? / What did you do yesterday after you ate breakfast? /After you ate breakfast yesterday, what did you do? / Yesterday, after you ate breakfast, what did you do?
7. Can you get up whenever you want to?
8. What kind of food do you prefer when you eat out? / When you eat out, what kind of food do you prefer?

B.

1. She canceled her doctor's appointment because she had to work that day.
2. He stopped drinking coffee because it made him nervous.
3. They called an ambulance because someone had a heart attack.
4. She went to a physical therapist because she hurt her shoulder.
5. He was late to work because he got stuck in rush hour traffic.

C.

Answers will vary.

D.

Answers will vary.

Application Lesson: Work, pages 52–53

A.

Wording of answers will vary.

1. Workers in the United States do NOT have the right to remove uncomfortable safety equipment.
2. Sprains and strains, usually involving the back, are the most common workplace injury.
3. False. Your boss cannot fire you for refusing to do unsafe work.
4. The construction industry has the most workplace fatalities.
5. False. Office workers DO have to worry about getting injured at work. Jobs that require repetitive motion such as typing or scanning groceries can cause serious injury to the hands and arms.

B.

Wording of answers will vary.

1. He fell fifty feet off a ladder.
2. The fall shattered his lower spine, and he was paralyzed from the waist down. He will be in a wheelchair for the rest of his life and is in a lot of pain.
3. James is twenty-four now.
4. Wright advises workers to tell their bosses if they don't feel safe and to ask for safety training.
5. Answers will vary.

Take It Outside

Answers will vary.

Take It Online

Answers will vary.

Application Lesson: Community, pages 54–55

A.

Wording of answers will vary.

1. An addiction is something you are dependent on.
2. She thought she was addicted to the computer because she couldn't stop using it, even though she knew she should have been doing her homework.
3. Answers will vary but may include bad grades, not enough sleep, not enough time with family or friends, sore eyes, hands, wrists
4. Answers will vary but may include sell your computer, limit the time you spend on the computer to an hour per day, do your homework and chores first before turning on the computer

B.

1. Alcohol is involved in <u>50%</u> of the fatalities on highways.
2. More than <u>83%</u> of the deaths in fires are alcohol related.
3. <u>75%</u> of the accidents at work are alcohol related.
4. Alcohol was involved in <u>40%</u> of the deaths of pedestrians.

C.

Answers will vary.

Take It Online

Answers will vary.

Review, pages 56–57

1. b	6. d
2. b	7. c
3. c	8. d
4. b	9. b
5. c	10. a

Spotlight: Reading, pages 58–59

A.

1. 1. extreme tiredness
2. 1. extreme tiredness
3. 3. the weakening of a material due to stress
4. 2. *plural* military clothes
5. 1. a written statement of the amount of money to be paid
6. 3. a written proposal for a new law
7. 2. a piece of paper money
8. 1. a written statement of the amount of money to be paid
9. 2. to present or act in a performance such as a play, concert, or dance.
10. 1. to carry out an action
11. 1. to carry out an action

B.

1. d	4. a
2. e	5. f
3. g	6. i

C.

1. smoking, alcohol consumption, and diet
2. exercise and maintain a normal body mass index (BMI)

Spotlight: Writing, pages 60–61

A.

People in the U.S. pay for their own medical care. Medical care is expensive *(comma)* so many people buy health insurance. You should get health insurance for yourself and your family as soon as possible.

Employers may offer health insurance as a benefit to their employees. Some employers pay all of your monthly health insurance fee *(comma)* and some pay only part of the fee. This monthly fee is called a "premium." You may need to pay part of the premium *(period.)* Usually *(comma)* employers will deduct the employee's part of the premium from their paycheck.

Doctors send their bills to your health insurance company. The health insurance company will pay for some or all of your medical bills. This is sometimes called a "co-payment. *(quotation mark")*

If you do not have health insurance *(comma)* you may be able to get federal or state health care assistance. In general *(comma)* most states provide some type of assistance to children and pregnant women. Check with the public health department of your state or town.

If you need urgent medical care *(comma)* you can go to the emergency room of the nearest hospital. Most hospitals are required by federal law to treat patients with a medical emergency even if the person cannot pay.

B.

Wording of answers will vary.
1. It's important to buy health insurance in the United States because health care is expensive.
2. A "co-payment" is when a health insurance company pays for some of your medical bills.
3. You should go to the emergency room of the nearest hospital.

C.

September 12 *(comma)* 2005
Dear Tricia *(comma)*

My apologies for not returning your book sooner *(period)* I enjoyed it a lot *(comma)* and I thank you for recommending it to me *(period)*
Sincerely *(comma)* Chandra

October 15 *(comma)* 2006
Dear Phil and Ben *(comma)*

Please forgive me for not writing sooner to thank you for the beautiful flowers you sent when I was in the hospital *(period)* It was very thoughtful of you to think of me *(comma)* and having the flowers cheered me up *(period)*
My best *(comma)* Oscar

D.

Answers will vary.

Unit 4

Lesson 1, pages 62–63

A.

1. T	5. F
2. F	6. T
3. F	7. F
4. T	8. F

B.

2. The White House is directly *north* of the Washington Monument.
3. To get from the White House to the Capitol building, you can go *east* on Pennsylvania Avenue.
7. To get from the Washington Monument to the White House, you *don't have to* cross Independence Avenue.
8. To get from the National Air and Space Museum to the National Museum of American History, you can go *west* on Jefferson Drive and then north on 14th street.

C.

1. What are the colors of the U.S. flag?
   Answer: d. red, white, and blue

2. How many stars are on the U.S. flag?
   Answer: e. 50

3. What color are the stars on the U.S. flag?
   Answer: h. white

4. What do the stars on the flag represent?
   Answer: a. the fifty states

5. How many stripes are on the flag?
   Answer: b. thirteen

6. What do the stripes on the flag represent?
   Answer: f. the original 13 colonies

7. What is the United States Capitol?
   Answer: g. the place where Congress meets

8. What is the capital of the United States?
   Answer: c. Washington, D.C.

D.

Wording of answers will vary.
the 1777 flag only: has thirteen stars; stars are in a circle

today's flag only: has fifty stars; stars are in rows

both flags: have stars and stripes; have thirteen stripes; have red, white and blue colors

Lesson 2, pages 64–65

A.

Except for questions 1 and 8, answers will vary.
1. In the United States, who has the authority to make new laws?
   Answer: In the United States, Congress has the authority to make new laws.

2. What is an example of unfair treatment of an employee by an employer?

3. How can you tell when someone isn't being honest?

4. Where in your city do large groups of people sometimes gather?

5. What is the closest religious building to your school?

6. Do you believe everything you read in the newspaper?

7. What kind of behavior is difficult to tolerate?

8. Can you register to vote by mail?
   Answer: Yes, you can.

9. When is the next presidential election?

10. How can young people show respect to older people?

B.

1. The Ninth Amendment
2. The First Amendment
3. The First Amendment
4. The First Amendment
5. The Fourth Amendment
6. The First Amendment

Lesson 3, pages 66–67

A.

Answers will vary.

B.

Wording of answers will vary.
1. I think so too. *or* So do I. *or* Me too. *or* I do too.
2. Neither do I. *or* I don't either.
3. I think so too. *or* So do I. *or* Me too. *or* I do too.
4. I think so too. *or* So do I. *or* Me too. *or* I do too.
5. Neither do I. *or* I don't either.
6. I think so too. *or* So do I. *or* Me too. *or* I do too.
7. So do I. *or* Me too. *or* I do too.
8. I think so too. *or* So do I. *or* Me too. *or* I do too.

C.

1. compulsory
2. peaceful
3. discriminatory
4. responsibility
5. participate
6. tolerate
7. policy
8. coeducational
9. honestly
10. requirements
11. encourage
12. protest

D.

Answers will vary.

Lesson 4, pages 68–69

A.

Wording of answers will vary.
1. What does the <u>acronym</u> FEMA stand for?
   Answer: Federal Emergency Management Agency
2. Why might an automobile company <u>recall</u> one of its cars?
   Answer: Answers will vary: if the car is unsafe; if the EPA tells them to
3. Which U.S. government agency works to stop <u>discrimination</u> at work?
   Answer: the Equal Employment Opportunity Commission (EEOC)
4. What kinds of <u>disasters</u> does the Federal Emergency Management Agency help communities recover from?
   Answer: disasters such as hurricanes, earthquakes, and floods
5. What is the acronym for the <u>Consumer</u> Product Safety Commission?
   Answer: CPSC
6. Which U.S. government agency <u>enforces</u> clean air laws?
   Answer: the Environmental Protection Agency (EPA)
7. Which U.S. agency <u>investigates</u> federal crimes?
   Answer: the Federal Bureau of Investigation (FBI)
8. Who makes sure that businesses <u>obey</u> the law?
   Answer: the Federal Trade Commission (FTC)

B.

Answers will vary.

C.

Wording of answers will vary.
1. Occupational Safety and Health Administration (OSHA)
2. He told him to get out because the trench was unsafe.
3. Workers on the tower did not have proper equipment to protect them from an 80-foot fall.
4. The employer needed to install a safety system to protect the workers from a fall.
5. The two workers were using the proper safety equipment, so they didn't fall to the ground.
6. Answers will vary but should include: The stories are about workplace safety; OSHA helped protect workers.
7. The workers and employer were following OSHA regulations.

Lesson 5, pages 70–71

A.

SIMPLE FORM	PAST FORM	PAST PARTICIPLE
1. write	wrote	written
2. call	called	called
3. sign	signed	signed
4. celebrate	celebrated	celebrated
5. elect	elected	elected
6. build	built	built
7. give	gave	given
8. allow	allowed	allowed

1. was written
2. were called
3. was signed
4. is celebrated
5. was elected
6. was built
7. were given
8. were allowed

B.
1. This letter was written by Adela.
2. My house was bought by someone from Florida.
3. This photograph was taken by my brother.
4. This sweater was made by my mother.
5. My taxes were paid on time by me.
6. He was treated unfairly by his landlord.
7. The song was sung by Marilyn.
8. My car was hit by a truck.
9. I was interviewed by someone from the newspaper.
10. The road was closed by the police.

C.

1. protects
2. is made up
3. is guaranteed
4. can be punished
5. was made up
6. were ruled
7. should govern
8. issued
9. said
10. wrote
11. was elected

Application Lesson: Family, pages 72–73

A.

1. landlord
2. landlord
3. tenant
4. landlord
5. landlord
6. tenant
7. tenant

B.

Wording of answers will vary.

1. **Problem:** Her landlord goes into apartments without asking.
   Possible response: She could tell her landlord that he must not enter the apartments without telling the tenants in advance, unless it is an emergency.
2. **Problem:** His landlord hasn't fixed the broken shower for three weeks.
   Possible response: He could write the landlord a letter by certified mail, ask for a return receipt, and keep a copy of the letter. If this doesn't help, he could complain to the building department.
3. **Problem:** The landlord turns off the electricity in summer.
   Possible response: He can tell the landlord that it's illegal to turn off the utilities unless he is making repairs. If this doesn't help, he could sue the landlord.

4. **Problem:** Her landlord promised to fix or replace the refrigerator two months ago.
   Possible response: Send the landlord a certified letter saying what he had promised to do. Ask for a return receipt, and keep a copy of the letter. If this doesn't help, she could complain to the building department.

Take It Online

Answers will vary.

Application Lesson: Community, pages 74–75

A.

1. 18 years old
2. Yes, you must.
3. Tuesday, November 8
4. No, you can't.
5. Mayela can't vote. Fernando and Lilian can vote.

B.

1. 9
2. 9
3. 3
4. 5
5. 7

Take It Online

Answers will vary.

Review, pages 76–77

1. b	6. c
2. d	7. c
3. d	8. c
4. c	9. c
5. b	10. a

Spotlight: Reading, pages 78–79

A.

1. The title is All About the U.S. Congress.
2. The headings are The U.S. House of Representatives and The U.S. Senate.
3. This reading is about the U.S. Congress.

B.

1. the House of Representatives; the Senate
2. 435 in the House; 100 in the Senate

C.

	The U.S. House of Representatives	The U.S. Senate
1. Total number	435	100
2. Number per state	depends on how many people live in that state	2
3. Length of term	2 years	6 years
4. Responsibilities	• make laws • make laws about taxes • decide if government officials accused of committing crimes against the U.S. should be impeached	• make laws • say "yes" or "no" to treaties • say "yes" or "no" to any person the President chooses for high-level jobs • hold trials for government officials accused of committing crimes against the U.S.

D.

Answers will vary.

Take It Online

Answers will vary.

Spotlight: Writing, pages 80–81

A.

1. to invite
2. to ask for help
3. to give information
4. to ask for information
5. to give an opinion
6. to persuade
7. to thank
8. to ask for help

B.

Wording of answer will vary.
The writer's purpose for writing this letter was to cancel her health insurance policy.

C.

1. Jacob Marden
2. Dear Senator Jones:
3. to give an opinion and to persuade
4. the use of all-terrain vehicles (ATVs) in parks
5. Sincerely,
6. Answers will vary.

Unit 5

Lesson 1, pages 82–83

A.

Wording of answers will vary.

1. You have to bring the ad in to Bob's Furniture.
2. You would pay $27.00 for a $30.00 sweater at Marden's.
3. You would pay $14.98 for two hairbrushes at Doogan's.
4. You can get the breakfast special at Jimmy's Diner between 3 A.M. and 5 A.M.
5. You would owe $49.50 for the car rental.

B.

Wording of answers will vary.

1. A misleading ad gives you information that is not exactly true or is true only under certain conditions.
2. The "bait and switch" sales technique is when a store advertises a product on sale to get you to go to the store, but it doesn't actually have the product in the store.
3. Answers will vary.
4. Answers may include: The conditions of the offer are in much smaller print than the word "free;" you have to buy 6 bagels to get one free; you only get 3 free bagels after 3:00 P.M. and only when you buy 6.

Take It Outside

Answers will vary.

Lesson 2, pages 84–85

A.

1. extend
2. suspect
3. profit
4. advertise
5. selection
6. purchase
7. expiration
8. impulse

Answers to formed questions will vary.

B.

1. ended up
2. extension
3. brand
4. out of stock
5. in bulk
6. time limit
7. store credit
8. expiration

C.

Answers will vary.

Lesson 3, pages 86–87

A.

Conversation A

1. Can I help you?
2. Yes, I'd like to pay for these.
3. Okay. How would you like to pay for them?
4. Do you take credit cards?
5. Yes, we do—as long as you have another form of identification.
6. Will a driver's license do?
7. Yes. That would be fine.

Conversation B

1. Can I help you?
2. Yes, I'd like to return this.
3. Do you have your receipt?
4. Yes, I do. Here it is.
5. Okay. I can give you store credit for that amount.
6. I'd rather get cash back.
7. I'm sorry, but we only give store credit.
8. Can I speak to the manager, please?
9. Yes, of course.

Conversation C

1. Can I help you?
2. Yes, can you tell me what the warranty is on the television sets?
3. Yes, of course. They come with a two-year warranty.
4. Did you say two years?
5. That's correct. But you can also buy an extended warranty.
6. No, thank you. I'm not interested in an extended warranty.
7. But it's only $5 a month. Really, it's a very good deal.
8. No, thank you. I'll take the television set, but I'm not interested in an extended warranty.

[Note: Sentences 6 and 8 could be reversed without changing the meaning.]

Conversation D

1. Can I help you?
2. Yes. Can I bring this back if it doesn't fit my husband?
3. Yes, of course. You can make an exchange or a return.
4. Is there a time limit?
5. Yes, you have 30 days to return something.
6. Can I get cash back?
7. Yes, of course. But be sure to bring the receipt with you.
8. That's good. I'll take this then.
9. And how would you like to pay for that?
10. By cash.

B.

Wording of answers will vary.

1. If a store accepts only cash or credit card, you cannot pay by <u>check.</u>

2. If something is nonreturnable, you can't <u>return it.</u>

3. If you lose the receipt for something you purchased, you can't <u>return or exchange it.</u>

4. Answers will vary.

5. If something comes with a warranty, you can <u>replace or repair it for free if it breaks before the warranty expires.</u>

6. If you buy things in bulk, you can <u>save money.</u>

7. Answers will vary.

8. Answers will vary.

C.

Wording of answers will vary.

1. One disadvantage of using cash to buy things is that <u>you have to carry around a lot of money.</u>

2. If you want to pay by personal check, you must <u>open a checking account at a bank and make sure you always have enough money in your account to cover your purchases.</u>

3. Credit card companies make money by <u>charging an interest rate.</u>

4. If you want to put something on layaway, you must first make <u>a down payment.</u>

5. One advantage of using a layaway program to buy something is that <u>the store holds the item for you/you usually have 30 to 90 days to pay for the item.</u>

Lesson 4, pages 88–89

A.

1. $2.50

2. $3.20

3. $0.80

4. $2.50

5. $162.00

B.

1. True
2. False
3. False
4. False
5. False
6. True
7. True
8. False
9. True
10. True
11. False
12. False

Lesson 5, pages 90–91

A.

1. f
2. h
3. j
4. b
5. i
6. c
7. a
8. d
9. e
10. g

B.

1. A: isn't it;
   B: wasn't it

2. isn't it

3. was there

4. could she

5. didn't he

6. didn't she

C.

1. Yes, he was.

2. Yes, it is.

3. Yes, it is.

4. No, it isn't.

5. Yes, it is.

6. No, it wasn't.

D.

1. No, it isn't.

2. No, it can't.

3. No, it isn't.

E.

Answers will vary.

Application Lesson: Work, pages 92–93

A.

1. c
2. b
3. a
4. b
5. c

B.

1. sewing supplies
2. cleaning; plumbing
3. 4; sports equipment
4. 6
5. 7; painting supplies
6. garden and yard
7. gift
8. No, I'm sorry, we don't.

Take It Outside

Answers will vary.

Application Lesson: Community, pages 94–95

A.

1. insure.com
2. The Federal Communications Commission (FCC)
   The Federal Trade Commission (FTC)
   The U.S. Department of Housing and Urban Development (HUD)
3. The Federal Trade Commission (FTC)
4. The U.S. Department of Housing and Urban Development
5. call 877-FTC-HELP
6. call a local ACLU office listed in your telephone directory

B.

1. The U.S. Department of Housing and Urban Development (HUD)
2. Better Business Bureaus (BBB)
3. The Federal Trade Commission (FTC)

C.

1. complain; complaint
2. protect
3. discrimination
4. inform
5. organization

Take It Outside

Answers will vary.

Take It Online

Answers will vary.

Review, pages 96–97

1. d	6. a
2. b	7. d
3. a	8. b
4. c	9. b
5. d	10. c

Spotlight: Reading, pages 98–99

A.

1. **Customer:** Do you have financing?
   Salesperson: Yes, we do.
2. **Customer:** Can I sell my car here for cash? or Can I sell my car for cash here?
   Salesperson: Yes, you can.
3. **Customer:** Do you have any trucks for sale?
   Salesperson: Yes, we do.
4. **Customer:** Do any of your cars come with a warranty?
   Salesperson: Yes, they do.

B.

1. c	5. h
2. e	6. b
3. d	7. g
4. f	8. a

C.

1. True	4. True
2. True	5. False
3. False	6. True

Spotlight: Writing, pages 100–101

A.

Answers will vary.

B.

1. decided
2. took
3. arrived
4. sent
5. tried
6. fit
7. was

C.

Wording of answers will vary.

2. Describe Reason(s)

The sweater was the wrong color.

The zipper on the jacket didn't work.

The shirt shrank when it was washed.

Reason Code	Qty.	Item #	Description	Size	Color	Price
18	1	075	sweater		blue	
22	1	862	jacket		black	
24	1	407	shirt		white	

Unit 6

Lesson 1, pages 102–103

A.

1. court reporter
2. judge
3. attorney
4. witness
5. jury member

B.

1. False
2. False
3. True
4. False
5. True

C.

Wording of answers will vary.

1. The defendant's name is James Harris.
2. The witness is Lynn Rogers.
3. The defendant is on trial for a hit-and-run accident.
4. A *hit-and-run accident* is when you cause a car accident and then leave the scene of the accident.

D.

Answers will vary.

Lesson 2, pages 104–105

A.

1. violate
2. imprisonment
3. punishment
4. convicted
5. robbery
6. commission
7. offended
8. convict
9. burglary
10. vandalism

B.

Answers will vary.

C.

1. d   4. a
2. b   5. d
3. a

Lesson 3, pages 106–107

A.

1. You have reached the Marriage License Division.
2. Premarital physicals are not required.
3. The marriage license is valid on the day it is issued and for 60 days thereafter.
4. The cost in cash is $50.
5. Applications are processed from 8:30 to 4:00.
6. It will take approximately 45 minutes to complete the application process.
7. You must have your Social Security number on the application.
8. You must bring a valid driver's license or photo ID with your date of birth.

B.

1. B: No, you don't need to have a physical exam.
2. B: It will take about 45 minutes to get the license.
3. B: No, you probably won't be finished in half an hour.
4. B: The hours are from 8:30 A.M. to 4:00 P.M.
5. B: No, it costs $50.
6. B: You should bring a photo ID with your date of birth.

C.

Answers will vary.

Lesson 4, pages 108–109

A.

Answers will vary.

B.

Wording of answers will vary.

a) don't argue; keep hands visible; don't move suddenly; be respectful and polite; stay calm; stay in control

b) the right to have rights read by the officer; the right to remain silent; the right to a lawyer; the right to make a phone call

c) get a judge-appointed lawyer for free; contact legal aid services

C.

1. False
2. False
3. False
4. True
5. False
6. True

D.

Answers will vary.

E.

Answers will vary.

Lesson 5, pages 110–111

A.

1. The house that was painted last month caught fire yesterday.
2. The car that Jaime bought was a great buy.
3. A man who witnessed the robbery is testifying today at the trial.
4. A young girl who was walking home from school was killed in the accident.
5. A lot of people who don't vote complain about the government anyway.

B.

Answers will vary.

C.

1. who
2. that
3. who / X / that
4. that
5. who
6. that
7. X
8. that
9. which
10. who
11. that
12. X

D.

Answers will vary.

Application Lesson: Family, pages 112–113

A.

1. The son missed school and stayed out late.
2. His parents locked him in his room for two days.
3. The parents have a record of suspected child abuse because the son's teacher learned about his punishment and reported them.

B.

1. False
2. False
3. True
4. True
5. True

C.

Physical Abuse: burning, kicking, shaking, slapping

Emotional Abuse: shaming, name calling

Neglect: failing to send to school, failing to take to the doctor, not feeding properly, not using a child seat for a baby in a car

Take It Outside

Answers will vary.

Take It Online

Answers will vary.

Application Lesson: Work, pages 114–115

A.

Answers will vary.

B.

Wording of answers will vary.

a) Sandra is wrong. The Fair Labor Standards Act (FLSA) does not limit the types of work employees age 18 and older may be asked to do.

b) Fong's friend is wrong. The FLSA does not require extra pay for weekend or night work.

c) Selena should be paid $475—forty hours at $10.00 per hour and 5 hours at $15.00 per hour. The FLSA requires time and one-half the employee's regular rate for time worked over 40 hours in a workweek.

d) Since she is under 14, Jesse may only deliver newspapers, perform in radio, television, movie, or theatre, work at businesses owned by her parents (unless it's dangerous), babysit, perform minor household chores, or gather evergreens to make wreaths.

e) Since he's over 14, Andy can legally do most jobs. However, in some states he might be prohibited from doing agricultural work.

Take It Online

Answers will vary.

Review, pages 116–117

1. d	6. b
2. c	7. c
3. a	8. d
4. b	9. a
5. c	10. b

Spotlight: Reading, pages 118–119

A.

1. **Cause:** He got three traffic tickets.
   Effect: He had to go to court.

2. **Cause:** The Republicans lost seats in the election.
   Effect: The Democrats took control of the Senate.

3. **Cause:** Gas prices rose.
   Effect: Bus ridership increased dramatically.

4. **Cause:** The murder rate decrease dramatically.
   Effect: The county saved $20,000 in the cost of prosecution last year.

5. **Cause:** The people in my neighborhood organized a community watch program.
   Effect: Crime in our neighborhood has gone down.

B.

Answers will vary.

C.

Answers may include:

1. **Cause:** Roosevelt contracted polio.
   Effect: He had difficulty walking for the rest of his life.

2. **Cause:** The United States was in a terrible economic depression.
   Effect: Roosevelt proposed the New Deal to help people.

3. **Cause:** Roosevelt proposed the New Deal.
   Effect: Businesses were helped economically, and relief was provided to thousands of unemployed people./Safety nets were set up and are still in effect today.

4. **Cause:** The Japanese attacked Pearl Harbor.
   Effect: The United States entered into World War II.

5. **Cause:** Roosevelt led the country through most of the war.
   Effect: He is remembered for his leadership.

D.

Answers will vary.

E.

1. Roosevelt had to use a wheelchair because he had polio as a child.
2. Roosevelt introduced the policies and programs of The New Deal because the United States was in an economic depression.
3. Roosevelt is one of the most well-known American presidents because he was president during World War II; he created Social Security; he created the New Deal.

Spotlight: Writing, pages 120–121
A.

1. Answers will vary, but "homelessness" should be in the "effect" box.
2. Answers will vary, but "violent crime" should be in the "cause" box.
3. Answers will vary.

B.

Answers will vary.

Unit 7

Lesson 1, pages 122–123
A.

Wording of answers will vary.
1. John and David are breaking rule 5 (ignoring work duties). Students may also say they are breaking rules 3 (violating safety rules) and 7 (using office equipment improperly).
2. Scott and Lenny are breaking rule 1 (fighting).
3. Sara, Meg, and Elise are breaking rule 7 (using office equipment improperly). Students may also say they are breaking rule 5 (ignoring work duties).

B.

Answers will vary.

C.

illegal; illiterate; illegible
improper; impossible; immature
inappropriate; incorrect; incapable
unnecessary; unacceptable; unusual
disorderly; disconnect; disagree

D.

Answers will vary.
1. improper, immature, inappropriate, unacceptable, *or* disorderly
2. improper, inappropriate, *or* unacceptable
3. incorrect, inappropriate, illegible, *or* unusual
4. illegal
5. disagree

E.

Answers will vary.

Lesson 2, pages 124–125
A.

1. assistance
2. courteous
3. disciplinary
4. ignore
5. possess
6. prefer
7. preparation
8. provide
9. recruit
10. resolve

Answers to formed questions will vary.

B.

Administrative Assistant Only: Maintains systems, procedures, and methods for record keeping; prepares budgets; interacts with vendors, member agencies, and the public to answer questions and to resolve account and billing discrepancies; writes reports; handles questions and concerns of employees, officials, and businesses; supervises volunteers and other support personnel

Chief Clerk Only: Edits reports; keeps records of leave and nontaxable wages; prepares and distributes pay checks; compiles information and records to prepare purchase orders; compares prices and specifications; maintains cost records on equipment

Both: Prepare reports; maintain personnel records; assist supervisor as needed

C.

Answers will vary.

Lesson 3, pages 126–127

A.

1. d
2. c
3. g
4. f
5. b
6. a
7. e

B.

Answers will vary.

C.

1. casual
2. casually
3. She's responsible.
4. She's too informal.
5. She's friendly.
6. She has good, creative ideas.
7. Answer will vary.

Lesson 4, pages 128–129

A.

1. b
2. a
3. c
4. a
5. d

B.

Answers will vary, but the employee should get good ratings for behavior, reliability, interpersonal skills, and job skills, and low ones for dependability, creativity, independence, and initiative.

Lesson 5, pages 130–131

A.

1. had just started
2. had already closed
3. had forgotten
4. had just received
5. had finally reached
6. had already deleted
7. had left

B.

1. was
2. moved
3. became
4. had won
5. made
6. had recently gotten
7. married
8. had already starred
9. acted
10. appointed
11. was elected

C.

1. had had
2. would not have married
3. hadn't rained
4. hadn't laid off
5. had arrived
6. hadn't moved
7. would have called
8. had left
9. had come
10. would have finished; had been
11. had voted
12. had thought
13. had gotten; would have earned
14. hadn't made; would have won

D.

1. am leaving
2. arrives *or* is arriving *or* is going to arrive *or* will arrive
3. didn't tell
4. had known
5. would have cleaned
6. looks
7. don't want
8. are
9. are
10. got
11. had already called

Application Lesson: Work, pages 132–133

A.

1. True
2. False
3. True
4. False
5. True

B.

1. b   3. a
2. c   4. c

C.

Answers will vary but should include the fact that jobs are expected to increase in both nursing and sales, and decrease in computers.

Take It Online

Answers will vary.

Application Lesson: Community, pages 134–135

A.

Answers will vary in column 2.

Column 3 (Wording of answers will vary.):

1. Lifelong learners are people who continue their education after becoming adults.
2. A GED (General Educational Development) certificate is the equivalent of a regular high school diploma.
3. You can get information about GED classes by looking in the phone book under "Adult Education" or calling your local school district office.
4. The most common reason for taking adult education courses is to learn work-related skills.

B.

1. True   4. True
2. False   5. False
3. True   6. True

Take It Outside

Answers will vary.

Take It Online

Answers will vary.

Review, pages 136–137

1. d   6. b
2. b   7. d
3. b   8. b
4. d   9. d
5. d   10. a

Spotlight: Reading, pages 138–139

A.

<u>Today</u> I decided to make a special dessert, nut meringue pie. <u>During</u> my childhood, my mother always made it for me on my birthday. So I called her and got the recipe. <u>After that</u> things started to go wrong. <u>First</u>, I drove to the store and had a flat tire. <u>After</u> I fixed the flat and went to the store, I found out I didn't have my checkbook. <u>Before</u> I could pay for the ingredients, I had to go all the way back home. <u>Meanwhile</u> it had started snowing and the streets were slippery. <u>When</u> I hit the brakes suddenly, the eggs flew out of the carton. <u>Then</u> I had to stop and clean up the eggs. Of course, I had to go back to the store for more eggs. <u>Finally</u>, I made it home with the ingredients, only to find the electricity was out!

B.

Wording of answers will vary.

- My mother always made nut meringue pie for me on my birthday.
- I decided to make a special dessert, nut meringue pie.
- So I called my mother and got the recipe.
- Things started to go wrong.
- I drove to the store and had a flat tire.
- I found out I didn't have my checkbook.
- I went all the way back home.
- It started snowing. [Note: this can come before or after "I paid for the ingredients."]
- I paid for the ingredients.
- The streets were slippery. [Note: this can come before or after "I paid for the ingredients."]
- I hit the brakes suddenly.
- The eggs flew out of the carton.
- I stopped and cleaned up the eggs.
- I went back to the store for more eggs.
- I made it home with the ingredients.
- I found the electricity was out.

C.

Once <u>when</u> a Lion was asleep a little Mouse began running up and down upon him; this <u>soon</u> wakened the Lion, who placed his huge paw upon him, and opened his big jaws to swallow him. "Pardon, O King," cried the little Mouse: "forgive me this time, I shall never forget it: who knows but what I may be able to do you a turn some of these days?" The Lion was so tickled at the idea of the Mouse being able to help him that he lifted up his paw and let him go. <u>Some time after</u> the Lion was caught in a trap, and the hunters, who desired to carry him alive to the King, tied him to a tree <u>while</u> they went in search of a wagon to carry him on. <u>Just then</u> the little Mouse happened to pass by, and seeing the sad plight in which the Lion was, went up to him and <u>soon</u> gnawed away the ropes that bound the King of the Beasts. "Was I not right?" said the little Mouse. "Little friends may prove great friends."

D.

Answers will vary.

Spotlight: Writing, pages 140–141

A.

1. Generate initial ideas through quick-writing.
2. Talk to one or more people about your ideas.
3. Organize your ideas through a mind-map or outline.
4. Write a first draft.
5. Exchange drafts with someone to get and give feedback.
6. Revise the draft to incorporate feedback and new ideas.

B.

Answers will vary but may include:

1. The topic is a fast-food restaurant where the writer eats breakfast.
2. The writer includes the details of a comfortable place, reading a newspaper while eating, having a conversation, and enjoying a cup of coffee.
3. Answers will vary.
4. The main topic—the restaurant—is introduced later, after some unconnected details about sleeping and cooking breakfast at home.
5. 1. Sentence #1: usually in the morning we ate breakfast → we eat breakfast
   2. Sentence #2: people has time → people have time
   3. Sentence #6: people can has → people can have
   4. Sentence #7: people may enjoy her coffee → people may enjoy their coffee

C.

Answers will vary.

Unit 8

Lesson 1, pages 142–143

A.

TRANSPORT	FOOD	ENTERTAIN.	MISC.	CLOTHING
5/1 bus pass $40.00	5/3 groceries $275.00	5/10 concert $32.00	5/5 books $33.80	5/6 skirt $38.00
5/16 parking $6.00	5/12 lunch $11.50	5/12 video $4.25	5/11 shampoo $3.00	5/6 T-shirt $15.00
5/24 taxi $7.30	5/22 groceries $25.00	5/26 video $4.25	5/16 cards $5.75	5/20 jacket $59.00
5/27 parking $2.50	5/27 milk $3.79	5/27 movie $8.50	5/27 book $6.75	5/27 running shoes $45.00
Total = $55.80	Total = $315.29	Total = $49.00	Total = $49.30	Total = $157.00

B.

Wording of answers will vary.
1. Sandy is just under budget for entertainment this month. So far she has spent $49.00.
2. To keep to her clothes budget, Sandy will have to spend no more than $43.00 on clothing for the rest of the month.
4. Answers will vary.
5. Approximately 50% of Sandy's total expenses this month have been spent on food.

C.

Fixed Expenses: mortgage payment, health insurance, school loan payments, rent, car payments, bus pass

Variable Expenses: gas, utilities, groceries, entertainment, clothing

[Note: Depending on students' situation, child care could be put in either category.]

D.

Answers are in italics.

Noun	Verb	Adjective
1. *entertaining*	entertain	entertaining
2. *utility*	utilize	XXXXX
3. *transportation*	transport	transportable
4. miscellany	XXXXX	*miscellaneous*
5. *clothing; clothes*	clothe	XXXXX
6. *investment*	invest	XXXXX
7. action	act	*active*

1. How much did you spend on <u>entertainment</u> last month?
2. Are your <u>utilities</u> higher or lower in the summer?
3. What form of <u>transportation</u> do you usually take to school?
4. What <u>miscellaneous</u> expenses did you have last week?
5. Who spends the most on <u>clothes *or* clothing</u> in your household?
6. What kind of <u>investments</u> do you have?
7. Is your <u>active</u> spending usually higher or lower than your goals?

Answers to formed questions will vary.

Lesson 2, pages 144–145

A.
1. The interest rate on a <u>certificate of deposit</u> is higher than on a regular savings account.
2. That new car <u>set</u> me <u>back</u> a few thousand dollars.
3. Although adjustable rate mortgages are cheaper right now, in the long run a <u>fixed</u> rate mortgage might save you more money and it's predictable.
4. There's a <u>penalty</u> for bouncing checks.
5. I couldn't buy the video game. I <u>maxed out</u> my credit card.
6. Downtown Bank is offering <u>perks</u> to customers who open accounts this month.
7. His grandparents left him <u>shares</u> of <u>stock</u> in a Fortune 500 company.

B.
1. What happens if you don't pay your credit card bill on time?
2. What are some differences between credit cards?
3. What are some advantages of a CD?
4. Why should you invest in an IRA?
5. When do governments have a deficit?

C.

Wording of answers will vary.

1. If you pay your credit card bill late, you will be charged a penalty fee.

2. Some credit cards charge an annual fee, some offer perks, and their interest rates vary.

3. A CD earns a fixed interest rate over a specific period of time. The interest rate is higher than a savings account, but you cannot use the money for a certain amount of time.

4. You should invest in an IRA because the money you invest doesn't count as part of your income so you don't have to pay taxes on it until you withdraw it. You can use this money after you retire.

5. Governments have a budget deficit when they spend more money than they collect in taxes.

D.

1. men
2. women
3. cash and money market
4. stock
5. men
6. stock

E.

Answers will vary.

Lesson 3, pages 146–147

A.

Conversation A: BankPlus

1. Hi. How can I help you?

2. Hi. I wanted to ask a few questions about opening a checking account.

3. Sure. What would you like to know?

4. Well, do you just have one type of checking account?

5. No, BankPlus actually offers two types of accounts, free checking and deluxe checking.

6. What are the differences?

7. With deluxe checking you get free checks and can earn interest, but you must have a minimum balance of $2,500 in your account.

8. Whoa. What about the free checking account?

9. Well, you don't earn interest, but there is no minimum balance and no monthly service fee.

10. I think I'll try that one.

Conversation B: Grand Bank

1. Excuse me. I'd like some information about checking accounts.

2. Sure. I'd be happy to answer your questions. What would you like to know?

3. Does Grand Bank offer free checks with checking accounts?

4. Yes, we do, with our Premium and Gold Star accounts. With basic checking the first 500 checks are free, but there is a charge for additional checks.

5. Is there a minimum balance on basic checking?

6. No. And there is no monthly service fee either. The other two charge fees when you drop below the minimums.

7. What are some other differences?

8. The Premium account requires a minimum balance of $1,500. With the Gold Star account, you need to maintain a minimum balance of $5,000, but you earn interest.

9. I think I'd like to open a Premium account.

B.

1. True
2. False
3. False
4. False
5. True

C.

Wording of answers will vary.

BankPlus Only: Offers two different kinds of accounts; requires a minimum balance of $2,500 for an interest-earning account and for free checks

Grand Bank Only: Offers three different kinds of accounts; offers 500 free checks with basic checking; offers unlimited free checks with a $1,500 minimum balance; requires a minimum balance of $5,000 for an interest-earning account

Both: Offer accounts that earn interest; no minimum balance or service fees for basic checking; offer free checks with some accounts

D.

Answers will vary but should include these phrases used to confirm information: *Did you say, You said, That was,* and *Was that.*

Lesson 4, pages 148–149

A.

The first, second, and fourth boxes should be checked.

B.

Immigrants may be more likely to become victims of <u>fraud</u> than other consumers because of language problems and unfamiliarity with the American market.

<u>Crooks</u> can take advantage of immigrants in the following areas.

Newcomers often need to establish <u>credit</u> so they can buy a car or rent an apartment.

Some so-called "agencies" provide <u>bogus</u> job listings for a fee.

Another way businesses take advantage of immigrants is to offer money transfers for very high <u>fees</u>.

Immigrants can best <u>guard</u> against these kinds of fraud by becoming educated.

C.

Answers will vary but may include:
1. Immigrants are frequent fraud victims because of their language difficulties and unfamiliarity with the American market.
2. Many immigrants use money-wiring services because they often send money to families in other countries and don't always have bank accounts.
3. Knowing more English can protect immigrants against fraud by giving them a clearer understanding of contracts and advertising written in English, making them appear more confident and less of an easy target, and making them better able to take legal action if they are defrauded.
4. Immigrants may be targeted by fraudulent credit offers, employment agencies, for-profit schools, money-wiring services, and used car sales.
5. Communities can provide immigrants with information about the dangers of fraud.

D.

Answers will vary.

Lesson 5, pages 150–151

A.

1. "I sure got in a lot of trouble at work," said Ming. "My boss was mad because I was late."
2. "That's too bad," said Paul.
3. Ming said, "Now I'm worried about taking the day off on Friday."
4. Paul said, "We should postpone our trip to the beach."
5. "That's a good idea," agreed Ming.
6. "Maybe we can go in a month," suggested Paul.
7. "Okay," said Ming. "I'm going to talk to my boss about it."
8. Paul said, "That's settled then. I'll change the reservations."

B.

Wording of answers will vary.
1. Ming says she sure got in a lot of trouble at work. She says her boss was mad because she was late.
2. Paul says that's too bad.
3. Ming says that now she's worried about taking the day off on Friday.
4. Paul says that they should postpone their trip to the beach.
5. Ming agrees that that's a good idea.
6. Paul suggests that they could go in a month.
7. Ming says she's going to talk to her boss about it.
8. Paul says that's settled then and that he's going to change the reservations.

C.

Wording of answers will vary.
1. Ming said she had sure gotten in a lot of trouble at work. She said her boss had been mad because she had been late.
2. Paul said that was too bad.
3. Ming said that now she was worried about taking the day off on Friday.
4. Paul said that they should postpone their trip to the beach.
5. Ming agreed that that was a good idea.
6. Paul suggested that they could go in a month.
7. Ming said she would talk to her boss about it.
8. Paul said that was settled then and that he would change the reservations.

D.

1. Yolanda said she couldn't come to the party.
2. Rob said they were going out later.
3. Mark said that he just bought a new car.
4. The bank officer said the interest rates on the Gold Star account were higher.
5. The teacher warned that we needed to protect ourselves against fraud.

E.

Answers will vary.

Application Lesson: Family, pages 152–153

A.

Wording of answers will vary.

1. They taught Alicia to be frugal, to live within her means, and to build up good credit.
2. They taught Alicia by the example of being frugal.
3. They never bought what they couldn't afford, and they kept perfect credit.
4. Answers will vary.
5. She taught her daughter to prioritize her purchases.
6. She gave her daughter a fixed amount of money to spend.

B.

Answers will vary.

C.

1. d
2. e
3. a
4. b
5. f
6. c

Take It Outside

Answers will vary.

Take It Online

Answers will vary.

Application Lesson: Community, pages 154–155

A.

Answers will vary.

B.

1. True
2. True
3. True
4. True
5. False

C.

1. a deficit
2. $200 billion
3. $4,500
4. Answers will vary but should reflect the chart: "debt is increasing," "debt increased most in the 1980s," "debt was stable from the 1950s to the 1970s"

Take It Online

Answers will vary but should reflect current National Debt Clock, found here: http://www.publicdebt.treas.gov/opd/opdpenny.htm

Review, pages 156–157

1. a
2. c
3. c
4. d
5. b
6. d
7. b
8. d
9. b
10. d

Spotlight: Reading, pages 158–159

A.

Wording of answers will vary.

1. The E.U. is a partnership of 25 member nations with a single economic system.
2. Europe adopted a single currency, the Euro, in 1992.
3. The E.U. has a higher unemployment rate.
4. The E.U. has a higher inflation rate.

B.

Comparison: also, while

Contrast: but, although, however, whereas

C.

Answers will vary but may include:

E.U. only: larger population, smaller size, higher inflation, higher unemployment, established in 1992, uses the Euro

U.S. only: smaller population, larger size, lower inflation, lower unemployment

Both: similar world export share

D.

Wording of answers will vary.

1. The U.S. has lower inflation and lower unemployment than the E.U.

2. The E.U. imports only a little more than it exports, while the U.S. imports a great deal more than it exports.

3. The creation of the E.U. established a single currency and eliminated barriers to trade and employment between its members, creating a single market that is more efficient than multiple economies.

Spotlight: Writing, pages 160–161

A.

To add information: also, besides, furthermore, too, and, in addition, moreover, further

To show order: second, third, first

To show cause and effect: therefore, due to, as a result, consequently, for this reason, so, because, thus

To give an example: for example, for instance, like, such as

To show a contrast: despite, in spite of, on the other hand, but, however, whereas, even though, though, yet, conversely, instead of, nevertheless

B.

Answers will vary.

1. word showing cause and effect (Because, Since, As)

2. word giving an example (such as, like).

3. word giving an example (For example, For instance, As an example)

4. word showing contrast (but)

5. word adding information (Moreover, Furthermore, In addition)

6. word showing contrast (Although, Even though)

7. word showing contrast (nevertheless)

8. word showing cause and effect (Thus, And so, Because of this)

9. word showing contrast (instead of, rather than)

C.

Answers will vary.

Name: _____ Date: _____ Score: _____

LISTENING: Listen to the conversation. Then choose the correct answer for each question.

Conversation 1 🎧

1. Who are the two speakers?
   A. two friends
   B. an employer and an employee
   C. a receptionist and a possible job applicant
   D. a landlord and a tenant

2. Why is the woman calling?
   A. to ask about a job
   B. to talk to her boss
   C. to get an apartment
   D. to order a newspaper

3. What is the caller's name?
   A. Sarah Abdi
   B. Sahara Abdi
   C. Lily Rogers
   D. Lily Johnson

4. What message should he write down?
   A. Please call back
   B. Will call again
   C. Returned your call
   D. Important

5. When will the caller be able to ask about the job?
   A. tomorrow
   B. later in the morning
   C. after two
   D. around one

GRAMMAR: Choose the correct answer to complete the sentences.

6. Do you know
   A. what is the time?
   B. if the time is?
   C. what time it is?
   D. time?

7. Can you tell me
   A. where we are meeting?
   B. where are we meeting?
   C. if are we meeting?
   D. if we meet?

8. Do you know
   A. if is Mary absent today?
   B. can Juan drive a car?
   C. if Tanya lives here?
   D. does Hugo have a truck?

9. Can you tell me
   A. when she will be home?
   B. why did he leave early?
   C. where is the bank?
   D. what day are we meeting?

10. Do you know
    A. what did he say?
    B. who called?
    C. why is it so late?
    D. when do we eat?

READING: Read the information below and choose the best response.

In today's workplace, employees should observe netiquette when they write emails. Netiquette is a term describing the manners, or rules of courtesy, that people observe on the Internet. Remember that your emails at work belong to your employer and may be read by supervisors. You should be polite when writing emails. Use mixed case because using all caps looks LIKE YOU ARE SHOUTING. If you receive an email as part of a group, don't hit "reply all" if you are really just replying to the sender. Remember that things in an email can be misunderstood, so be especially clear and diplomatic.

11. This article is intended for:
    A. friends
    B. family members
    C. workers
    D. students

12. Netiquette is:
    A. a set of rules
    B. a type of email
    C. an Internet service
    D. a office document

13. Your emails at work belong to:
    A. you
    B. your company
    C. the person you are emailing
    D. the Internet

14. *Mixed case* probably means:
    A. confusing words
    B. emails with different sources
    C. reply all
    D. capital and lower-case letters

15. You probably shouldn't hit "reply all" every time because:
    A. your mailbox will get too full
    B. the response may not be for everyone
    C. it will repeat the original email
    D. it will send a response to all the emails you have received

VOCABULARY: Choose the word or phrase that is closest in meaning to the bold-faced words.

16. It is **essential** that we meet today.
    A. convenient
    B. lucky
    C. important
    D. sad

17. My supervisor said I **was very cooperative**.
    A. worked very well with others
    B. was very punctual
    C. solved problems very well
    D. was a very proficient writer.

18. The report was very **concise**.
    A. accurate
    B. long

19. Some articles are difficult to **comprehend**.
    A. pronounce
    B. understand
    C. remember
    D. rewrite

20. I couldn't **concentrate** in class today.
    A. pay attention
    B. understand
    C. remember
    D. listen

C. short and to the point
D. confusing

Name: _____ Date: _____ Score: _____

LISTENING: Listen to the conversation. Then choose the correct answer for each question.

Conversation 1 🎧

1. Who are the two speakers?
   A. two friends
   B. an employer and an employee
   C. a customer and a travel agent
   D. a customer and a ticket agent

2. Where does the woman want to go?
   A. Miami
   B. Newark
   C. New York
   D. Newtown

3. When is the woman going to depart?
   A. 11:30
   B. 10:00
   C. 3:20
   D. 9:05

4. Where are the speakers?
   A. at a travel agency
   B. at an airport
   C. at a bus station
   D. at a train station

5. What time is it now (in the conversation)?
   A. 11:30
   B. 11:45
   C. 9:00
   D. 3:20

GRAMMAR: Choose the correct answer to complete the sentences.

6. He _____ so late. Now he'll never make it on time.
   A. could have left
   B. should have left
   C. couldn't have left
   D. shouldn't have left

7. I'm surprised she took the bus. She _____ and gotten here yesterday.
   A. could have flown
   B. could fly
   C. should fly
   D. shouldn't have flown

8. Yesterday was Nick's birthday. I _____ him a card.
   A. shouldn't have bought
   B. couldn't have bought
   C. should have bought
   D. shouldn't buy

9. Linda had an accident. She _____ when it started raining
   A. shouldn't have slowed down
   B. couldn't have slowed down
   C. should have slowed down
   D. should have been speeding

10. We _____ there by 9:00. The bus didn't even leave until 9:15.
    A. could have arrived
    B. couldn't have arrived
    C. should have arrived
    D. shouldn't have arrived

READING: Read the information below and choose the best response.

```
⊠ ⊟ ⊞                                    ▤
┌──────────┬──────────┬───────────┬──────────┬──────────┬──────────┐
│  INBOX   │  REPLY   │ REPLY ALL │ FORWARD  │  PRINT   │  DELETE  │ ▲
└──────────┴──────────┴───────────┴──────────┴──────────┴──────────┘
```

FROM: GRAY, YOLANDA <GRAYOL@VESPER.NET   TO: MR. HARPER <HARPER77@SUNCAST.NET   CC:
SUBJECT: MEXICO TRIP

Mr. Harper,

I am attaching the itinerary for your upcoming trip to Mexico. I haven't quite figured out the best way to get you to the Agua Minerales resort for your 4-night stay. You will be in Mexico City the night before. There are several options. I could book you a flight from Mexico City, but there is only one flight per day into the local airport, so you wouldn't arrive until 11 P.M. the cost would be about 200 American dollars. The bus system in Mexico is excellent, and I can get you a ticket on an express bus for about $30. The trip is 5 hours, and you would arrive at the resort at 4 P.M. Another option is to get a rental car. That would allow you the most flexibility in arrival time, and is a reasonable price, just $10 a day, but once you are at the resort, you may not need the car at all. The disadvantage is that the car needs to be returned to Mexico City. Please let me know which option you would prefer and I will finalize the plans.

Sincerely,
Yolanda Gray

11. What is the topic of the email?
   A. a trip   B. a resort   C. a car   D. Mexico City

12. What is the relationship between Mr. Harper and Ms. Gray?
   A. two friends   C. a customer and a travel agent
   B. two coworkers   D. a customer and a car rental agent

13. To get to Agua Minerales, which option would be the most expensive?
   A. a flight   B. the bus   C. a rental car   D. a train

14. Which option is the most flexible in terms of when Mr. Harper could go?
   A. a flight   B. the bus   C. a rental car   D. a train

15. Which option has the fewest disadvantages?
   A. a flight   B. the bus   C. a rental car   D. a train

VOCABULARY: Choose the word or phrase that best completes the sentence.

16. Her insurance isn't very expensive, but she has a very high _____.
   A. deductible   B. annual   C. motorist   D. collision

17. It wasn't my fault, but the other _____ was uninsured.
   A. claim   B. premium   C. motorist   D. collision

18. This new rate will become _____ on April 15.
   A. annual   B. effective   C. deductible   D. uninsured

19. He got a check as _____ for his expenses.
   A. reimbursement   B. policy   C. claim   D. premium

20. When you turn left, you need to pay attention to _____ traffic.
   A. motorist   B. oncoming   C. shoulder   D. collision

Name: _____ Date: _____ Score: _____

LISTENING: Listen to the conversation. Then choose the correct answer for each question.

Conversation 1 🎧

1. Who are the two speakers?
   A. a receptionist and a job applicant
   B. a receptionist and a customer
   C. a receptionist and a patient
   D. a hair stylist and a customer

2. Why is the man calling?
   A. to make an appointment
   B. to reschedule an appointment
   C. to cancel an appointment
   D. to ask about a bill

3. What is the caller's name?
   A. Ted Land
   B. Ted Porter
   C. Ted Lang
   D. Fred Porter

4. When will he come in?
   A. today at 4:00
   B. today at 2:00
   C. the 16th at 9:30
   D. the 15th at 9:30

5. Where is he now?
   A. at work
   B. at home
   C. out of town
   D. downtown

GRAMMAR: Choose the best answer to complete the sentences.

6. The nurse gave him some medicine
   _____ he started to feel pain.
   A. as soon as
   B. until
   C. before
   D. while

7. _____ I feel nausea, I take
   some ginger and honey.
   A. Until
   B. Before
   C. Whenever
   D. Since

8. He is going to start an exercise program _____
   his doctor has given permission.
   A. although
   B. even though
   C. now that
   D. so that

9. _____ she is overweight,
   her blood pressure is not high.
   A. Because
   B. Since
   C. Even though
   D. Now that

10. We loved teaching there _____
    we didn't make much money.
    A. since
    B. although
    C. now that
    D. because

READING: Read the information below and choose the best response.

It's very important to help your child get ready for school. One of the most important steps you can take is to schedule a physical exam. The examining physician should check vision and hearing, as well as make sure immunizations are up to date.

State laws require certain immunizations before a child can begin kindergarten. These immunization requirements provide a safety net in case children were not immunized as infants or small children. Immunizations prevent the spread of potentially devastating diseases.

Most states offer exemptions to the immunization requirements, especially if the immunization itself would cause medical problems. Some states offer exemptions based on religious or personal beliefs. If you do not want your child to be immunized, you must ask for an exemption before you enroll your child in school.

11. This article is intended for:
   A. parents   B. teachers   C. workers   D. students

12. A doctor should check:
   A. vision   B. hearing   C. immunizations   D. all of the above

13. *Exemption* probably means:
   A. requirement   B. exception to the rule   C. immunization   D. vaccine

14. You may not need to have your child immunized if:
   A. your child is too young   C. you just moved here
   B. you aren't religious   D. it would cause health problems

15. Immunizations are required:
   A. by laws in all states   C. by school regulations
   B. by federal law   D. by local communities

VOCABULARY: Choose the word or phrase that the sentence describes.

16. She is a medical doctor that treats common health problems.
   A. cardiologist   B. general practitioner   C. obstetrician/gynecologist   D. dermatologist

17. He treats skin problems and diseases.
   A. cardiologist   B. general practitioner   C. obstetrician/gynecologist   D. dermatologist

18. Patients go to this specialist for heart problems.
   A. cardiologist   B. general practitioner   C. obstetrician/gynecologist   D. dermatologist

19. Children are usually treated by this type of medical doctor.
   A. dermatologist   B. gynecologist   C. pediatrician   D. cardiologist

20. This doctor often delivers babies.
   A. obstetrician   B. pediatrician   C. dermatologist   D. general practitioner

Name: _____   Date: _____   Score: _____

LISTENING: Listen to the conversation. Then choose the correct answer for each question.

Conversation 1 🎧

1. Who are the two speakers?
   A. a parent and a child
   B. two friends
   C. a teacher and a student
   D. two coworkers

2. What are they talking about?
   A. a teacher
   B. girls
   C. a math class
   D. whether boys or girls are smarter

3. Why is the class single gender?
   A. because boys are smarter than girls
   B. to help girls become more confident in math
   C. to help boys compete with girls
   D. because girls answer all the questions

4. Which sentence is correct?
   A. The two speakers agree about single gender classes.
   B. The two speakers disagree about math class.
   C. The two speakers disagree about single gender classes.
   D. The two speakers agree about girls' intelligence.

5. What is one argument for coeducational classes made in the conversation?
   A. Boys are smarter than girls.
   B. Girls are less confident than boys.
   C. Girls and boys are equally intelligent.
   D. Girls and boys will have to compete in classes eventually.

GRAMMAR: Choose the correct passive form of the sentences below.

6. John Wilkes Booth shot President Lincoln in 1865.
   A. President Lincoln shot John Wilkes Booth in 1865.
   B. President Lincoln was shot by John Wilkes Booth in 1865.
   C. President Lincoln is shot by John Wilkes Booth in 1865.
   D. President Lincoln was shoot John Wilkes Booth in 1865.

7. People re-elected George W. Bush in 2004.
   A. George W. Bush re-elected people in 2004.
   B. George W. Bush is re-elected in 2004.
   C. George W. Bush was re-elected in 2004.
   D. People were re-elected in 2004.

8. The Constitution protects the rights of citizens and non-citizens alike.
   A. The rights of citizens and non-citizens alike are protected by the Constitution.
   B. The rights of citizens and non-citizens alike is protected by the Constitution.
   C. The rights of citizens and non-citizens alike protected by the Constitution.
   D. The rights of citizens and non-citizens alike protect the Constitution.

9. People speak English in the United States.
   A. English is spoken in the United States.
   B. English was spoken in the United States.
   C. English is spoke in the United States.
   D. English people speak in the United States.

10. Someone invented the wheel a long time ago.
    A. The wheel invented someone a long time ago.
    B. The wheel is invented a long time ago.
    C. The wheel is invented by someone a long time ago.
    D. The wheel was invented a long time ago.

READING: Read the information below and choose the best response.

The Food and Drug Administration is part of the U.S. Department of Health and Human Services. It is responsible for regulating food, drugs, medical products, biological products, food and drugs for animals, and cosmetics. The FDA tests products and gives approval for those it determines are safe. The FDA also recalls products that pose a safety risk. Consumers can report problems with products to the FDA. The FDA also advises consumers on health and nutrition through information campaigns such as the food pyramid.

11. Which product would the FDA probably regulate?
    A. aspirin   B. cars   C. toys   D. hair dryers

12. Which agency is the FDA most similar to in terms of its responsibilities?
    A. the FBI   B. the FTC   c. the CPSC   D. the EEOC

13. What does the FDA promote?
    A. saving money   B. health and nutrition   C. emergency preparedness   D. fairness

14. What does *risk* probably mean?
    A. insurance   B. the FTC   C. danger   D. enforcement

15. What do the products the FDA regulates have in common?
    A. They are all food products.
    B. They are all products you can buy at a supermarket.
    C. They are all products containing drugs.
    D. They are all products that may be used on or in the body.

VOCABULARY: Choose the word or phrase that is closest in meaning to the bold-faced words.

16. **Discrimination** because of national origin is illegal.
    A. unfair treatment   B. arrest   C. disagreement   D. tolerance

17. You should report any problems to the **authorities**.
    A. company   B. customer service C. people in charge   D. counselor

18. The EPA works to clean up **harmful** products in the air and water.
    A. unsafe   B. chemical   C. waste   D. required

19. Attendance at the meeting tomorrow is **compulsory**.
    A. optional   B. helpful   C. difficult   D. required

20. You should **participate** in local government.
    A. protest   B. take part   C. agree   D. march

Name: _____   Date: _____   Score: _____

LISTENING: Listen to the conversation. Then choose the correct answer for each question.

Conversation 1 🎧

1. Who are the two speakers?
   A. two customers
   B. a customer and an employee
   C. a manager and a customer
   D. a supervisor and an employee

2. Where are the speakers?
   A. in an office
   B. at a printing company
   C. in an office supply store
   D. at a supermarket

3. What does the woman want?
   A. a fax machine
   B. a photocopier
   C. a printer for photos
   D. a printer for documents

4. Where are the laptops?
   A. next to the fax machines
   B. in aisle 3
   C. across from the printers
   D. in aisle 2

5. Why is the man unsure about the printer?
   A. He only works with fax machines.
   B. He's new.
   C. He works in a different department.
   D. He doesn't work there.

GRAMMAR: Choose the correct tag to complete the questions.

6. He likes that store,
   A. does he?   C. did he?
   B. doesn't he?   D. didn't he?

7. They had a sale last week,
   A. had they?   C. did they?
   B. hadn't they?   D. didn't they?

8. We can't drop by after the game,
   A. can't we?   C. are we?
   B. can we?   D. aren't we?

9. That price was really good,
   A. isn't it?   C. is it?
   B. wasn't it?   D. was it?

10. I shouldn't eat that,
    A. do I?   C. should I?
    B. don't I?   D. shouldn't I?

READING: Read the information below and choose the best response.

Make this the holiday you don't overspend. If you are like most holiday shoppers, you disrupt your entire budget during the holidays, not only by purchasing gifts, but also with extra travel and decorating. Make this year different. Plan ahead of time how much you will spend on the special season, say $750. Try to buy gifts throughout the year, not just in November and December. Look for items when they are on sale, rather than at the height of the season. Ornaments, for example, will be much cheaper in January than in December. Also, avoid using your credit cards to pay for all the extras. With the interest on credit card purchases, you may end up paying much more than you bargained for.

11. This article is intended for:
    A. consumers   B. family members   C. employees   D. religious people

12. *Say* in this context probably means:
    A. tell   B. talk   C. for example   D. but

13. You should probably buy Christmas decorations:
    A. in November   B. in December   C. in January   D. on credit

14. One reason you shouldn't use credit cards is:
    A. you need to show ID   C. your purchases are probably cheap
    B. most stores don't accept them   D. you may pay a lot in interest

15. Holiday spending is disruptive because we spend too much on:
    A. gifts   B. travel   C. decorating   D. all of the above

VOCABULARY: Choose the word or phrase that is closest in meaning to the bold-faced words.

16. The **selection** at that store is really good.
    A. quality   B. variety of choices   C. price   D. service

17. His **purchases** were very unusual.
    A. things he bought   B. plans   C. brands   D. consignments

18. All returned **merchandise** should be put over there.
    A. products   B. warranties   C. consignments   D. shopping carts

19. The microwaves were **out of stock**.
    A. a good price   B. in bulk   C. sold out   D. recalled

20. I get **a commission** on each sale.
    A. some money   B. a warranty   C. a policy   D. a brand

Name: _____ Date: _____ Score: _____

LISTENING: Listen to the conversation. Then choose the correct answer for each question.

Message 1 🎧

1. What information does the caller want?
   A. traffic court   C. marriage licenses
   B. jury duty   D. civil proceedings

2. What should the caller press for information about traffic court?
   A. 1   C. 3
   B. 2   D. 4

3. What days are applications processed?
   A. Monday and Thursday
   B. Monday through Thursday
   C. Monday, Thursday, and Friday
   D. Monday through Friday

4. How long will it take to complete the application process?
   A. an hour   C. 40 minutes
   B. a half-hour   D. 50 minutes

5. What do you need to bring?
   A. $50
   B. a Social Security card and a photo
   C. a Social Security card, a picture ID, and $50
   D. a federal ID and $50

GRAMMAR: Identify the boldfaced pronoun at the beginning of each adjective clause as either a subject or an object.

6. The witness **who** will testify next is a police officer.
   A. subject   B. object

7. The car **that** I hit was towed away.
   A. subject   B. object

8. She'll never forget the man **that** she saw in the parking lot.
   A. subject   B. object

9. The jury believed the man **that** was working at the gas station that day.
   A. subject   B. object

10. I described Bigmart, **which** was the scene of the crime.
    A. subject   B. object

READING: Read the information below and choose the best response.

Traffic court

Traffic "infractions," such as speeding, driving a vehicle needing repair, or driving with an expired license or tag, are handled by traffic court. Usually you are issued a citation and have to pay a fine. You do not face any jail or prison time.

In addition to any fine you may have to pay as a result of the infraction, you are subject to court fees, such as photocopying and record searches.

More serious driving violations, such as reckless driving, vehicular manslaughter or driving while under the influence of alcohol or drugs, are misdemeanors or felonies and are handled in criminal court. These charges are subject to more serious punishment, including imprisonment.

11. The purpose of this information is:
    A. to persuade B. to educate C. to give advice D. to invite

12. An example of an infraction is:
    A. driving with an expired tag C. driving while under the influence of alcohol
    B. reckless driving D. vehicular manslaughter

13. *Citation* probably means:
    A. violation B. fee C. charge D. ticket

14. If you are guilty of an infraction, you may have to pay:
    A. for criminal court fees C. for photocopying
    B. for repair of your vehicle D. for a new license

15. If you are driving a car with a broken brake light, you may be charged with:
    A. an infraction B. a misdemeanor C. a felony D. a serious offense

VOCABULARY: Choose the best word or phrase to complete the sentences.

16. When you steal something from a house, it is known as:
    A. vandalism B. a violation C. assault D. burglary

17. An infraction is a:
    A. minor offense B. felony C. trespass D. rape

18. An example of a misdemeanor is:
    A. murder B. rape C. arson D. vandalism

19. An example of a felony is:
    A. vandalism B. jaywalking C. arson D. littering

20. When you are found guilty of a crime, you are:
    A. punishable B. convicted C. violated D. aggravated

Name: _____ Date: _____ Score: _____

LISTENING: Listen to the conversation. Then choose the correct answer for each question.

Conversation 1 🎧

1. What is the relationship between the two speakers?
   A. two coworkers
   B. a supervisor and an employee
   C. an interviewer and a job applicant
   D. an applicant and a receptionist

2. What is the woman's name?
   A. Matt Leavitt
   B. Anna Park
   C. Lee Grange
   D. Carolina Pace

3. What is one of her strengths?
   A. responsibility
   B. organization
   C. supervisory experience
   D. attention to detail

4. What is one of her weaknesses?
   A. undependable
   B. poor organization skills
   C. lack of supervisory experience
   D. customers complain about her

5. Which of the following is true?
   A. The woman wants a job with more responsibility.
   B. The woman wants a higher salary.
   C. The woman wants to travel.
   D. The woman prefers to work alone.

GRAMMAR: Choose the best response to complete the sentences.

6. I got a promotion last year even though I _____ several poor ratings on my evaluation.
   A. receive
   B. would have received
   C. had received
   D. have received

7. By the time the police arrived, he _____ away.
   A. had already run
   B. already ran
   C. has already run
   D. already run

8. I _____ if they had given me a raise.
   A. would quit
   B. wouldn't have quit
   C. won't quit
   D. hadn't quit

9. If she _____ the position, she would have applied.
   A. wanted
   B. would have wanted
   C. wants
   D. had wanted

10. If the building _____, we wouldn't have gotten in.
    A. had locked
    B. had been locked
    C. have locked
    D. have been locked

READING: Read the information below and choose the best response.

Our latest survey regarding family-friendly companies did not provide surprising results. As in past years, many companies in the computer software industry were found to be very family-friendly, but some of the companies that were the most supportive of family needs were in retail and hospitality. Our readers rated companies on a variety of policies, including family leave, health benefits, tuition reimbursement, flextime, telecommuting, and job sharing. We found that flexibility (in scheduling, location of work, and hours per week) was the most important issue for families with young children, whereas families with older children rated health and dental insurance as more important.

11. You would probably find this information:
    A. in a textbook   B. in a magazine   C. on a government website   D. in a work memo

12. A *survey* is probably:
    A. a test   B. a report   C. a questionnaire   D. discussion

13. According to the article, some companies that are family friendly are:
    A. stores   B. transportation companies   C. construction companies   D. factories

14. One inference that could be made about the survey results is that:
    A. parents with older children get sicker
    B. parents with younger children have more concerns about childcare
    C. all parents worry about college tuition
    D. people who read this information are single

15. *Supportive* probably means:
    A. unfriendly   B. casual   C. reliable   D. caring

VOCABULARY: Choose the word or phrase that is closest in meaning to the bold-faced word.

16. There are certain qualities you must **possess** to do well in this job.
    A. obtain   B. develop   C. improve   D. have

17. He is very **courteous**.
    A. polite   B. dependable   C. punctual   D. independent

18. Her supervisor doesn't think she is very **reliable**.
    A. independent   B. dependable   C. creative   D. cooperative

19. He faces **dismissal** for his performance at work yesterday.
    A. a promotion   B. a warning   C. a raise   D. firing

20. She is known for her responsible **behavior**.
    A. actions   B. appearance   C. comprehension   D. speech

Name: _____   Date: _____   Score: _____

LISTENING: Listen to the conversation. Then choose the correct answer for each question.

Conversation 1 🎧

1. What is the relationship between the two speakers?
   A. a customer and a bank officer
   B. two coworkers
   C. a supervisor and an employee
   D. a customer and a store employee

2. How many types of checking accounts do they discuss?
   A. one   C. three
   B. two   D. four

3. Which account requires the highest minimum balance?
   A. Basic   C. Optimum
   B. Preferred   D. Online

4. Which account does he choose?
   A. Basic   C. Optimum
   B. Preferred   D. Online

5. Why does he probably make that choice?
   A. He wants free checks.
   B. He wants a low monthly fee.
   C. He prefers to bank online.
   D. He thinks the minimum balances are too high.

GRAMMAR: Choose the reported speech that best represents the quoted speech.

6. "I'm leaving soon," said Tom last week.
   A. I'm leaving soon said Tom.   C. Tom said he's leaving soon.
   B. Tom said I'm leaving soon.   D. Tom said he was leaving soon.

7. Linda said, "You're late."
   A. Linda said I was late.   C. Linda said I'm late.
   B. Linda said she was late.   D. Linda said you're late.

8. Jose said, "It hasn't arrived."
   A. Jose said it hadn't arrived.   C. Jose said it isn't arrived.
   B. Jose said it didn't arrive.   D. Jose said it couldn't arrive.

9. "Maria, you can't leave yet," said the teacher.
   A. Maria can't leave yet said the teacher. C. The teacher said you can't leave yet.
   B. The teacher said Maria couldn't leave yet. D. The teacher said I couldn't leave yet.

10. "You two will have to finish," said our supervisor.
    A. Our supervisor said you two will have to finish.   C. Our supervisor said we would have to finish.
    B. Our supervisor said we have finished.   D. You will have to finish said our supervisor.

© McGraw-Hill

READING: Read the information below and choose the best response.

According to the FTC, many telemarketers are fraudulent, although some do represent legitimate causes or businesses. Fraudulent telemarketers frequently call to make certain kinds of pitches, including credit card loss protection offers and advanced fee loan offers. Consumers don't really need to pay for protection in case their credit cards are lost or stolen. Laws restrict consumer liability for charges made on the stolen card to $50. When telemarketers offer a loan for a fee in advance, they are breaking the law. Lawful loan offers do not require a fee paid in advance. As a consumer, you should be wary of telemarketers who do not listen when you tell them not to call and telemarketers who call before 8 in the morning or after 9 at night. These telemarketers are breaking the law. Legitimate telemarketers respect your time and won't pressure you into sending a payment.

11. The purpose of this information is:
   A. to give a definition of telemarketing
   B. to warn consumers about telemarketing fraud
   C. to describe lawful telemarketing offers
   D. to persuade readers to listen to telemarketers

12. *Fraudulent* probably means:
   A. lawful   B. fair   C. crooked   D. fast

13. Telemarketers shouldn't call after 9 P.M. because:
   A. it's rude
   B. most people are asleep
   C. people are more likely to listen then
   D. it's illegal

14. If someone steals your credit card, you will have to pay:
   A. for up to $50 worth of charges
   B. for everything charged between 8 A.M. and 9 P.M.
   C. for all charges made before you reported the theft
   D. nothing

15. You should be careful of telemarketers who:
   A. offer to call back at a more convenient time
   B. call between 8 A.M. and 9 P.M.
   C. do not require a fee in advance
   D. want you to send a payment right away

VOCABULARY: Choose the word or phrase that is closest in meaning to the bold-faced word.

16. The address he gave us was **bogus**.
   A. real   B. fake   C. specific   D. unclear

17. **Fortunately**, I just got here.
   A. luckily   B. punctually   C. sadly   D. obviously

18. The terms of the contract can **vary**.
   A. confuse   B. maintain   C. specify   D. change

19. He is a **crook**.
   A. manager   B. banker   C. criminal   D. telemarketer

20. They provide a lot of **perks**.
   A. benefits   B. disadvantages   C. choices   D. checks

UNIT 1 TEST

Conversation 1

Male: Good morning. Johnson Realty.

Female: Hi. I'm calling about the job advertised in today's newspaper.

Male: Do you mean the sales associate position?

Female: Yes, that's the one.

Male: You need to speak with Lily Rogers, and she's not in this morning.

Female: When do you expect her?

Male: Around two. Would you like to call back or leave a message?

Female: I'd like to leave a message. Would you say that Sahara Abdi called about the position?

Male: Sure. Is Abdi A-B-D-I?

Female: Yes, it is. And Sahara is spelled S-A-H-A-R-A.

Male: Would you like Ms. Rogers to call you back?

Female: No, I'll call back after two.

Male: Okay, I've got it.

Female: Thanks a lot.

UNIT 2 TEST

Conversation 1

Male: Good morning. How can I help you?

Female: I'd like to buy a ticket for Newark.

Male: Will that be one way or round trip?

Female: One way, but I need to get there by 9 P.M. When's the next train?

Male: Just a moment. It looks like one left 15 minutes ago at 11:30. The next one isn't until 3:20.

Female: Wow. That's pretty late. Will I get there in time?

Male: Well, it'll be close. It's due to arrive at 9:05. We only have 3 trains running to Newark a day. The next one isn't until 10 tonight.

Female: Okay. I'll buy a ticket for the 3:20.

Male: That'll be $79.90 for one ticket on the #12 at 3:20. You can wait right over there.

Female: Here you go. Thanks.

UNIT 3 TEST

Conversation 1

Female:	Dr. Porter's office. How can I help you?
Male:	Hi. This is Ted Lang. I need to reschedule my appointment.
Female:	Okay, Mr. Land. When was your appointment?
Male:	I'm sorry. It's Ted Lang, not Land. I think I was supposed to come in today at 2, but I can't make it.
Female:	Oh, I see, Mr. Lang. Your appointment is actually today at 4 P.M. Do you still need to reschedule?
Male:	Hmm. Let me think. Yes, I think I should. I'm out of town, and I don't think I can get there in time.
Female:	Okay. When did you want to make the new appointment?
Male:	Do you have any openings in the morning next week?
Female:	Let me look. Yes, you could come on the 15th at 9:30. Would that work?
Male:	The 16th at 9:30? Yes, I think so.
Female:	That was the 15th at 9:30, not the 16th.
Male:	Yes, I can make that.

UNIT 4 TEST

Conversation 1

Male (teen):	How are your classes?
Female (teen):	Pretty good. How about yours?
Male:	Okay, I guess. I like math the best.
Female:	I do too, although it's strange being in an all-girl class.
Male:	Why is it all girls?
Female:	The school is hoping that the girls will feel more comfortable and confident in a single-gender class. I think it's a good idea.
Male:	Really? Why is that?
Female:	Well, sometimes the guys in a math class answer all the questions or act like girls aren't as smart.
Male:	I'm not sure it's such a good idea. I mean, some time you're going to have to compete with guys, even in math.

UNIT 5 TEST

Conversation 1

Female:	Excuse me. Could you tell me where the printers are?
Male:	Yes, I can. They're in aisle 3, next to the laptops.
Female:	Great. Also, do you know which printers are best for photos?
Male:	I think Printpro is pretty good.
Female:	You're not sure? Is there something else you'd recommend?
Male:	Well, actually, I don't really know much about the printers.
Female:	Can you tell me who would know?
Male:	Probably someone who works here.
Female:	You're not an employee?
Male:	No, sorry. I'm shopping for a fax machine.

UNIT 6 LISTENING SCRIPT

Message 1

Welcome to the Martin County Courthouse. Please listen to the following options. For information about traffic court, press 1. For information about civil proceedings, press 2. For information about jury duty, press 3. For information regarding marriage licenses, press 4. For all other inquiries, press 5. To speak to an operator, press 0. [beep for pressing 4]. Marriage license applications are processed Monday through Thursday, 9 to 4, and Friday 9 to 2. You no longer need a blood test to get a license. Forms are available online or at the registrar's office on the 3rd floor of the County Courthouse. The application process will take approximately 30 minutes. The fee is $50. You will need a valid Social Security card and a federal or state-issued photo ID, such as a driver's license.

UNIT 7 TEST

Conversation 1

Male:	Anna Park? Hi, I'm Matt Leavitt. Nice to meet you. Please have a seat.
Female:	Hello, Mr. Leavitt. It's nice to meet you, too.
Male:	Did you have any trouble finding the office?
Female:	Not at all. The directions were great.
Male:	Would you like coffee or anything?
Female:	No, thank you. I'm fine.
Male:	Okay, then. I see that you are applying for the position of senior sales associate. Why are you looking for a job change?
Female:	Well, as you can see on my resume, I've been a sales associate at Lee Grange for several years, and although I've received several salary increases and bonuses, I would really like more responsibility.
Male:	Tell me about your experience at your present job.
Female:	I am the sales representative for the southeast district, so I travel a lot and work with many customers. I've increased sales in my district every year.
Male:	That's great. Why do you think you've been so successful?
Female:	I have good people skills, and I'm very organized. I resolve customer complaints immediately and provide excellent customer service.
Male:	What areas of job performance do you think you need to improve?
Female:	Well, I don't really have any supervisory experience, and that's one reason why this position at Carolina Pace is so attractive to me.

UNIT 8 TEST

Conversation 1

Male:	Hi, I'd like to talk to someone about opening a checking account.
Female:	Sure, I can help you with that. What would you like to know?
Male:	Well, do you have different types of checking accounts?
Female:	Yes, we do. Our Basic Checking requires no minimum balance, although you do need $50 to open the account.
Male:	And is there a monthly fee?
Female:	Yes, it's $5 a month. Also, you pay for your checks.
Male:	Do you have any checking accounts that provide free checks?
Female:	Yes, both the Preferred Checking and the Optimum Checking provide free checks. They also have no monthly fee if you maintain a certain balance in your account. However, if you go below that minimum balance, Preferred Checking charges a $5 fee, and Optimum checking charges $15.
Male:	What minimum balances are required for the two accounts?
Female:	$2,000 in Preferred Checking and $5,000 in Optimum Checking.
Male:	Whoa. I think I'll stick with the Basic account.

UNIT 1 TEST

1. c; 2. a; 3. b; 4. b; 5. c; 6. c; 7. a; 8. c; 9. a; 10. b; 11. c; 12. a; 13. b; 14. d; 15. b; 16. c; 17. a; 18. c; 19. b; 20. a

UNIT 2 TEST

1. d; 2. b; 3. c; 4. d; 5. b; 6. d; 7. a; 8. c; 9. c; 10. b; 11. a; 12. c; 13. a; 14. c; 15. b; 16. a; 17. c; 18. b; 19. a; 20. b

UNIT 3 TEST

1. c; 2. b; 3. c; 4. d; 5. c; 6. a; 7. c; 8. c; 9. c; 10. b; 11. a; 12. d; 13. b; 14. d; 15. a; 16. b; 17. d; 18. a; 19. c; 20. a

UNIT 4 TEST

1. b; 2. c; 3. b; 4. c; 5. d; 6. b; 7. c; 8. a; 9. a; 10. d; 11. a; 12. c; 13. b; 14. c; 15. d; 16. a; 17. c; 18. a; 19. d; 20. b

UNIT 5 TEST

1. a; 2. c; 3. c; 4. b; 5. d; 6. b; 7. d; 8. b; 9. b; 10. c; 11. a; 12. c; 13. c; 14. d; 15. d; 16. b; 17. a; 18. a; 19. c; 20. a

UNIT 6 TEST

1. c; 2. a; 3. b; 4. b; 5. c; 6. a; 7. b; 8. b; 9. a; 10. a; 11. b; 12. a; 13. d; 14. c; 15. a; 16. d; 17. a; 18. d; 19. c; 20. b

UNIT 7 TEST

1. c; 2. b; 3. b; 4. c; 5. a; 6. c; 7. a; 8. b; 9. d; 10. b; 11. b; 12. c; 13. a; 14. b; 15. d; 16. d; 17. a; 18. b; 19. d; 20. a

UNIT 8 TEST

1. a; 2. c; 3. c; 4. a; 5. d; 6. d; 7. a; 8. a; 9. b; 10. c; 11. b; 12. c; 13. d; 14. a; 15. d; 16. b; 17. a; 18. d; 19. c; 20. a